# Introduction to Financial and Business Administration in Public Education

DR. WILLIAM T. REBORE
*St. Louis University*

DR. RONALD W. REBORE
*St. Louis University*

ALLYN AND BACON
Boston  London  Toronto  Sydney  Tokyo  Singapore

Dedication:
To   Joyce, Kim, and Bill
      Sandy, Ron, and Lisa

**Series Editor**: Ray Short
**Production Administrator**: Marjorie Payne
**Editorial-Production Service**: Cynthia Newby, Chestnut Hill Enterprises, Inc.
**Cover Administrator**: Linda Dickinson
**Composition Buyer**: Linda Cox
**Manufacturing Buyer**: Megan Cochran

Copyright © 1993 by Allyn & Bacon
A Division of Simon & Schuster, Inc.
160 Gould Street
Needham Heights, MA 02194

**Library of Congress Cataloging-in-Publication Data**

Rebore, William T.
    Introduction to financial and business administration in public education / Willlam T. Rebore, Ronald W. Rebore.
        p.   cm.
    Includes bibliographical references and index.
    ISBN 0-205-13509-9
    1. Public  schools—United  States—Business  management.
2. Education—United States—Finance.    I. Rebore, Ronald W.
II. Title.
LB2825.R39   1993
371.2'00973—dc20                                              92-5862
                                                              CIP


Printed in the United States of America

10  9  8  7  6  5  4  3  2  1     98  97  96  95  94  93

# BRIEF CONTENTS

# CONTENTS

# PREFACE

The 1990s will certainly be remembered as a decade of challenge and change for our public school districts. Confusion and concern have become two constant aspects in the lives of school board members and educators. The federal government under the leadership of Lamar Alexander, secretary of education, has come forth with a new public policy on education. It was on April 18, 1991, when President Bush released *AMERICA 2000: An Education Strategy*, a long-range plan for achieving national educational goals that were adopted by the President and the state governors in 1990.

The following national goals have been established by President Bush:

**1.** By the year 2000, all children in the United States will start school ready to learn;

**2.** By the year 2000, the high school graduation rate will increase to at least 90 percent;

**3.** By the year 2000, American students will leave grades four, eight, and twelve having demonstrated competency in challenging subject matter including English, mathematics, science, history, and geography; and every school in the United States will ensure that all students learn to use their minds well, so that they may be prepared for responsible citizenship, further learning, and productive employment in our modern economy;

**4.** By the year 2000, U.S. students will be first in the world in science and mathematics achievement;

**5.** By the year 2000, every adult American will be literate and will possess the knowledge and skills necessary to compete in a global economy and to exercise the rights and responsibilities of citizenship;

**6.** By the year 2000, every school in the United States will be free of drugs and violence and will offer a disciplined environment conducive to learning.

No educator would disagree with these lofty goals but attaining them will certainly be problematic. Economic, cultural, and social variables will come together for good or ill as school districts attempt to implement the goals. For example, even though the 1980s was a period of intense public concern about education (which was reflected in the fact that education received approximately 2.5 percent of the federal budget), the education budget entered the 1990s with approximately 9 billion dollars less than anticipated.

The general state of the economy and the taxpayers revolt have resulted in the failure of tax levy elections and in decreased state aid to school districts. In many states, the entire system of financing public education is under scrutiny. Depending on a person's economic perspective concerning whether the country is experiencing a recession, the fact remains that businesses are restructuring and this has resulted in personnel layoffs that have further impacted the economy.

Because revenues are not keeping pace with inflation, administrators have been faced with reevaluating the scope and content of the programs that constitute a free public education.

*Introduction to Financial and Business Administration in Public Education* is concerned with business and financial administration in public education and, thus, cultural and social considerations are not addressed. Economic considerations are the major concerns herein but these considerations are addressed from a perspective of the accountable management of fiscal resources without regard to the public policy of our country. In other words, this book will be relevant even if the public policy changes with the next presidential election.

The point is, however, that financial issues will always occupy a central importance in education. Thus, this book is intended to meet the needs of professors who teach educational business and finance administration courses and should also meet the needs of superintendents of schools, building level principals, central office administrators, teachers, and staff members who want to update their knowledge of educational business and financial administration. Each chapter is written from a technical perspective and identifies those processes, procedures, and techniques necessary to effective business and financial administration. Many chapters also contain extensive exhibits and appendices that highlight the concepts presented in those chapters. This is a practical and comprehensive treatment of educational business and financial administration that bridges the gap between theory and practice.

The authors bring a wealth of experience in educational administration to the contents of this book. Both were assistant superintendents for business and superintendents of schools in school districts located in metropolitan areas. In addition, both authors have taught educational business and finance administration courses at major universities located in metropolitan areas.

Finally, there are few books that treat educational business and finance administration from both a theoretical and a practical perspective. Most treat either theory or practice, and others consist of edited works with chapters that lack the comprehensive nature presented here.

The authors wish to acknowledge the contribution of the reviewers of this book: Dr. Richard Rossmiller, University of Wisconsin, and Dr. Jerry Pulley, Pan American University.

The authors want to dedicate this book to their wives Joyce and Sandy whose understanding and encouragement have made the writing of this book possible.

William T. Rebore
Ronald W. Rebore

# ABOUT THE AUTHORS

Ronald W. Rebore, Sr., Ph.D., has had extensive experience in the field of educational administration. He is currently the superintendent of schools for an intermediate suburban school district in the St. Louis Metropolitan Area. The district serves approximately twenty thousand students with an operating budget of approximately $130 million, and it employs approximately three thousand people.

Dr. Rebore has had seventeen years experience as a central office administrator. For eight of these years he has served as a superintendent of schools and for nine years as an assistant superintendent for business and finance.

Dr. Rebore was the President of the Missouri Association of School Business Officials during the 1990–1991 academic year. He has taught graduate courses in educational administration as an adjunct professor for fifteen years both at the University of Missouri-St. Louis and at St. Louis University.

Dr. Rebore has written many articles and four books on educational administration that have been published by Prentice-Hall, Inc. His book *Personnel Administration in Education: A Management Approach* is in its third edition.


William T. Rebore, Ph.D., has had extensive experience both as a school administrator and as a professor of educational administration in the St. Louis Metropolitan Area. He served as an assistant superintendent for business and as superintendent of two school districts. In his capacity as superintendent, he was responsible for the administration of a school district of 11,500 students and 900 employees, with an annual budget of approximately $50 million.

Since 1987, Dr. Rebore has chaired the Division of Educational Administration at St. Louis University. He is directly responsible for the coordination of approximately 250 students at both the master and doctoral degree levels. His teaching responsibilities include graduate courses in the areas of school finance and school business management.

During the past two years, Dr. Rebore has worked with the National Association of School Business Officials in the development of a "Model Preparation Program" for school business administrators. He was directly responsible for authoring four of the six content areas included in the Model. This effort included the writing and development of objectives, resources, and strategies in the areas of *Financial Resource Management, Human Resource Management, Information Management,* and *Educational Management.* The Model has been approved by the Association's Board of Directors and is currently in the implementation stage.

# 1

# The Financial Structure of Public Education

The financial structure of a public school district is not substantially different from the business and financial operations of private-sector commercial and industrial companies. In fact it is very important for educational administrators to understand the similarity between the public and private sectors. Without this understanding, public school administrators might fail to utilize the business and financial strategies that have proved to be successful when employed by private-sector companies.

The following classification of organizations will serve as a point of reference for the financial structures of a public school district. Most organizations fall into one of two categories: service rendering or production. The former can be further divided into private-sector and public-sector organizations. The criteria for classifying an organization are its mission and the manner in which it is financed.

The overall mission of the Chrysler Corporation is to manufacture automobiles. The company generates a profit through the sale of these automobiles. Thus, Chrysler Corporation is also classified as a *private-sector production organization*. Arthur Andersen and Company is a firm that provides auditing services and generates a profit by charging fees for such services. Therefore, Arthur Andersen and Company is classified as a *private-sector service rendering organization*.

Public school districts provide educational services to children. School districts are financed primarily through the taxing authority of the federal

1

government, the state government, and the local school district. For these reasons, school districts are classified as *public-sector service rendering organizations*. This same designation can be applied to municipal governments, sewer districts, water districts, and fire districts because they all provide public services financed by some form of taxation.

All these organizations perform similar kinds of business and financial operations. The payroll operation is exactly the same at the Chrysler Corporation as it is at the Dade County Public School District in Miami, Florida: federal income tax is deducted; some employees are paid hourly while others are salaried; and fringe benefit programs are available with payroll deduction. In fact, it would be difficult to observe any difference in the job description of a payroll clerk either at the Chrysler Corporation or at the Dade County Public School District. Differences are usually found only with respect to the organization's mission and manner of financing.

It sounds trite to say that a price tag is attached to everything, but some school board members, teachers, and even administrators tend to forget this maxim when they plan for new programs or the expansion of existing services. However, many other board members, teachers, and administrators have felt the pain associated with cutting programs, activities, and personnel because of rising costs and shrinking fund balances and revenues.

The financial crunch that has hit many school districts over the last decade has heightened awareness of the importance of the business and finance divisions in school districts across the nation. However, most citizens and parents focus more on the service, education, that is rendered, rather than on the business operations of a district. This is never more apparent than when a school district places a tax increase proposition before the voters. Educators are sometimes stunned when such proposals are defeated, and they are unbelieving when taxpayers verbalize their opinion that more money is not needed.

This chapter will focus on two dimensions of public school districts. The first section will review the impact of education on the national economy, and the second section will concentrate on the management structure of the business and finance components of public school districts.

## Education and the National Economy

Much has been written lately regarding the value of education in the United States. School districts are constantly being pressured to justify and demonstrate their accountability for preparing the nation's youth to take their rightful place in the future of the country. Societal and technological changes in the past forty years have transformed the U.S. labor force from predominantly blue-collar industrial and manufacturing toward service industries. Within the recent past, the United States appears to have lost its competitive position in steel, automobiles, and textiles.[1] As a result, financial ramifications regarding the funding of educational programs are more crucial today than at any other time in the history of the country. Although the first seventy-five years of the twentieth century witnessed continual steady growth of the power of the United States and an increase in the standard of living of its citizens, the last seventeen years have seen an eroding of productivity and the loss of both jobs and entire industries to foreign competition. The lower costs of labor and productivity in Third World Countries have driven some U.S. industries to produce goods there in order to maintain competitiveness in the world economy.[2]

Within this context, the impact of financing education should be analyzed in two ways:

1. The contribution of American education as a provider of jobs and purchaser of goods and services in the community
2. The contribution of American Education in preparing the nation's youth to meet the challenges of a changing society whose economic base is moving from industrial and manufacturing toward service industries

Although it is customary to discuss education costs in light of federal and state subsidies as well as the impact of property taxes collected by local school districts, it is also useful to examine the spending side as it impacts the local community in particular and the nation in general.

## Impact of Educational Spending

The rate of unemployment is always one of the most significant factors affecting the welfare of a nation. Jobs create prosperity for all levels of society. As the decade of the 1980s was emerging, the nation was plagued with a recession, and by 1982 approximately 12 million Americans were out of work, which represented almost 11 percent of the labor force.[3] Many economists believed that the private sector was the most important vehicle for taking the country out of the recession through the creation of jobs. Government was asked to provide the necessary incentives through stimulation of economic growth in the private sector.[4] To this end, the Reagan Administration sought to reduce taxes in order to increase disposable income and cut government spending. Although these changes did stimulate development of the private sector, they ignored the importance of government in creating jobs directly in the public and private sectors. The number of people employed in public elementary and secondary education grew from 1.3 million in 1950 to 4.2 million by the fall of 1986.[5] During the same period, total expenditures for public education increased from $5.8 billion to $148.6 billion,[6] representing 4.1 percent of the U.S. Gross National Product.[7] The GNP represents the current market value of all goods and services produced in a given year. It consists of personal consumption expenditures, gross private domestic investment, government spending, and net exports (exports minus imports).[8]

One of the most significant characteristics of public education is its heavy dependence on local communities to provide the labor force. Although it is common for large metropolitan and suburban districts to recruit nationally for administrative and instructional staff, the vast majority of districts employ teachers and administrators from their local communities. Non-instructional staff, including secretaries, bus drivers, cooks, custodians, and maintenance personnel come almost exclusively from the local area regardless of the size and location of the district. In many of these communities, the local school district ranks among the largest employers in the area. In addition to jobs, these districts reinvest financial resources in the local and state business community through the spending of tax dollars for supplies, materials, utilities, and equipment. Because education is a labor-intensive industry, the average local school district budget allocates approximately 78.7 percent of all funds received for salaries, retirement contributions and fringe benefits. Of the remaining 21.3 percent, 3 percent is used for the payment of principal and interest on debt and 18.3 percent for all other operating expenses.[9] Therefore, at an annual expenditure of $148.6 billion in 1986, $116.95 billion was invested in salaries and related expenses, $4.46 billion for principal and interest and $27.19 billion for all other operating costs.

The impact of government and private spending on jobs was investigated by Rumberger in 1983. His research focused on the number of jobs generated by each billion dollars of government and private spending.[10] The data indicates that government spending, with the exception of transfer payments, produces more jobs per billion dollars spent than the same amount spent by the private-sector. Transfer spending refers to social security, unemployment compensation, and other social programs that provide direct aid to individuals. One of the most productive generators of jobs was found in expenditures by state and local governments (49,100 jobs per billion dollars), which included local school districts.

## Enrollment

The economic impact of school district spending, especially in the local community, can be affected by changes in student enrollment. From 1950 through 1971, enrollment grew rapidly as a result of the "baby boom" years immediately after World War II. By the 1971-72 school year, student enrollment in the elementary and secondary schools reached its peak of 46,081,000, then declined to a low of 39,352,000 during the 1984-85 school year. School districts experienced difficulty during those declining years adjusting to fewer students and increased cost per pupil.[11] For the first time in the history of U.S. education, districts were forced to reduce staff and close schools. The economic impact of this change in student population affected the respective communities in the same way as would the loss of jobs in the private sector. Since most state distribution programs were based on an allocation per pupil or percentage of budget, districts with rapidly declining enrollment faced the severe loss of state funds. In order to alleviate the financial strain, many states implemented "hold harmless clauses" allowing districts to claim an average loss of students over a period of time, rather than the actual loss each year. This gave districts time to adjust to the changing patterns of student enrollment. The decline in students did not necessarily correspond to an equal reduction in cost. Obviously, the costs of maintaining the school buildings, utilities, maintenance, and repairs were not drastically modified by fewer students in the building. Likewise, personnel costs did not immediately decrease. The ultimate decline from a class of thirty-five to twenty-five reduced the student-teacher ratio, but not the costs.

Enrollment began to shift once again during the 1985-86 school year, with slow steady growth from the low of 39,352,000 to 40,196,000 during the 1987-88 school year. Current projections are that enrollment in both private and public schools will grow steadily through the end of the century. By the year 2000, public elementary and secondary schools can expect an enrollment of 43,835,000. Private elementary and secondary schools can expect an enrollment of 5,695,000.[12]

Districts will experience a much easier time adjusting to slight increases in enrollment. Overall, per pupil expenditures will decrease, since existing personnel will easily handle slight increases. From 1983 through 1988, the western and southern states experienced the largest growth, while the eastern states experienced a loss of students during this five-year period.[13]

### Impact of Education on the Future Economy

The importance of education to the national economy was reviewed by Hornsby in his paper "Education and the Economy."[14]

> *Virtual unanimity exists among business, government and education that the industrial and manufacturing segments of the United States economy are in serious trouble. More importantly, the nation cannot maintain its present level of prosperity without them. No nation can prosper in a purely service economy.*[15]

Hornsby attributes the tremendous economic success of the United States during the twentieth century to the flexibility and innovation of U.S. education. The educational system produced a productive work force that led the world in technological development and innovation.

The present sophistication of the world economy demands that the educational system continue to produce the needed changes in technology to allow the United States to develop and maintain a competitiveness in the world market. The nation cannot sustain large numbers of people dependent on welfare with the base of contributions diminishing.[16] Approximately 28 percent of high school aged students dropped out of school in 1986. When compared with the 50 percent dropout rate in the 1950s, it would appear that the educational community is slowly resolving the problem. However, the nation was in a much more favorable position to accommodate that dropout rate in the 1950s than it is today. The complexity of the technology needed in today's market cannot tolerate a 28 percent undereducated work force. Enough jobs do not and will not exist to accommodate this number of the workers at that level. Therefore, the majority will have to depend on social programs for existence.[17]

The importance of education to economic development, economic growth and productivity growth was synthesized by Hornsby.

> *In all countries, at any stage of development, the share of resources allocated to education is an important factor in determining the rate and extent of economic development. Education may be the most significant factor in the rate of advance of scientific and technical knowledge; as well as in the speed and effectiveness with which research and development findings can become diffused and adopted by the productive units that make up the economy.*[18]

## The Business and Financial Components of School Districts

The business and finance division of a school district should be managed by an administrator who shares the superintendency. In other words, this person should be an assistant superintendent. Of course, other titles, such as *business manager*, may be used, but this position should be vested with that level of authority exercised by an assistant superintendent.

The size of the school district obviously will have a role in deciding who performs the business and financial services. In a very small school district, the superintendent will probably perform these operations. Further, the organizational structure of the business and finance division will depend on the size of the school district. The detailed organizational charts in Figures 1-1 to 1-7 show possible structural options for a large school district of approximately twenty-five thousand students.

It is important to keep in mind that all operations are common to all school districts. However, the smaller the district, the fewer people needed to perform business and financial services.

## Job Description for the Assistant Superintendent for Business

To begin this explanation of the business operation of a public school district, the job description of the administrator charged with managing this division is covered first.

### Position Summary

The assistant superintendent for business is responsible for the school district's administrative support program. The support program includes the establishment and maintenance of effective two-way communications with other divisions. The business operation affects all other operations in the school district. This will become more apparent as the organizational structure of a business and finance division is explained. As a preview, it should be sufficient to state that all employees receive a salary that is processed through the payroll department. Further, the assistant superintendent is responsible for the formulation, recommendation, and management of the district's business and finance policies and procedures.

### Organizational Relationship

The assistant superintendent for business has a line relationship with the superintendent of schools and reports directly to that position, serving as the chief advisor to the superintendent on business and financial matters. The assistant superintendent has a staff relationship with other administrators, which means that he or she must provide help and support to them. The assistant superintendent, of course, has a line relationship with his or her immediate staff and is responsible for evaluating their performance.[19]

### Organizational Tasks

The assistant superintendent is responsible for establishing and managing the policies, processes, and procedures necessary to carry out the business and financial services of the school district. This includes the following tasks: accounting, auditing, banking, budgeting, custodial services management, data processing management, inventory control, materials warehousing and distribution, payroll management, purchasing, and pupil transportation management.

### Experience and Education Requirements

There are a number of opinions concerning the minimal type and scope of experience and education that are appropriate for the position of assistant superintendent for business and finance. This author's position is as follows:

> A doctorate in educational administration
> A formal course of study in the areas of accounting, data processing, facility management, finance, school district administration, and school law
> Five years' experience in a central office administrative position

From time to time, the opinion emerges that the chief business and finance position in a school district should be occupied by a person with education in business administration rather than educational administration. Thus, the person should have the professional business degree of Master of Business Administration (M.B.A.) rather than the Doctor of Philosophy (Ph.D.) or Doctor of Education (Ed.D.) degree in educational administration.

This opinion is contrary to the current trend in other disciplines. A master's degree in public administration (M.P.A.) is a desired credential for the person seeking a position in municipal and state governmental agencies. Likewise, a master's degree in Hospital Administration (M.H.A.) is an example of a growing number of degree programs that recognize the importance of teaching management skills in the context of the unique needs of specialized organizations in our society.

This author firmly subscribes to the above premise. Public-sector educational service organizations, public school districts, require university-level administrator educational programs that are geared to the unique business and finance requirements of this type of organization.

The other administrators reporting to the assistant superintendent for business may have experience in public- or private-sector organizations and college or university degrees in private- or public-sector business disciplines such as a bachelor's degree in accounting.

## Departments of the Business and Finance Division

This section will identify the departments within the business and finance division. The caveat mentioned before still applies. Different school districts will have different organizational charts, but all districts perform the operations that will be described.

Each of the departments should be managed by a person who possesses not only the necessary technical skills, but also those supervisory skills that are necessary to lead the staff. Although it is not the intent of this book to examine human relations skills, it is important to understand that many problems in business divisions stem from poor interpersonal relations rather than from lack of technical expertise.

The following section presents a short overview of the organizational structure of the various departments in the business division and briefly describes the type of personnel specialists that each department requires.

### Accounting and Related Services Department

Figure 1-1 schematically presents the line relationship of the personnel in this department to the assistant superintendent and the director of accounting and related services. Further, it names the types of personnel specialists that usually work in such a department.

FIGURE 1-1 • *Organizational Chart of the Accounting and Related Services Department*

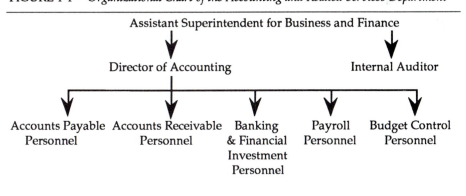

In larger districts, the director should be a certified public accountant (C.P.A.). In a small district, at least a bachelor's degree in accounting would be the minimal standard. A certified public accountant is more likely to have the background needed to understand the requirements expected by auditing firms examining public school districts. The demand of taxpayers for accountability makes it necessary for school districts to maintain *audit trails* that will ensure appropriate financial transactions.

The *accounts payable* staff is charged with paying invoices for purchased services, supplies, textbooks, equipment, and so on. This is typically accomplished by presenting to the board of education, at least once each month, a listing of the invoices to be paid. Most states require formal approval of this list by the board at an open meeting.

The *accounts receivable* staff monitors and records the revenue that the district is entitled to receive from local, state, and federal sources. The *banking and financial investment* staff manages the banking associated with the district's funds. This staff is usually responsible for investing those funds that are not immediately needed to satisfy the financial responsibilities of the district. The *payroll* staff carries out the procedures that are required in order to pay the salaries of the school district's employees. This includes all federal and state deductions and those deductions for fringe benefits programs that are not paid by the district. Monitoring the receipts and expenditures that have been budgeted is the responsibility of the *budget* control staff. Cash flow is the primary concern for the budget control staff, because the receiving of revenue and the paying of invoices are not always in balance. Thus, the district must develop a budget calendar to reflect this situation.

There is another staff member listed on the organizational chart who reports directly to the assistant superintendent and who does not supervise staff members: the *internal auditor*. This person's responsibility centers around monitoring the compliance of administrative procedures with board of education policies and with state and federal regulations. The complexity of operations in large school districts demands such a position because the usual checks and balances may not disclose problems until major harm has been done to the district. In small districts, the superintendent will perform this function.

### Purchasing and Materials Management Department
Figure 1-2 schematically presents the line relationship of the personnel in this department to the assistant superintendent and the director of purchasing and materials management.

FIGURE 1-2 • *Organizational Chart of the Purchasing and Materials Management*
*Department*

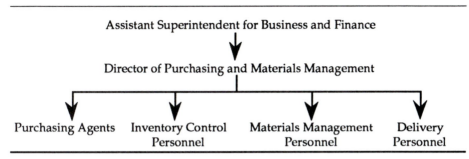

The director of purchasing and materials management is a key person in the support services area. Many school administrators and board of education members fail to understand the importance of this position. In fact, in districts with a pupil enrollment of over 10,000 students, the director should be a specialist in purchasing and materials management. This means that the person hired for such a position should have a college degree with a major in purchasing and materials management or significant experience in purchasing.

A well-organized school district will involve the director not only in the procurement process (purchasing supplies, materials, equipment, and services), but also in the materials management process (warehousing and delivery of supplies, materials, and equipment).

The *purchase of services* component refers to the process that is used to hire architects, attorneys, auditors, engineers, land surveyors, and so on. This process will be fully explained in Chapter 6. It is sufficient to say that many school districts overlook the talents of professional purchasing administrators.

The four components that comprise the purchasing and materials management department are purchasing, asset inventory control, warehousing, and delivery. Purchasing staff members are usually referred to as *purchasing agents*. They are charged with the responsibility of implementing the board of education policy and administrative procedures dealing with the taking of bids or quotations for supplies, materials, and equipment. Further, they are responsible for handling problems that might arise, such as the delivery of incomplete orders.

The *inventory control* staff has the responsibility of recording and keeping track of all equipment that belongs to the school district. There are numerous computerized fixed asset programs that can be purchased which also allow for entering a description of each item by means of a bar code that is scanned by an optical reader.

The purchasing and materials management model presented here is a centralized mode. Purchasing, receiving, and warehousing are under the control of a central office administrator.

The receiving, storage, and delivery of items are under the supervision of a *materials manager*. The warehouse staff receives the items and prepares them for delivery; the delivery staff brings them to the school and other buildings in the district.

### The Buildings and Grounds Department

Figure 1-3 presents the organizational chart for the buildings and grounds department. Like other departments, a director oversees the operations of the department and has a line relationship to the assistant superintendent. The components of the buildings and grounds department are: custodial services, grounds keeping, maintenance, parts, and inventory.

Everyone who has experience in teaching knows the importance of the buildings and grounds department. The teaching/learning process is either enhanced or hindered by the level of maintenance and custodial services available in a school district. Also, preventative maintenance pays off by saving the district a considerable amount of money in the future. For example, if replacement of a roof is delayed until multiple leaks cause damage to the structure itself and to equipment and furniture, the costs could amount to as much as twice the cost of the roof being replaced in a timely manner. Too often, schools defer maintenance of facilities especially if there is pressure from internal and external groups to raise the salaries of teachers and other employees beyond the limits the district can afford without cutting into non-personnel budgets.

FIGURE 1-3 • *Organizational Chart of the Buildings and Grounds Department*

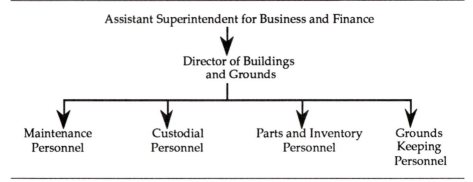

The *director of buildings and grounds* should have a university degree in architecture or engineering. The director will supervise *maintenance* staff members who should be skilled in such areas as carpentry, plumbing, and electrical work. Most large school districts will have a *parts and inventory* component, because much time is expended in ordering replacement parts. If the mechanical systems in district facilities such as the heating-ventilation-air conditioning (HVAC) system have been standardized, a supply of replacement parts can be readily available.

The *grounds keeping* crew not only cuts grass but also maintains shrubbery and trees. In states that experience winters with snowfall, the grounds keeping crew will be responsible for snow removal.

### The Data Processing Department

The organizational chart for this department is exhibited in Figure 1-4. Everyone employed in the data processing department will require some college training, and most should have at least a bachelor's degree in data processing. There are four categories of specialists that report to the director of data processing: programmer operator, programmer analyst, computer operator, and database analyst. Typically, this type of staff would not be needed if a given school district utilized microcomputers.

Rather, this organization of a data processing department is necessary where the school district is large enough to use a mainframe with software that computerizes all administrative functions and networks computer terminals at remote sites. For example, the supplies and materials budget for each school could be stored on-line in the mainframe. A principal could bring up the building budget and check the status of a supply order on a remote terminal located in the office.

FIGURE 1-4 • *Organizational Chart of the Data Processing Department*

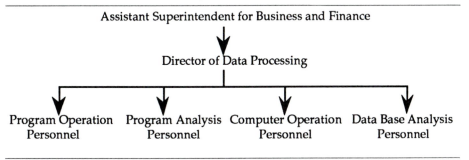

The entire staff in a data processing department performs operations that are completely interrelated. For the most part, this is also true in other departments, but not to the extent that it occurs in data processing. The *programmer analyst* is concerned with refining the software that is used to operate computer programs.  Operating the programs is the responsibility of the *programmer operator*. The *computer operator* needs to have a thorough understanding of how the computer hardware works, and the *database analyst* is concerned with the identification, input, and merging of different information that can be used to develop reports.

### The Pupil Transportation Department

The pupil transportation operation has come to the forefront in recent years for the same reason that air travel, railroads, and truck transportation have received such extensive coverage in the newspapers and on television. That reason is *safety*. Human error has been the cause of many accidents that resulted in the lost of human life. To compound the situation, drug use has been identified as a leading cause of human error. Thus, the testing of employees for drug abuse has become a major issue.

The organizational chart in Figure 1-5 presents the major components of a pupil transportation department. The *director of transportation* position has developed in scope and responsibility to the point that medium to large school districts have hired individuals with college degrees in transit or transportation management.

The hiring of *bus drivers* and *bus aides* now requires *transportation supervisors* to check thoroughly the backgrounds of prospective drivers and aides. Thus, supervisors need sharpened skills as they engage in the interviewing and selection process.

FIGURE 1-5 • *Organizational Chart of the Pupil Transportation Department*

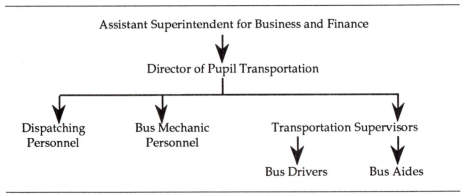

FIGURE 1-6 • *Organizational Chart of the Food Services Department*

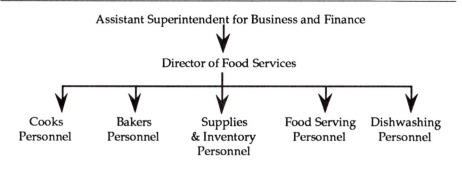

Other specialists in the transportation department include *bus mechanics* and *dispatching* personnel. The complexity of safety features on buses and the opportunity to utilize computerized routing have raised the qualifications for these positions.

### Food Services Department

Figure 1-6 represents an organizational chart for a typical food services department. A *director* supervises *cooks, bakers, food serving personnel, dish washing personnel, supplies,* and *inventory personnel.* Federal, state, and local governments have enacted regulations that tightly control food services activities. Sanitation in the preparation of food and the storage of supplies should be a concern of every staff member in this department. The controlling of costs and the setting of food prices are two concerns of every food services director, because these factors will determine the solvency of the food services program.

### Risk Management Department

Most school districts have not established a risk management department. The reasons for this are numerous. Perhaps the two most obvious reasons arise out of antiquated concepts about the insurance industry. School district administrators traditionally relegated the responsibility for protecting the district's fixed assets to insurance companies. Premium costs for policies were relatively low for the amount of protection desired by boards and administrators.

That all changed when premiums skyrocketed in the early eighties. School districts were faced with premiums that doubled, tripled, and even quadrupled over a few years. In fact, some districts with a small number of claims were dropped by companies for no apparent reason except that school districts posed a potential risk that insurance companies were no longer willing to assume. To meet this challenge, school district administrators began to take a hard look at the levels of liability that were uninsured. This examination provided the impetus to create risk management programs.

Figure 1-7 presents the organizational structure of a risk management department. Whenever money and availability allow, the *director of risk management* must be a professional with formal education in risk management and experience in the insurance industry. This area of responsibility is very complex, and improper procedures may involve the school district in claims amounting to millions of dollars.

There are six components to the risk management department developed for this presentation. Many administrators perceive risk management in a very narrow sense and do not understand the scope of such a program.

Perhaps the most critical position is that of *safety specialist.* This person is responsible for evaluating every aspect of district operations in order to identify potential risks. When potential risks have been identified, this staff member is responsible for finding ways of reducing the risk. For example, auditory fire alarms may not be heard by industrial arts classes when equipment is in use. Thus, a flashing light alarm should be installed in each industrial arts classroom. This would reduce the risk of injury to teachers and students due to an undetected fire.

*Security* personnel are concerned with protecting school district property and protecting students and staff members from possible harm. They may hire security guards or contract with a security company to patrol the district at night to deter vandalism and theft. The level of security needed depends on the type of community that the school district serves. A high crime area demands more extensive security measures.

FIGURE 1-7 • *Organizational Chart of the Risk Management Department*

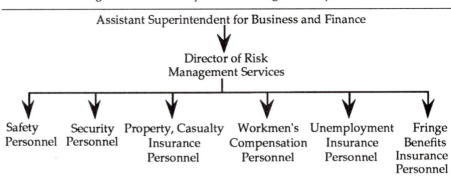

The *coordinator of property, casualty, and liability insurance* will be responsible for the procedures that are developed in reporting injuries and property damage or theft. Some large districts may find that *self insurance* is the most economical method of insuring against these risks. Thus, this person will be responsible for ensuring that proper procedures are followed in investigating claims and in reaching settlements.

In like manner, the staff members responsible for the *unemployment insurance* program and the *workers' compensation* program will be concerned with investigating claims and reaching settlements. The workers' compensation staff should work closely with the safety specialists in developing safety programs that will minimize the risk of accidents on the job.

Finally, the *fringe benefits* insurance specialists are responsible for monitoring the medical, hospitalization, dental, life insurance, retirement insurance, and similar programs. This has also become an area of particular concern. For example, the Internal Revenue Service has extensive regulations on Section 125 cafeteria fringe benefits plans. The loss ratio of a school district will determine the premiums that a district must pay and the amount of funds that the district must set aside in the budget for substitute workers. Investigating options for insurance coverage and packaging these options has become very important to school boards and administrators as they deal with the rising levels of health and other fringe benefit costs.

Once again it is important to remember that this presentation sets forth the obligations of the assistant superintendent for business along with the responsibilities of other administrators and personnel for a large school district in the business and finance division. Small and medium-size school districts have all these responsibilities but will not have the size staff so presented. Thus, these responsibilities will be collapsed into the job descriptions of fewer central office administrators and will probably become the responsibility of the superintendent in small districts.[20]

## Summary

Education will continue to occupy a major role in the economy of the United States. As a provider of jobs in the community and purchaser of goods and services, education impacts directly the economic well-being of local communities in both the public and private sectors. As this country moves into the twenty-first century, education is the only vehicle for preparing a productive work force for the tremendous technological changes necessary to maintain a competitive position in the world economy. This new economy cannot support the undereducated, as it has in the past, through low-level jobs.

The business and financial operations of public school districts are not substantially different from the business and financial operations of private-sector commercial and industrial companies. The financial crunch that has hit many school districts over the last decade has heightened awareness of the importance of the business and finance divisions in school districts across the nation.

The assistant superintendent for business is responsible for the school district's administrative support program. This person is responsible for establishing and managing the policies, processes, and procedures which are necessary to carry out the business and financial operations of the school district. These operations include the following tasks: accounting, auditing, banking, budgeting, custodial services management, data processing management, facility maintenance management, financial investing, food service management, insurance management, inventory control, materials warehousing and distribution, payroll management, purchasing, and pupil transportation management. Thus, departments are created within the business and finance division for the purpose of carrying out these tasks. Each department is staffed with people who have work experience and formal education appropriate for the execution of the tasks.

## Endnotes

1. H. Heyward Hornsby, "Education and the Economy," Paper presented at the Annual Meeting of the Southern Regional Council for Educational Administration (Gatlinburg, Tennessee: 1987), p. 2.

2. Russell W. Rumberger, *The Employment Impact of Government Spending* (Washington, D.C.: National Institute of Education, 1983), p. 1.

3. *Ibid.*

4. *Ibid.*

5. National Center For Educational Statistics, *Digest of Education Statistics, 1988*. Washington, D.C.: United States Department of Education, p. 83.

6. *Ibid.*, p. 31.

7. *Ibid.*, p. 29.

8. Jae K. Shim and Joel G. Siegel, *Encyclopedic Dictionary of Accounting and Finance* (Englewood Cliffs, New Jersey: Prentice-Hall, 1989), p. 218.

9. Glen E. Robinson and Nancy Protheroe, "Local School Budget Profiles Study," *School Business Affairs* (Vol. 57, No.9, September 1991), pp. 12-13.

10. Rumberger, *The Employment Impact of Government Spending*, p. 25.

11. *Digest of Educational Statistics*, Table 1.

12. *Ibid.*

13. *Ibid.*, Figure 9.
14. Hornsby, "Education and the Economy."
15. *Ibid.*, p.1.
16. *Ibid.*, p.1.
17. Ben Brodinsky and Katherine E. Keough, *Students at Risk: Problems and Solutions* (Arlington, Virginia: American Association of School Administrators, 1989), p. 19.
18. Hornsby, "Education and the Economy," p. 5.
19. Frederick W. Hill, *The School Business Administrator* (Reston, Virginia: Association of School Business Officials International, 1982), pp. 28-32.
20. *Ibid.*, pp. 18-27.

## Selected Bibliography

Association of School Business Officials International, *Major Topics of School Management in the Mid-1980's* (Reston, Virginia: The Association, 1984).

Association of School Business Officials International, *Management Techniques for School Districts* (Reston, Virginia: The Association, 1985).

Candoli, Carl, Walter G. Hack, John R. Ray, and Dewey H. Stollar, *School Business Administration: A Planning Approach* (Rockleigh, New Jersey: Allyn and Bacon, Inc., 1984).

Haverman, Robert, and Barbara Wolfe, *Education, Productivity, and Well-Being: On Defining and Measuring the Economic Characteristics of Schooling* (Washington, D.C.: National Institute of Education, 1982).

Hentschke, Gilbert C., *School Business Administration: Comparative Perspective* (Berkeley, California: McCutchan Publishing Corporation, 1986).

Hill, F. W., *The School Business Administrator*, 3rd ed. (Reston, Virginia: Association of School Business Officials International, 1982).

McGuffey, C. W., *Competencies Needed by Chief School Business Administrators* (Reston, Virginia: Association of School Business Officials International, 1980).

McNamara, Kevin T., and Brady J. Deaton, *Educational Expenditures and Education Measures* (Blacksburg, Virginia: Virginia Polytechnic Institute and State University, 1985).

Miles, F. Mike, "Introduction to School Business Management," in *Principles of School Business Management* (Reston, Virginia: Association of School Business Officials International, 1986),. pp. 13-22.

Morphet, Edgar L., Roe L. Johns, and Theodore L. Reller, *Educational Organizations and Administration: Concepts, Practices, and Issues*, 4th ed. (Englewood Cliffs, New Jersey: Prentice-Hall), 1982.

Rebore, Ronald W., *Educational Administration: A Management Approach* (Englewood Cliffs, New Jersey: Prentice-Hall, 1985).

Robbins, Stephen P., *Organization Theory: The Structure and Design of Organizations* (Englewood Cliffs, New Jersey: Prentice-Hall, 1983).

# 2

# Federal and State Aid to Education

The financing of public education in the United States is a cooperative effort between the federal government, the state government, and the local school district. Exhibit 2-1 is a summary of the historical funding of education by source from the 1919-20 school year through the 1986-87 school year.[1] During that period, federal and state subsidies increased substantially while local sources declined. Since 1919, the federal government has increased funding for education from .03 percent of the total education budget to 6.4 percent of a total expenditure from all sources of $158.8 billion during the 1986-87 school year. During the same period, state contributions increased from 16.5 percent to 49.8 percent, while local and intermediate sources of revenue decreased from 83.2 percent to 43.9 percent by the 1986-87 school year. Preliminary estimates for the 1989-90 school year indicate little change, with federal revenue at 6.3 percent, state revenue at 49.4 percent, and local revenue at 44.3 percent.

   This gradual increase in funding by both federal and state government was accompanied by an increase in control of education by the respective agencies on both levels. In exchange for dollars received, national and state agendas for education moved gradually from essentially a "hands-off" approach to significant control of both curricular and non-curricular programs. Although the specific subsidies by federal and state sources

EXHIBIT 2-1 • *Educational Funding by Source*

| Year | Total | Federal | State | Local | Total | Fed. | St. | Loc. |
|------|------:|--------:|------:|------:|------:|-----:|----:|----:|
| | | (Dollars in 000s) | | | | (Percent) | | |
| 1919-20 | 970,121 | 2,475 | 160,085 | 807,561 | 100.0 | 0.3 | 16.5 | 83.2 |
| 1929-30 | 2,088,557 | 7,334 | 353,670 | 1,727,553 | 100.0 | 0.4 | 16.9 | 82.7 |
| 1939-40 | 2,260,527 | 38,810 | 684,354 | 1,536,363 | 100.0 | 1.8 | 30.3 | 68.0 |
| 1949-50 | 4,311,534 | 155,848 | 2,165,689 | 3,105,507 | 100.0 | 2.9 | 39.8 | 57.3 |
| 1959-60 | 14,746,618 | 651,639 | 5,768,047 | 8,326,932 | 100.0 | 4.4 | 39.1 | 56.5 |
| 1969-70 | 40,266,923 | 3,219,557 | 16,062,776 | 20,984,589 | 100.0 | 8.0 | 39.9 | 52.1 |
| 1979-80 | 96,881,165 | 9,503,537 | 45,348,814 | 42,028,813 | 100.0 | 9.8 | 46.8 | 43.4 |
| 1986-87 | 158,827,473 | 10,145,899 | 79,022,572 | 69,659,003 | 100.0 | 6.4 | 49.8 | 43.9 |

varied by state, all states, with the exception of Hawaii, experienced greater dominance by these two levels of government. Hawaii, since statehood, has maintained a state school system with no local independent districts.

The most significant loss of local control of education occurred during the 1980s. On the heels of what began as a federal report on the need for educational reform, "A Nation at Risk" spurred several state reform movements with funding for specific programs aimed at increasing the productivity of local schools.[2] Local schools were required either through legislation or maintenance of state subsidies to modify curricular programs, increase testing requirements, or even change the organizational structure of the local school district.

Another significant occurrence of the late 1970s and early 1980s was the increase in litigation regarding the desegregation of public schools through either a mandated or voluntary interdistrict movement of school children to affect a racial balance in the schools. For the most part, the federal courts required the states to accept responsibility for desegregating the schools and funding the necessary programs (busing, magnet schools, etc.) to meet federal guidelines for racially balanced programs.

This chapter will briefly review the role of federal and state governmental aid to education. Although some historical review is necessary to understand the dynamics of change, the previous ten years will form the basis of the discussion.

## Federal Aid to Education

Although the U.S. Constitution makes no direct mention of education, interpretation of the Tenth Amendment forms the basis for the legal control of public education by the states. The Tenth Amendment provides that states are responsible for all matters not delegated to the federal government or specifically prohibited to the states. As a result, from 1787 through the first half of the twentieth century, the federal government provided little attention to education, except for property allocations and vocational programs. From this initial origin of planned neglect, federal intrusion into public education has gradually accelerated over the past thirty years.

Definite changes in the scope and administration of federal programs can be identified during two distinct periods from 1960 through 1990. A detailed analysis of educational programs in the 1960's and 1970's will reveal massive increases in categorical aid, while the period between 1980 through 1990 will be characterized by federal retrenchment and an overall decrease in funding, considering the necessary adjustments for inflation.

## Categorical Aid

During the 1960s and 1970s, several categorical aid programs were passed by Congress. In 1965, the Elementary and Secondary School Act (ESEA), with its various titles, doubled the amount of federal aid to education. Title I was a compensatory program for educationally deprived children from low-income families. This program, later to be known as Chapter 1, survived the major restructuring of federal aid to education under the Reagan Administration.

The Vocational Education Act of 1963, replaced by the Carl D. Perkins Act of 1984, moved beyond the rigid requirements of previous legislation by providing additional funding and expanding the categories of eligible participants. Under this legislation, individuals attending high school, those who had completed high school, those employed who needed additional training, and handicapped students previously prohibited from participation in vocational programs were now eligible for assistance. Funding for vocational programs increased from $225,000,000 in 1966 to $908,781,000 in 1987.[3] Vocational education retained its categorical prominence through the eighties and expanded its funding to single parents and homemakers.

In 1975 Congress passed Public Law 94-142, the Education for All Handicapped Children Act. This act required access to public education for all handicapped children. As with most federal programs, the local school districts receive funds through their respective state departments of education. Each district is required to identify all handicapped children and provide services appropriate to the handicapping condition. States receive a flat grant for each child identified as handicapped. The maximum grant available to each state is equal to its number of handicapped children served multiplied by 40 percent of the average per-pupil expenditure in the United States.[4] In order to discourage over-identification, a cap of 12 percent of the student enrollment was instituted as the maximum number of handicapped student funding within a district. Discretionary funding for handicapped 3- to 5-year-olds and early intervention services for handicapped children from birth through age 2 were added in the 1980s. Funding has increased from $250 million at its inception to over $3.3 billion in 1987. In 1991, the "Education for All Handicapped Children Act" was renamed the "Individuals with Disabilities Education Act."

With increased funding for categorical programs, the federal government's control over education increased steadily between 1960 and 1980. Federal regulations mandated that funding to one program within a school district subjected any other program or activity to regulation. Therefore, school districts spent considerable time and effort preparing necessary forms to indicate compliance with all federal regulations. "Increased federal activity involved a manifold increase in regulatory behavior, standards, and procedures imposed by various governmental agencies pertaining to the enforcement of the law (Office of Civil Rights, Equal Opportunity Commission, Environmental Protection Agency, etc.)."[5]

## Education Consolidation and Improvement Act (ECIA)

In 1981, President Reagan signed the Educational Consolidation and Improvement Act (ECIA), which eliminated many of the categorical grant programs under the Elementary and Secondary School Act in favor of block grants. Although the Reagan Administration was successful in restructuring federal aid to schools, Title I programs (identified as Chapter 1 under ECIA) for disadvantaged children and aid to handicapped children escaped the consolidation strategy.

President Reagan initially sought to consolidate forty-four specific education programs, including Title I and aid to handicapped children, into block grants, and to cut the total funding by 25 percent.[6] The administration expressed the belief that state and local school districts were in the best position to determine how to spend federal funds. The block grant approach would eliminate "burdensome federal regulations and paperwork, which educators had long complained about."[7] It was suggested that the 25 percent reduction would be offset by savings through dismantling the bureaucracy needed to regulate the categorical programs. The critics of this approach argued that without sufficient federal safeguards, proponents of specific programs would literally fight among themselves for the reduced available aid, with poor school districts losing the most. As a result, the administration was able to replace only some forty-four small categorical programs with block grants, while retaining the large compensatory programs under Chapter 1, Aid to the Handicapped, Vocational Education, and what was known as Part B of the Impact Aid Programs (to be discussed later). Federal funding was appropriated through 1988.

## Omnibus Education Act of 1988

Congress approved an $8.3 billion re-authorization bill of federal aid to elementary and secondary schools in 1988. This legislation retained both the compensatory and block grant programs initially passed in 1981 with few modifications. The major provisions of the act are summarized below by program.

### Compensatory Education (Chapter 1)

This program was reauthorized through 1993 to help educationally deprived children from low-income families. Remedial reading and mathematics programs comprised the basis for most Chapter 1 programs throughout the United States. The following is a summary of the significant features of this program.

A. *Basic Grants* Distribute funds to state departments of Education for allocation to local districts based on the number of children ages 5 through 17 from families below the poverty level. A minimum number of ten children must be identified for the district to receive basic grant funds.

B. *Concentration Grants* School districts with high concentrations of students from low-income families receive additional funds. Any district enrolling more than 6500 qualified students or where low-income students represented at least fifteen percent of the total enrollment would qualify for additional funds. This funding was to be available only for Congressional appropriation between $3.9 billion and $4.3 billion. Appropriations exceeding $4.3 billion would result in 10 percent of the total appropriation available for concentration grants.

C. *Use of Funds* Chapter 1 funds were reserved for schools with the highest concentration of low-income children. If the available funds did not meet the needs within the district, schools with the highest concentration would be serviced first. School districts are required to conduct an annual needs assessment identifying educationally deprived children and the areas that Chapter 1 programs should entail.

D. *Parental Involvement* Chapter 1 requires the local district to involve parents in the planning and implementation of programs. The district must present the Chapter 1 application and description of services to a parent advisory panel for approval. If necessary, language must be modified to allow complete understanding of the proposed program.

E. *Private Schools* Specific allocations of funds are reserved for Chapter 1 programs for educationally deprived children enrolled in private and parochial schools. These funds were designed for capital expenses such as mobile units and computer equipment.[8]

F. *Even Start* This program was created to extend Chapter 1 services to children from ages 1 through 7. Federal government program costs were limited to 90 percent in the first year, 80 percent in the second, 70 percent in the third, and 60 percent in all succeeding years.

G. *Secondary Schools* By authorization through 1993, Congress provided funds for the development of dropout prevention programs and basic skill improvement of educationally deprived secondary school students. Local districts were required to allocate these funds to those schools within the district with the highest number of poverty level students and dropout rates.

### Block Grants (Chapter 2)

The 1988 legislation retained the program of block grants established in 1981 and authorized funding of $610 million in 1990 to $706 million in 1993.[9] Like Chapter 1, funds are allocated to the local districts through the state. Up to 20 percent of the funds may be retained by the state for administration of the program, with 80 percent distributed to local districts. Chapter 2 funds are limited to the following six areas:

1. Programs for at-risk students most likely to drop out of school.
2. Purchase of instructional materials including library resources, computer software, and so on.
3. Innovative programs for district-wide improvement programs, including "effective schools." Twenty percent of the authorized funds are earmarked specifically for effective school programs emphasizing system-wide planning and improvement of the academic achievement of students.
4. In-service programs for instructional personnel.
5. Programs for personal excellence, such as classes in ethics, performing and creative arts, physical fitness, and health.
6. Innovative programs for gifted and talented students, early childhood programs, and suicide prevention strategies.

Chapter 2 funds were also authorized to continue the National Diffusion Network, the Inexpensive Book Distribution Program (Reading Is Fundamental), Arts in Education, Law Related Education, and the creation of a new program called "Blue Ribbon Schools" to recognize excellent elementary and secondary schools throughout the country. The legislation required funding at 5 percent above the 1987 level.

### Math and Science
The 1988 legislation authorized $250 million for grants to state and local educational agencies to strengthen the skills of teachers in the area of math and science. The distribution formula of the funds to the states incorporated both a flat grant based on enrollment and Chapter 1 eligibility. Of the available funds, 50 percent are distributed to the states on a per pupil basis. The remaining 50 percent are distributed based on the Chapter 1 poverty guidelines. Twenty-five percent of the authorization was earmarked for establishing preparation programs at colleges and universities for new teachers majoring in math or science.

### Satellite Technology
Over a five-year period, $100 million was authorized to introduce satellite technology into the classroom. State education agencies, local school districts, consortiums, and universities are allowed to prepare grant proposals for equipment purchases and instructional programming.

### Magnet Schools
School districts participating in a desegregation plan to attract students of diverse racial and social backgrounds were eligible for funds to develop magnet schools specializing in one or more academic programs. While some discussion centered on making funds available to any district, the current authorization limits funding to desegregation programs. The act authorized $165 million in 1989 for this purpose.

### Drug Education
The act re-authorized the Drug Free Schools and Communities Act through 1993 at a funding level of $250 million. In addition to local districts, 50 percent of the funds were made available to public and private non-profit organizations for drug and alcohol education, prevention and early intervention programs; training programs for teachers, parents, and local public service personnel; and a youth suicide prevention program. The remaining fifty percent were to be targeted to community based programs for high-risk youths such as dropouts and children of drug and alcohol abusers.[10]

### Special Programs

In addition to the programs mentioned above, the Omnibus Education Act provided funds for new programs concerning the needs of gifted and talented students, alternative schools, and child development programs.

The gifted and talented authorization provided grants to be used for preparing teachers, creating model programs, and providing technical assistance in the areas of data collection and evaluation. Funds for alternative curriculum programs were developed to provide grants to local districts not eligible for magnet schools funding. Grant proposals were limited to school districts with at least 65 percent minority population, and schools within the district with a 50 percent minority enrollment. Child development program funds were authorized for parenting classes, child care, and nutrition programs. However, funding for these programs during the first two years would only occur if Head Start was funded at 104 percent of the 1988 appropriation.

## Other Federal Programs for Education

### Federal Impact Aid

In 1950, Congress passed P.L. 81-874, providing funds for school districts with large concentrations of federal employees and federal installations. The aid was designed to replace the revenue lost to school districts as a result of tax-exempt federal property within the boundaries of the school district. The law is divided into the following two categories:

*Part A.* Provides funds for maintenance and operations of school facilities where enrollments and local revenue are adversely affected by federal activities such as military bases, government offices, Indian Lands, and low-rent public housing.

*Part B.* Provides funds to school districts who educate children whose parents either work or live on federal property.

The original act identified sixteen categories of students creating eligibility for Impact Aid. The Education Consolidation and Improvement Act of 1981 contained a provision eliminating Impact Aid by 1984 to district students whose parents either lived or worked on federal property, but not both. The Omnibus Education Act of 1988 retained Part A funds and extended Part B until 1993.

Since its inception, Impact Aid has continuously been the target for cost-conscious legislators. Part B funds have reached a point that most school districts often incur more expenses to collect the necessary data than they receive in the allocation.

**Nutrition Programs**

*National School Lunch Act of 1946*
The school lunch program was established by Congress in 1946. By 1980, it was providing federal support for 4.4 billion lunches served each school year to 27 million students in elementary and secondary schools. Although several changes have been made over the years, it still remains the one federal aid program most used by the majority of public and private schools in the United States. Children of families earning less than 130 percent above the poverty level are entitled to a free lunch. Reduced-price lunches are available to families with incomes up to 185 percent above the poverty level. All paid lunches are subsidized through direct payment for each lunch served, as well as food commodities delivered to the schools. The Department of Agriculture requires that each lunch include at least one half pint of milk, a slice of bread, two ounces of meat or other protein-rich food, and three-quarters of a cup of fruits and vegetables. Subsequent changes in the requirements allowed some substitutions, as long as the overall meal was nutritiously balanced. In 1981, schools were allowed to give elementary students the option of refusing food they did not intend to eat.

*Child Nutrition Act of 1966*
A school breakfast program was established through a method similar to the lunch program in the Child Nutrition Act of 1966. On July 1, 1989, new breakfast regulations were implemented. Four food items must now be offered rather than only three. Each breakfast must contain one half pint of milk and one half cup of fruit, vegetable, or juice. In addition, one of the following options must be offered to meet minimum requirements:

> Two servings of bread or bread alternate; or
> Two servings of meat or meat alternate; or
> One serving of bread or bread alternate and one serving of meat or meat alternate.

Exhibit 2-2 represents the current reimbursement rates for the 1989-90 school year.

Schools serving 60 percent or more of free and reduced lunches receive larger subsidies than districts with less than 60 percent. The maximum charge for reduced lunches is 40 cents and for breakfast is 30 cents. Direct commodity distribution averages approximately an equivalent of 20 cents per lunch.

EXHIBIT 2-2 • *Reimbursement Rates*

| *School Lunch Program* | | *Effective July 1, 1989* |
|---|---|---|
| Districts serving less | Paid | $0.1475 |
| than 60 percent free and | Reduced | 1.1325 |
| reduced lunches in 1987-88 | Free | 1.5325 |
| Districts serving | Paid | 0.1675 |
| 60 percent or more free | Reduced | 1.1525 |
| and reduced | Free | 1.5525 |
| lunches in 1987-88 | | |
| *Maximum Reduced Price Charge* | | *40 Cents* |
| *Special Milk Program* | | |
| Schools and split- | Reduced | .1025 |
| session kindergarten | Free | Actual Cost |
| classes not in lunch | | |
| and/or breakfast program. | | |
| *School Breakfast Program* | | |
| Schools that served less | Paid | 0.1750 |
| than 40 percent free and reduced | Reduced | 0.5600 |
| lunches in 1987-88 | Free | 0.8600 |
| Schools that served | Paid | 0.1750 |
| 40 percent or more free and | Reduced | 0.7200 |
| reduced lunches in 1987-88 | Free | 1.0200 |
| Maximum Reduced Price Charge | 30 Cents | |
| *Food Distribution Program* | | |
| Total value of open-order commodities | 20 cents per lunch | |

*Special Milk Program* Included in the Child Nutrition Act of 1966 was a special milk program offering subsidies for milk purchases by all students. However, in 1988, the program was changed to provide milk subsidies only to children eligible for free or reduced lunch or to students without access to a lunch program. In most schools, children attending half-day kindergarten classes qualify for the subsidy. Districts receive the actual cost of a half pint of milk for each child who qualifies for a free lunch and 10.25 cents for each child who qualifies for reduced lunch.

Federal funding for education grew significantly between 1965 and 1989, with the greatest increase occurring between 1965 and 1975. During this period, federal funds for elementary and secondary education rose 189 percent (adjusted for inflation). While federal funding remained relatively stable from 1975 through 1980, it decreased 17 percent from 1981 through 1989.[11]

The *Digest of Education Statistics* provides the following analysis concerning federal aid to education for fiscal years 1980 through 1989.

> *Between fiscal years 1980 and 1989, Department of Education obligations rose by about 14 percent, after adjustment for inflation. Funds for student financial assistance increased to $10.5 billion in 1989, a rise of 37 percent. Funds for elementary and secondary education stood at an estimated $6.1 billion in 1989, a decline of about 3 percent since 1980.*[12]

Federal aid to education will continue to provide significant funding through categorical and block-grant programs. However, it appears that although the present administration contends that education is a priority, dramatic increases, except for small, high-impact programs such as drug prevention, will not be forthcoming.

## State Aid to Education

Throughout the history of public education, revenue sources available to state government and local school districts have provided the primary funding for the delivery of educational services to the local community. Even though the federal government is often portrayed as a significant source of funds, federal aid only accounts for approximately 6 percent of all revenue available to local districts. State expenditures for education, on the other hand, increased from 16 percent during the 1919–20 school year to approximately 49 percent during the 1986-87 school year. The traditional role of state government as the provider of public education has grown substantially from little funding and governance to large expenditures and closer control of local school districts. This control was heightened during the 1980s as a result of public interest in education introduced by the Reagan Administration's publication of "A Nation at Risk." State legislators, feeling the pressure from constituents, introduced legislation in almost every state aimed at strengthening curricular programs and instituting statewide testing programs to measure student achievement. Governors, representing the fifty states, formed an alliance to address the failure of public education to meet the needs of today's youth. Programs were identified and studied with the hopes of correcting many of the deficiencies attributed to present educational programs.[13] With a few notable exceptions, professional educators found themselves outside the "reform movement" and forced into a posture of reacting to the changes being developed through state and federal agendas.

Within this environment of close scrutiny of public education, many states mandated new programs without additional funding sources. A corollary of the "reform movement" contended that improved educational services did not mean additional dollars to education, but a restructuring of the present programs to effect a more efficient use of public funds. As a result, many of the basic grant or foundation programs designed to guarantee equity of educational opportunity were "watered down" in order to find dollars to implement new programs. This approach was set in motion by the federal agenda to reduce rather than increase taxes to fund government services. This philosophy of taxation became one of the most influential campaign promises of many national and state candidates for public office. As a whole, the country was not interested in tax increases to fund changes and additional programs.

This section examines the state sources of revenue, the states' role in funding education, and the fiscal issues of the reform movement.

## State Sources of Revenue

States rely heavily on sales and use, income, gasoline, and cigarette taxes to finance all government services. With the exception of Alaska, Delaware, Montana, New Hampshire, and Oregon, which levy no sales taxes, this tax represents approximately 37 percent of all state revenue sources. The income tax, both individual and corporate, amounts to 28 percent of revenue. As of 1988, Nevada, South Dakota, Texas, Washington, and Wyoming did not levy any corporate or individual income taxes. Alaska and Florida collect corporate income taxes but have no individual income tax requirements. All states currently collect taxes on gasoline and the sale of tobacco.[14]

## State Distribution Formulas

Every state distributes funds to local school districts to provide educational services to the community. The basis of this distribution is to provide a degree of equity of educational opportunity to all students within the state. Although each state applies its own concept of equity to the funding process, several patterns have emerged that allow some comparison and classification of funding mechanisms. Essentially, the following three basic methods, or a combination of them, have been developed by the states to finance the basic educational programs of local school districts:

1. Foundation Programs
2. Power Equalizing Programs
3. Full State Funding[15]

## Foundation Programs

The concept of equity of educational opportunity implies that each student within a state is guaranteed an educational program designed to meet the student's needs. However, since many students require programs above and beyond the normal curriculum, states have had to complement their funding through specific mechanisms designed to provide more dollars for these programs. Program funding for special education, vocational education and gifted programs allows districts to offer programs for students meeting specialized criteria. These programs will be discussed in detail later in the chapter. As a result of the many needs of today's students, foundation programs have evolved from the theoretical dimension of guaranteeing equal educational programs to all students to equal dollars spent per student or instructional unit in regular educational programs. Since most states do not have enough revenue to fully fund foundation programs, formulas have been developed that combine state funding with local revenue generated by a minimal required fixed tax rate. The state requires the district to levy a specific tax rate on all property within the district, and the state allocation is the difference between the amount raised by the local district and the amount of dollars guaranteed by the state to each pupil or instructional unit.[16] The equalizing component of the formula ensures equity of dollars regardless of the wealth of the local district. Theoretically, a wealthy district with a large tax base will receive less state aid because the minimal required tax rate will raise significantly more funds than a district with a lower tax base. Thus, each district will receive the same amount per pupil or instructional unit, with the state contributing more dollars in the less wealthy districts. If this formula is taken to its logical conclusion, an extremely wealthy district collecting more than the state guarantee through the minimal tax levy should rebate the excess amount back to the state for redistribution to other districts. This is referred to as the recaptured cost.[17] However, states are reluctant to require districts to allocate locally generated funds to the state. Therefore, the district is usually allowed to retain all locally generated funds. In some states, local districts are even guaranteed a minimum state allocation regardless of the total local revenue. These factors, although contrary to the concept of equity, are the political realities of financing education. As a result, equalizing mechanisms work only to the extent that the required local revenue is less than the state guarantee.

Example 2-1 may clarify this funding approach. If State A guarantees $2,000 per pupil and requires each district to levy a tax rate of $1.25 (12.5 mills for each one hundred dollars of assessed valuation), the calculation shown in the example would determine the state allocation.

*Equalized Funding Per Pupil* Twenty-four states currently allocate state funds through a foundation program on a per pupil basis. Each requires a minimum local levy that is subtracted from the state guaranteed amount per pupil. In all instances, state expenditures through the foundation program are offset by a required levy often referred to as "local effort."

*Equalized Instructional Units* As of the 1988-89 school year, seven states distribute funds to local districts by equalized instructional units. Similar to per pupil funding, districts receive the difference between the state guaranteed amount per units and the local revenue received from a required local levy.

### Power Equalizing Programs

Unlike foundation programs aimed at equalizing funds allocated on a per pupil or per instructional unit basis, power equalizing concentrates on the ability of the local district to support the programs offered to the community. As a result, power equalizing provides a structure for equalizing the local districts ability to raise funds. The total amount of funds raised is left to the local district.[18] Guaranteed tax base, guaranteed yield, and percentage equalizing are three variations of power equalizing currently used by some states.

*Guaranteed Tax Base* This mechanism for funding local district programs guarantees each district the same assessed valuation per pupil. The district constructs its budget based on the guaranteed tax base and then levies a tax rate on the district's actual assessed valuation. The difference between local revenue generated by the district's actual assessed valuation and the guaranteed tax base is paid by the state. Example 2-2 provides the basic computation of this approach.

*Guaranteed Tax Yield* Another form of power equalizing is the guaranteed tax yield. The state guarantees a per pupil yield for each penny or mill levied. For example, a state may guarantee $100 per pupil for each 10 cents or 1 mill levied by the district. The state funds the difference between local revenue received from the levy and the state guarantee. Example 2-3 demonstrates a district's allocation by this method.

EXAMPLE 2-1

District A
    State Aid = $2000 Per Pupil—Local Tax Revenue
    Assessed Valuation = $100,000,000

$$\frac{\$100,000,000}{100} \cdot 1.25 = \$1,250,000$$

or

$$\frac{\$100,000,000}{100} \cdot \frac{12.50}{10} \text{ mills} = \$1,250,000$$

Pupils = 1000

$$\frac{\$1,250,000}{1000} = \$1250 \text{ Per Pupil}$$

State Aid   = $2000 – 1250.
          = $750.00 · 1000 Pupils
          = $750,000

District B
    State Aid = $2000 Per Pupil—Local Tax Revenue
    Assessed Valuation = $150,000,000

$$\frac{\$150,000,000}{100} \cdot 1.25 = \$1,875,000$$

or

$$\frac{\$150,000,000}{100} \cdot \frac{12.50}{10} \text{ mills} = \$1,875,000$$

Pupils = 1000

$$\frac{\$1,875,000}{1000} = \$1875 \text{ Per Pupil}$$

State Aid   = $2000 - 1875
          = $125 · 1000 Pupils
          = $125,000

District C
    State Aid = $2000—Local Tax Revenue
    Assessed Valuation = $200,000,000

$$\frac{\$200,000,000}{100} \cdot 1.25 = \$2,500,000$$

or

$$\frac{\$200,000,000}{100} \cdot \frac{12.50}{10} \text{ mills} = \$2,500,000$$

Pupils = 1000

$$\frac{\$2,500,000}{1000} = \$2500 \text{ Per Pupil}$$

State Aid  = 00—Current local revenue per pupil is higher than the state guarantee.

If state law provides that no district will receive less than $100 per pupil, District C would receive $100,000, even though local revenue is above the current state guarantee.

---

*EXAMPLE 2-2*

---

Guaranteed tax base = $300,000 Per Pupil
Total number of pupils = 1000
The district's budget will reflect revenue equal to an assessed valuation of $300,000,000 (1000 · 300,000).
District tax rate $1.25 or 12.5 mills
District assessed valuation = $200,000,000

Guaranteed tax base = $\dfrac{\$300,000,000}{100} \cdot \$1.25 \text{ or } \dfrac{12.5}{10} \text{ mills}$

Total guaranteed revenue = $3,750,000

Guaranteed revenue per pupil = $\dfrac{\$3,750,000}{1000} = 3750$

Local revenue = $\dfrac{\$200,000,000}{100} \cdot 1.25 \text{ or } \dfrac{12.5}{10} \text{ mills}$

Local revenue = $2,500,000

Local revenue per pupil = $\dfrac{\$2,500,000}{1000} = \$2500$

State aid = $3750 – $2500 = $1250 Per Pupil
Total state aid = $1250 · 1000 Pupils = $1,250,000

---

*EXAMPLE 2-3*

---

Guaranteed yield $100 per pupil for each 1 mill or each 10 cents levied.
Total pupils = 1000
Guaranteed yield = 1000 · $100.00 = $100,000
District assessed valuation = $80,000,000
District local revenue per 1 mill or 10 cents per $100 of assessed valuation.

$$\text{District revenue yield} = \frac{\$80,000,000}{100} \cdot \frac{1\,mill}{10} = \$80,000$$

or

$$\text{District revenue yield} = \frac{\$80,000,000}{100} \cdot .10 = \$80,000$$

$$\text{Per student yield} = \frac{\$80,000}{1000} = \$80$$

State allocation = $100 – $80 = $20 Per Student
Total state allocation = $20 · 1000 = $20,000

---

*Percentage Equalizing*  A third variation of power equalization is percentage equalizing, which allows each district to develop its own budget with the state paying a percentage of the budget based on the district's aid ratio. The ratio is determined by the district's assessed valuation per pupil in relation to the average assessed valuation per pupil in the state. Example 2-4 is an illustration of the percentage equalizing technique.

New York and Rhode Island currently use percentage equalization as the basic funding of local school districts. During the 1989-90 school year, a district of average wealth in New York received 36 percent of its budget from the state; Rhode Island guarantees a state allocation of no less than 28.5 percent regardless of wealth.[19]

### Full State Funding

Only one state, Hawaii, has full state funding. There are no local districts. Education is the total responsibility of the state, and all public schools are completely funded at that level.

### Pupil Weighting

As noted above, the basic tenet of both foundation and power equalizing programs is to provide equal dollars for educational programs. However,

EXAMPLE 2-4

---

District assessed valuation = $80,000,000
Total pupils = 1000

District assessed valuation per pupil = $\dfrac{80,000,000}{1000}$

District assessed valuation per pupil = $80,000
District aid ratio = .50
State average assessed valuation per pupil = $108,000

Percentage Equalization = $\dfrac{80,000}{108,000} \cdot .50 = 37\%$

The district will fund 37% of the budget from local revenue and the state will fund 63% through a state allocation.

---

some students require programs to meet specialized needs, and these programs often require additional expenditures. One way to provide for these differences is to assign a weighting factor to these students by counting them as more than one pupil. This mechanism provides additional funding through either the foundation programs or any of the power equalizing methods. Weighting systems are not based on actual expenditures of the local district; they assume that district costs will exceed the per pupil or per instructional unit cost of the regular programs. Therefore, districts receive the funds based on the number of pupils in each category times the weighted factor. Weighting is most common for special education programs, vocational programs, gifted programs, compensatory programs for the economically deprived, and grade level differences. The advantages of weighting distributions is the recognition that specialized programs will require higher per pupil or program costs. While many of these programs, such as special education, are required by law, some programs are left to district discretion. The weighted factors provide a necessary incentive for district participation. The disadvantages of the pupil weighting mechanism are limited to basically two areas. First, the additional revenue is not directly related to actual costs incurred by the district. As a result, there is a normal tendency to develop the programs based on the available dollars, whether or not the funds are sufficient to adequately offer the service. Second, the individual weights must be continually updated to account for any changes in the program. Often, specialized program costs increase at a faster rate than regular program costs.

*Special Education*  Twenty-one states currently use a weighting system to fund special education programs. In most cases, each handicapping condition is weighted differently. Exhibit 2-3 is an example of the weighting units assigned to special education students. Each special education pupil is counted times the weighting factor. The weighting factor is determined by the anticipated cost of each program. From the weights assigned, for example, it can be assumed that a hearing-impaired student will require a program costing approximately 2.3 times the cost for a regular student.

*Grade Level Differences*  Twenty-eight states currently differentiate between grade levels, assigning a higher weight to specific grade configurations. In a few instances, the weighting is restricted to half-day kindergarten students counted as 0.5 of a full-day student. In other instances, differences are specified between elementary, junior high, and senior high school students. An illustration of grade weights assigned to students is presented in Exhibit 2-4.

The underlying assumption is that the cost of educational programs increases as the student moves from a self contained classroom in the elementary schools to a departmentalized curriculum in junior high school and to a more specialized curriculum in high school.

*Compensatory Educational Programs*  Many states provide additional funds for compensatory programs for both the economically and educationally deprived students. Weighting is usually limited to those students on free or reduced lunch, receiving Chapter 1 services, receiving aid to dependent children, and scoring below statewide standards in reading and/or mathematics.

EXHIBIT 2-3 • *Special Education Program Weights*

| Category | Weight |
|---|---|
| Hearing Impaired | 2.312 |
| Multiple Handicapped (Resource) | 0.762 |
| Multiple Handicapped (Self-Contained) | 2.368 |
| Physically Handicapped (Resource) | 0.603 |
| Physically Handicapped (Self-Contained) | 2.648 |
| Trainable Mentally Handicapped | 2.042 |
| Visually Handicapped | 2.900 |
| Multiple Handicapped (Severe Sensory Impaired) | 4.000 |
| Severely Emotionally Handicapped | 1.500 |

EXHIBIT 2-4 • *Grade Level Per Pupil Weighting*

| Grade | Weight |
|-------|--------|
| K | 0.5 |
| 1-6 | 1.0 |
| 7-8 | 1.2 |
| 9-12 | 1.4 |

*Vocational and Gifted Programs*  The final category of programs most often funded through a weighted mechanism are vocational and gifted programs. The reliance of vocational programs on changes in technology requires additional funding. In addition to the cost of equipment, these programs are often limited in enrollment and require specialized physical facilities. Gifted programs are usually characterized by a low student/teacher ratio and, in some cases, a more significant use of technology.

### Reimbursement Programs

Another common method of funding specialized programs is to reimburse local districts for either the actual cost or a percentage of the cost of the program. The advantage of this type of funding is that actual program costs are known before the funding is provided. Unlike weighting mechanisms, which assume that each program will incur the same costs in each district, reimbursement funding acknowledges that the costs of the same service may vary from district to district. Although many of the same programs funded in some states through a weighting process are funded in others through reimbursement, the most common reimbursement programs are in special education, transportation, capital outlay, and vocational programs. Exhibit 2-5 is an example of reimbursable costs offered by several states.

EXHIBIT 2-5 • *Reimbursable Rates*

| Category | Reimbursable Rate |
|----------|-------------------|
| Capital Outlay | 60 percent of Approved Projects |
| Transportation | 80 percent of Allowable Costs |
| Special Education | 75 percent of Actual Salaries |
| Vocational Education | 80 percent of Actual Costs |

The disadvantage of reimbursement programs is directly related to the efficiency of the district's operation. A reimbursement program not tied to a measure of efficiency provides no incentive for districts to operate the programs in the most cost-efficient manner. As a result, many states have restricted reimbursement to those programs operating usually within a specified level related to the state average. For example, Missouri will only reimburse transportation costs at 80 percent if a district's operating costs are below 125 percent of the state average. Approximately nine states currently reimburse districts for capital outlay, thirty nine reimburse transportation costs, fifteen offer varying reimbursement for special education, and twelve provide reimbursement for vocational education.

### Flat Grants

The final method of financing local district programs is a flat grant by the state. These grants have some of the same characteristics of weighted programs. Since they are not directly related to actual costs, the district is limited to the same amount received by all districts regardless of local wealth. As a result, the grants have to be continually revised to account for increases in costs associated with the specific programs. Capital outlay and special education programs are the most common vehicles for flat grants distributed by states.

## The Reform Movement

The issue of equity of educational programs and dollars has been the primary focus of both federal and state funding programs for local school districts. During the 1960s and 1970s, federal compensatory and categorical programs were structured to provide services to the most needy students in school districts that did not have the wealth to offer these programs. State foundation programs and power equalizing systems were implemented to provide equal financial resources to guarantee a basic educational program. However, during the 1980s, educational reform overshadowed equity issues. What has become known as the "excellence" movement shifted attention away from equal opportunity for all students and stressed the outcomes of education as a means of strengthening the nation's economy.[20]

During the decade of the 1980s, every state responded to this new emphasis on reform. Graduation requirements were enhanced, statewide testing programs were implemented, programs designed to strengthen teacher preparation programs as well as in-service requirements for practicing teachers were mandated, and many states ended the practice of issuing life certifications. Of the fifty states implementing at least one reform measure during the past decade, only thirteen provided additional funding to implement the programs in the local district. For the most part, these programs were funded through the regular budget or through existing state formulas.[21]

Proponents of the reform moment argued that the emphasis on equity had failed to resolve the two most pressing educational issues of the last two decades: student achievement and school dropouts. With student scores on standardized achievement tests declining and dropout rates on the rise, the reformers concluded that equity programs and increased funding were not the answer. As a result, the states looked toward increasing standards for both students and teachers and developing alternative programs for "at risk" students. One means of attacking these problems was to tie the business community directly to the school. School/business partnerships were encouraged, with the underlying thought that better business practices in schools would both increase efficiency and impact the employability of students after graduation.

The arrival of the "excellence movement" and the trend away from increased funding for education were not mere coincidences. The restructuring of federal support and subsequent decrease in federal dollars for education, as well as the end of substantial increases in state dollars to fund new programs, became synonymous with reform. The underlying principle of school finance in the reform era was better utilization and more efficient use of tax dollars for education. Both federal and state leaders embraced the notion that improved outcomes did not require additional dollars but better use of existing funds. For the first time in history, education occupied a central position at both the federal and state level. However, instead of using this emphasis to fund significant reform, the dollars either remained constant or declined. This emphasis was further noted at the local level. Local communities were unwilling to increase local revenue to offset the greater demands placed on school districts. As education moves into the last decade of the twentieth century, the issues of equity and reform will retain their prominence in seeking to resolve each without one impinging on the other.

## Summary

The prominence of the state in the funding of local education has steadily increased during the latter half of the twentieth century. From providing less than 20 percent of total education dollars to becoming the majority funding agent in many states, state legislators and officials are now the dominant force in controlling local educational programs. The most significant trend from 1950 through 1980 was the development of foundation programs and equalizing schemes to provide equal educational dollars for all programs within the state. These equity programs changed significantly as new demands emerged for specialized programs to meet the needs of students. As a result, handicapped, vocational, and gifted programs required additional financing to become adequately funded. To meet this challenge, states created weighting, reimbursement, and flat grant plans aimed at implementing these programs at the local level. The transportation of pupils and increased costs between elementary, junior high, and senior high students were also funded at different levels in many states.

This increased funding of local districts was accompanied by more control of educational programs by the state. State legislatures and departments of education required specific curricular programs and close monitoring of costs at the local level in order to continue state funding. As a result, local boards of education were forced to relinquish much of their traditional control over local programs. Budget decisions for some programs were completely removed from the local level. For example, special education programs were mandated by both the federal and state level. These mandates identified maximum class size, teacher preparation, and parental involvement necessary for district participation.

The "excellence" movement of the 1980s further eroded the local control of education. School districts were required, in some states, to implement statewide testing programs, new curricular programs, increased graduation requirements, and programs for improving instruction. Additional funding by the state was not in proportion to the enhanced requirements.

The trend of increased state involvement in local school districts appears to be intensifying in the final decade of the twentieth century. As a result, local autonomy will continue to erode in favor of state control. The politics of education at the state level appear to be stronger today than at any time in the history of U.S. education.

## Endnotes

1. Digest of Education Statistics, 1988 (Washington, D.C.: National Center for Education Statistics), p. 148.
2. National Commission on Excellence in Education, *A Nation at Risk: The Imperative for Educational Reform* (Washington, D.C.: United States Printing Office, 1983).

3. *Congressional Quarterly Almanac, 1988* (Washington, D.C.: United States Printing Office), p. 325.

4. *Directory of Federal Domestic Assistance* (Washington, D.C.: United States Printing Office).

5. *Congressional Quarterly Almanac, 1988*, p. 331.

6. *Congressional Quarterly Almanac, 1981* (Washington, D.C.: United States Printing Office), p. 499.

7. *Ibid.*

8. *Congressional Quarterly Almanac, 1988*, p. 330.

9. *Ibid.*, p. 331.

10. *Ibid.*, p. 332.

11. Digest of Education Statistics, p. 354.

12. *Ibid.*, p. 332.

13. National Governors' Association, *Time for Results* (Washington, D.C.: 1986).

14. Sumner N. Levine, ed., *The Dow Jones-Irwin Business and Investment Almanac* (Homewood, Illinois: Dow Jones-Irwin, 1989), p. 553.

15. Deborah A. Verstegen, *School Finance at a Glance* (Denver, Colorado: Education Commission of the State and National Conference of State Legislatures, 1990), p. 2.

16. James W. Guthrie, Walter I. Garms, and Lawrence C. Pierce, *School Finance and Education Policy: Enhancing Educational Efficiency, Equality, and Choice,* 3rd ed. (Englewood Cliffs, New Jersey: Prentice-Hall, 1988), p. 135.

17. *Ibid.*, p. 136.

18. *Ibid.*, p. 138.

19. Finance at a Glance, pp. 11, 13.

20. Robert Berne, "Equity Issues in School Finance," *Journal of Education Finance* (Vol. 14, Fall 1988), p. 168.

21. K. Forbis and M. Mckeown, "State Funding for Education Reform: False Hopes and Unfulfilled Expectations," *Journal of Education Finance* (Vol. 14, Summer 1988), p. 28.

## Selected Bibliography

Boyer, Ernest L., *High School: A Report on Secondary Education in America* (New York: Harper & Row, 1983).

Break, George F., *Financing Government in a Federal System* (Washington D.C.: Brookings Institution, 1980).

Coons, John E., William H. Clune III, and Stephen D. Sugarman, *Private Wealth and Public Education* (Cambridge, Massachusetts: Harvard University Press, Belknap Press, 1970).

Fisher, Ronald C., *State and Local Public Finance* (Glenview Illinois: Scott, Foresman and Company, 1988).

Goodlad, John, *A Place Called School* (New York: McGraw-Hill, 1984).

Kaestle, Carl, and Marshall Smith, "The Federal Role in Elementary and Secondary Education," *Harvard Educational Review*, Vol. 52 (1982), 389.

Timpane, Michael, *The Federal Interest in School Financing* (Cambridge, Massachusetts: Ballinger Publishing Company, 1978).

United States Government Printing Office, *Directory of Federal Domestic Assistance* (Washington, D.C., 1989).

# 3

---

# Taxation

Historically, public schools have been financed through the levying of a property tax at the local level. In fact, many school districts receive over 50 percent of their revenue from the property tax. State government also shares in the responsibility of financing education. The manner in which the states fulfill this obligation differs widely. However, for the most part, each state appropriates a portion of its "general revenue" to help finance the schools. General revenue is generated primarily through corporate income tax, personal income tax, license tax, sales tax, and other consumption taxes. Thus, many state taxing systems do not earmark a certain tax for the support of education.[1] The state of Michigan is one of the exceptions. That state's constitution mandates that 60 percent of the net revenue generated from the sales tax be used for K-12 public education. This is the same method used by the federal government, which appropriates funds generated from general revenue for specific educational programs created by Congress. In the federal sector, general revenue is obtained primarily through the corporate income tax, personal income tax, excise tax, estate and gift tax, custom duty, etc. Chapters 4 and 5 provide a detailed explanation of federal and state aid to education.

## Definitions

For the sake of clarity, it will be useful to set forth a few key definitions. Although *taxes* are a constant obsession with politicians, the news media, and the general public, few people thoroughly understand the concepts associated with taxation.

A *tax* is a compulsory charge levied by a governmental entity for the purpose of financing a service. This service must be performed for the common good and not to benefit a particular person or persons. In like manner, a tax is not for services rendered only to those paying the levy.[2] For example, charges levied by a sewer or water district only against those receiving the service cannot be considered a tax.

A property *tax roll* is an official list that indicates the amount of taxes levied against property owners on each parcel of property owned. The tax roll is maintained by each school district unless the district is located within the boundaries of a county or municipal government. In such a situation, a county or municipal governmental agency is usually responsible for collecting the taxes levied by other local governmental entities. Thus, the *collector of revenue* office appears in such counties or municipalities. A *tax deed* is a written document by which title to property is unconditionally transferred to a purchaser. The definition of *tax roll* is meaningful only in conjunction with the terms *tax rate* and *assessed valuation*.

The *tax rate* is the amount that is levied against a percentage of the fair market value of property. This percentage is termed the *assessed valuation*. This is also the origin of the term *ad majorem tax* which means "in proportion to value."

## Basic Concepts Concerning Taxation[3]

The first and most fundamental concept concerning taxation centers on the *social benefit theory*. Paying taxes is not an option; rather, it is an obligation. Under this theory, there should be no expectation on the part of the taxpayer of immediate or direct benefit from paying taxes. For example, a taxpayer without children still must pay taxes to the local school district. From a broader perspective, it is recognized by all responsible people that paying taxes to support education will result in a more competent citizenry, which, in turn, will increase the probability of enhancing the quality of life in a given community and beyond.

The second concept is the *ability-to-pay* standard. In most cases, ability is defined in terms of income. People who earn the most money usually have a greater ability to pay taxes. That which is taxed is called the *tax base*. For example, land and buildings are the tax base for the property tax. Some tax bases are better indicators than others of the ability-to-pay principle. The cigarette tax, for example, is not the best indicator of this principle; the income tax is one of the best examples.

This leads into a discussion concerning the usual classification of taxes as being *progressive, proportional,* or *regressive.* The federal individual income tax is a good example of a progressive tax, because each person pays taxes according to an increasing ratio schedule. Thus, the ratio of taxes due in relation to income is higher for those who earn more money than is the ratio of taxes due in relation to income for those who earn less.

A proportional tax is levied at a constant ratio. For example, some cities tax people working within the city boundaries at a percentage rate levied against earnings. If the percentage is 1 percent, a person earning $25,000 would pay $250 and a person earning $50,000 would pay $500.

A regressive tax is levied at a constant rate rather than a ratio. The sales tax is a good example of a regressive tax. For example, if 2 cents are collected as a tax on every dollar spent to purchase products, a person who earns $25,000 per year is paying a higher percentage of income to purchase products than a person who earns $50,000.

The third concept is called *shifting.* This phenomenon is often observed when a property tax is increased. The *impact* of the tax will fall on the owners of real property, including the owners of rental property. The owner will probably pass on the increase to tenants. The *incidence* of the tax, thus, falls on a person other than the person who first paid the tax. It is interesting that the incidence of all taxes ultimately falls to individuals. Corporations pay income taxes, but like the owners of rental property, the incidence of corporate taxes will be shifted ultimately to consumers. In some situations, the employees of a company experience a shifting when their wages and benefits are altered to absorb corporate taxes.

The fourth concept is *tax capitalization.* When property taxes are increased, the owner of a house may find that the property has decreased in value to prospective buyers because of the higher taxes. Conversely, when taxes are contained, as with Proposition 13 in California, property will probably increase in value.

Economists use the term *elasticity* when speaking about the phenomenon that is the fifth concept. When a governmental entity experiences a change in revenue faster than a change in personal income, the yield from a particular tax to income is *elastic. Elasticity of unity* takes place when changes in personal income and tax yield have a one-to-one relationship. If changes in personal income are greater than changes in the yield from a tax, then *inelasticity* has occurred. The significance of this phenomenon has practical application when analyzing taxes. Boards of education are generally concerned about the relationship of the personal income of taxpayers to the yield of the district's tax levy.

The sixth concept pertains more to the progressive nature of taxes such as the income tax. The concept of *marginality* speaks, to the last unit among similar units in a series. Certainly, this concept was formulated with a deep understanding of human psychology. People tend to value the last units in a series less than they value the preceding unit. For example, a person owning three automobiles probably feels that he or she needs the first automobile more than the second and the second more than the third.

Thus, *diminishing marginal utility of income* means that a person probably values the first few thousand dollars of income more than the last few thousand dollars of income. This leads the way to higher marginal (progressive) rates of taxation—the income tax brackets!

The seventh concept is *equity*, which deals with fairness. There is a great divergence of opinion about equity in all aspects of human existence. Here the focus is on equity in taxation. This, of course, must be considered in the light of *standard of living*. In the United States, it is shameful that some people cannot maintain a standard of living beyond mere subsistence. Equity militates against regressive taxation because regressive taxes adversely effect the standard of living. However, the proportional and progressive tax structures present a greater challenge to those in control of levying taxes. It is not easy to analyze the effect of proportional and progressive taxes on the standard of living and consequently on the concept of equity in taxation.

## Major Types of Taxes

Although this chapter is concerned primarily with the local property tax as the major vehicle for financing education, it is important to understand other types of taxes not only to avoid confusion but also because they are significant sources of revenue used by the state and federal governments in fulfilling their obligation to support education.

### Individual Income Tax

There are two categories of income tax, individual and corporate. Both categories are used not only by the federal government but also by virtually every state. The structure of this tax is relatively simple. The individual taxpayer or corporation adds up all income from every source, subtracts certain deductions, exemptions, and credits, and then applies the tax rates to the difference. It is interesting to note that credits, exemptions, and deductions are used by the federal and states governments to foster certain values.

For individual taxpayers, governments allow exemptions for children and other dependents. Theoretically, this type of exemption is meant to ensure a minimal standard of living for families where income must support not only the taxpayer but also other people.

Both corporations and individuals are allowed deductions by the federal government and state governments. The major type of deduction allowed to corporations is the *cost of doing business.* This deduction helps to foster business development, which in turn may produce economic development in a given community resulting in higher wages for individuals. In this scenario, federal and state governments realize greater yield from the income tax.

Further, individuals can receive a deduction for extraordinary medical expenses, for losses due to casualty, and for interest on debts. These types of deductions help individuals recover from economically detrimental situations. Deductions for charitable contributions are desirable because such contributions help relieve government from providing increased services to those in need.

Tax credits are similar to deductions and exemptions. However, credits are reductions from the income tax that would otherwise be payable. This results in the same dollar savings to all individuals or corporations regardless of income. For example, the Revenue Act of 1978 allowed a 10 percent investment credit for the cost of rehabilitating historic buildings provided that at least 75 percent of the existing external walls of the building were left standing.

The income tax is clearly the best example of a progressive tax. The personal income tax does not allow for the phenomenon of shifting, although the corporate income tax does experience this to some degree. There is still a debate among economists as to whom the shifting affects.[4]

## Sales Tax

There are two broad categories of sales taxes, general and excise. A general sales tax is levied against nearly all products and services. An excise tax is levied against specific products such as tobacco, alcoholic beverages, and petroleum. In the United States, sales taxes are usually levied at the retail level. However, the selective excise tax is usually levied on the producer, distributor, or wholesaler.

The general sales tax is used by most of the states, and this tax vehicle has consistently remained at the state level. The excise tax is levied not only at the state level but also at the federal and local levels.

Food and medicine are usually exempt from the general sales tax. There are some states that exempt clothing and other necessities. The general sales tax is roughly proportional in nature. However, because the poor spend most of their income on exempt items, this tax is somewhat progressive for them. For wealthy people who spend a great deal of their income on non-exempt items, the general sales tax is slightly regressive.

In general, the excise tax is regressive in nature. The consensus of economists is that the excise tax is shifted to the consumer when it is paid by the producer, distributor, or wholesaler. In addition, the excise tax is considered to be inelastic, because the consumption of taxed products usually remains the same regardless of changes in personal income. The contrary is true of the general sales tax, which usually experiences an elasticity of unity.[5]

## Property Tax

As the name indicates, the tax base for this revenue source is property, and the tax is collected from the property owner. Public education in the United States has used this source of revenue from its earliest history. This source accounts for approximately 40 percent of the revenue that supports public education in the United States. Because this type of tax is applied at the local level, there are many variations in how it is applied. Traditionally, the property tax is levied without regard to the owner's equity in the property. Rather, the tax is levied in accordance with the value of the property with no consideration given to any mortgages. The legal basis for the property tax is found in individual state constitutions or statutes. This tax is also used by other local governments, which, of course, include municipalities.

### Definitions

Land and buildings are the most basic units subject to the property tax. Land and buildings are commonly referred to as *real property.* In many states, personal property is also subject to the property tax. There are two categories of personal property, tangible and intangible. *Tangible personal property* usually includes farm animals and equipment, motor vehicles, boats and other recreational vehicles, business equipment and inventory, household goods, clothing, and jewelry. *Intangible personal property* usually includes stocks, bonds, bank deposits, and accounts receivable. Intangible personal property is difficult to assess. For this reason, there has been a decline in the number of states that apply a property tax to this category.

### *Assessment of Property*

The valuation of real property is the central issue in relation to the property tax. Because this tax generates the largest portion of local revenue and because historically it has been so basic to the financing of public education, it is treated in many state constitutions and is also found in state statutes. When describing the value of property, the phrase "fair market value" is commonly employed. It refers to the price that would prevail if a sale occurred between a buyer and seller. In litigation involving property, the courts have accepted the concept of fair market value. When a building exists on a parcel of land that is involved in litigation, the courts have consistently interpreted the fair market value of such buildings to mean the replacement cost minus depreciation.

The separation of land value from building value persists in the methods used by assessors throughout the United States. Buildings are commonly referred to as "improvements" to property. Arriving at the fair market value is not as easy as the phrase may imply. In fact, most states have established boards or panels empowered to review and make modification in the assessments of local assessors. In other words, a taxpayer who believes that an assessment is incorrect may appeal to such a board in hope that the assessment will be altered. Of course, every taxpayer has the right to appeal to the state court system if dissatisfied with the decision of the assessment board.

Although assessment practices vary from location to location, practically all assessors perform their responsibility with the help of preestablished tables that set forth standardized measures of value for land and buildings. For example, in estimating the value of a lot in an urban area, an assessor would first calculate the value per "front foot." Adjustments are then made with respect to width, depth, gradation, etc., which would be obtained from standard tables. There will be situations that do not conform to table standards. This is especially true with regards to large commercial and industrial properties. When this occurs, assessors may use a variety of techniques and, in a few cases, negotiations between the owner and the assessor may bring about the only solution.

The great variation in assessment techniques creates a problem when comparing assessments even within a given state. Further, the fact that assessors are elected in some cities and counties also creates a problem. The pleasure of the electorate with assessments will certainly affect a person's chances of being reelected. To compensate for possible inequities, every state uses a fractional assessment against which the property tax rate is levied. What this fractional assessment accomplishes is the flexibility to make adjustments which would not be possible if "fair market value" constituted the assessment.

Within many states, such as Missouri, properties also are assessed at different fractional measure depending on their use. For example, residential property is assessed at approximately 20 percent. Farm property is assessed at approximately 12 percent, and commercial property at approximately 32 percent of market value. This approach, of course, bespeaks of social benefit theory. In essence, the government is encouraging farming and house ownership. The owners of commercial property will certainly shift the burden of property taxes to the consumer, but the distribution will be spread over a larger portion of the population.

Some economists believe that fractional assessment has a neutral effect. "A low ratio of assessment would imply simply higher tax rates, and vice versa." This is one viewpoint that is difficult to prove. However, the most serious concern arises in those states that incorporate the assessed valuation of each school district into a formula for distributing state aid. In this situation, if assessments are not equitable throughout a given state, certain school districts could be penalized for having accurate and proper assessments.

Further, taxpayers in some states are concerned about reassessment. The problem is that a person in one of these states who owns a tract of land with a house on it will be taxed on the original assessment regardless of whether the land and house increase in market value over a period of years. A person who buys a similar house on a comparable lot might pay twice as much in taxes as another property owner just because his or her property was assessed at a more recent date, probably when the house was purchased. It is common practice for a reassessment to occur when a deed is transferred, as is the case when property is purchased. However, there are a few states where the original assessment does not change even if a house or other property is sold. The trend is in the opposite direction. Thus, many states have statutes that require a reassessment of property on a regular basis, perhaps every two years.

### Setting the Tax Rate[6]

The total assessed valuation of a school district is simply the sum total of all the assessments within the boundaries of the district. The board of education is empowered to levy a tax on this assessment. From an operational framework, the superintendent of schools presents a budget to the board of education for approval that sets forth projected revenues and recommended expenditure. In order to determine the amount of revenue that will be needed from the property tax, other sources of revenue are added together and subtracted from the total expenditures. The remainder is the amount to be raised from the property tax. Thus, if the recommended expenditures equal $50 million and revenues from the state and federal governments equal $25 million, an additional $25 million would be needed from the property tax.

Every state has statutes that operationalize the property tax through a tax-rate setting process. For example, the tax rate is usually expressed in terms of a mill or a penny. A *mill* is a monetary unit equalling .001 of a dollar. Thus, a tax rate of 500 mills equals 50 cents. For ease of explanation, examples of tax rates will be presented using the penny as the monetary unit. Because the tax rate is an *ad valorem* tax, it is levied on only a percent of the fair market value of the property. The Missouri residential property is assessed at approximately 20 percent of fair market value. Further, Missouri levies the property tax against this assessment in units of $100. If a certain house has a fair market value of $100,000, it would be assessed at $20,000 for tax purposes. This $20,000 is then divided by 100 units and multiplied by the tax rate. If the tax rate is 50 pennies, this taxpayer would pay $100 in property taxes.

Now to return to the tax-rate setting process used by the board of education. In the example above, the board of education would need to raise $25 million from the property tax. If the total assessed valuation of a school district is $500 million, this amount would be divided by 100 units and multiplied by a tax rate of $5 per $100 of assessed valuation. Therefore, the taxpayer with a house assessed at $20,000 would pay a tax of $1000. The calculation is as follows: $20,000 is divided by 100 units and multiplied by a $5 tax rate which equals $1000 in taxes.

### State Limitations on the Property Tax

Every state places some limitations on the property tax. The most common limitation is the setting of a tax ceiling. If a board of education wishes to increase the tax rate above a statutory limit, a referendum election must be held, thereby giving citizens final authority over rate increases. A simple majority is required in most states to increase the rate. However, there are other limitations that have become more numerous over the last decade.

Perhaps the most publicized attempt to control property tax increases was Proposition 13, an amendment to the California State Constitution.

> *Specifically, the amendment provided for (1) property taxes to be limited to 1 percent of full cash value plus the rate needed to service bonded indebtedness approved by the voters before 1978-79; (2) assessed values to be rolled back to 1975-76 levels, with increases of only 2 percent annually, to reflect inflation (newly sold property could be assessed at market value exceeding the 1975-76 levels); (3) statutes to increase state taxes to be approved by two-thirds of each of the two houses of the legislature and no new ad valorem, sales, or transaction taxes on real property to be levied; (4) special local taxes, taxes on real property, to be approved by two-thirds of the jurisdiction's voters.[7]*

The most widely used method of controlling property tax increases is the homestead exemption. It provides an exemption from taxation of a certain amount of homestead value. This is similar to the personal exemptions used with income taxes. For example, Kentucky allows an exemption of $16,100 of assessed valuation for elderly and disabled homeowners. This was enacted in 1985 with the provision that every two years an adjustment would be made for inflation. Forty-two states have similar laws.

The second most widely used method of controlling property tax increases is commonly called a "circuit breaker." Thirty-two states use this mechanism, which is a state government financed credit or rebate for property taxes paid to school districts and local government. Typically, the credit or rebate is provided in relation to the state income tax and usually applies to specific taxpayers such as the elderly or disabled. Further, the credit or rebate is usually applied to property taxes that exceed a specific percentage of a taxpayer's income. For this reason, such measures are called "circuit breakers."[8]

### Suitability of the Property Tax

Although there are disadvantages to the property tax, it is still the most suitable tax for the local financing of public education. This suitability is based on the stability of the property tax. School districts can depend upon the yield produced by this tax in both the best and worst of economic times. Personal income can rise and fall within a community but once property and improvements have been placed on the tax rolls, the tax yield will remain stable for years to come.

Stability of income is critical, of course, not only for the present delivery of educational services but also for the future. Planning would be difficult if a school district's income could change drastically over a short period of time. In fact, those conditions that bring about the loss of personal income in a community can usually be corrected through education. For example, the use of robotics in industry has displaced unskilled workers. For most of these individuals, education will be the only way in which they can acquire the skills necessary to once again become wage earners.

### Administration and Compliance with the Property Tax[9]

It is easy to locate property—and the owners of property—because these are matters of public record. In like manner, compliance with a property tax law is relatively simple. Tax bills can be mailed to property owners once or twice a year, and keeping track of delinquent taxpayers is a routine procedure. Thus, the administration of and compliance with property tax laws are usually not problematic, except in relation to assessment.

The major problem with assessment stems from the political influence exercised in the assessment process. This can occur in those communities where assessors are either elected or politically appointed. One solution to this problem is obvious but very difficult to engineer. Assessors should be appointed by a bipartisan commission with equal membership from the two major political parties. Of course, there are other ways in which to accomplish a certain amount of impartiality in the assessment practice. The bipartisan commission is only one example of a way to minimize political influence.

## Litigation Concerning Taxation and Equity[10]

This section will review a few court cases in which funding disparities existed within a region or state. More specifically, these cases occurred when differing tax bases resulted in unequal revenues to school districts. The most significant case was *San Antonio Independent School District* v. *Rodriguez*, 93 S.Ct. 1278 (1973). This U.S. Supreme Court case originated in Texas where a public school financing system was based on ad valorem taxation, which is the situation throughout the nation. This system created disparities between school districts in terms of revenue. The Supreme Court ruled that such a system did not create a disadvantage to any group or class of citizens because the disparity occurred only between school districts. The wealth of any family in the district was not the root cause of the disparity. Consequently, economically poor citizens were not disadvantaged as a class. Further, the Supreme Court stated that education was not a fundamental right guaranteed by the U.S. Constitution, even though it is of the utmost importance to the welfare of the nation.

In *Forward* v. *Webster Central School District*, 526 N.Y.S.2d 870 (A.D.4d Dep't 1988), the New York Appellate Court reversed the decision of a lower trial court. A school district levied different tax rates within the same school district but because of assessed valuation differentials, the individual taxpayers affected did not pay additional taxes. The lower court stated that this was unconstitutional.

In a South Carolina case, that state's supreme court ruled that the state constitution delegated broad powers to the state assembly to devise a means for funding education. Thus, a shared funding plan was a constitutional means of equalizing educational opportunity among the state's public school districts. See *Richard Country* v. *Campbell*, 364 S.E.2d 470 (S.C.1988).

A North Carolina court of appeals ruled that the state constitutional provision to provide equal opportunity for all students only applied to racial discrimination. North Carolina provided flat rate grants to school districts based solely upon the number of students in attendance. Thus school districts with a larger tax base had larger per pupil expenditures since the flat grants did not compensate for the disparity in local funding. See *Britt* v. *North Carolina State Board of Education,* 357 S.E.2d 432 (N.C.App.1987).

The questions of equal expenditures per child as a means of providing equal educational opportunity was addressed by the Oklahoma Supreme Court in *Fair School Finance Counsel of Oklahoma* v. *State,* 746 P.2d 1135 (Okl.1987). Because the children were receiving a basic and adequate education, stated the court, the Oklahoma school finance system was constitutional even though there was a great variance in assessed valuation and, therefore, a variance in revenues received by the different school districts.

The question of equality in funding education through taxation and how this relates to equal educational opportunity has remained a concern since the San Antonio case. Also, taxation and how it affects equality in funding is a matter to be handled by the states.

## Summary

Public school districts historically have been financed through the levying of a property tax at the local level. Many districts receive over 50 percent of their revenue from the property tax. State governments and the federal government also provide revenue to school districts through their general revenue. Corporate income tax, personal income tax, and a variety of other taxes are the sources from which general revenue is generated.

A tax is a compulsory charge levied by a governmental entity for the purpose of financing a service that is performed for the common good. A property tax roll is an official list showing the amount of taxes levied against each person on each parcel of property owned. A tax deed is a written document by which the title to a property is unconditionally transferred to a purchaser upon foreclosure for failure to pay taxes by the original owner. A tax rate is the amount that is levied against a percentage of the fair market value of property; the percentage is termed the assessed valuation.

There are seven fundamental concepts concerning taxation. The most fundamental concept centers around the *social benefit theory*. This theory explains that paying taxes is not an option but an obligation, and taxpayers should not expect to directly or immediately benefit from paying taxes.

A second concept is the *ability-to-pay* standard. It is best understood within the context of the usual classification of taxes as being progressive, proportional, or regressive.

A third concept is called *shifting*. This phenomenon is often observed when property taxes are increased. The owners of property usually pass on this increase in taxes to their tenants.

A fourth concept is called *tax capitalization*. An owner of a house may find that the property has decreased in value because of high property taxes.

Economists use the term *elasticity* when speaking about the phenomenon that occurs when a governmental entity experiences a change in revenue faster than the taxpayer experiences a change in personal income. Elasticity is the fifth concept.

The sixth concept is concerned with *marginality*, which is commonly understood to mean that people tend to value the last unit in a series less than they value the preceding unit.

The last concept is *equity*, which deals with the fairness of a given tax in relation to the standard of living among taxpayers.

There are two categories of income taxes, corporate and individual. The mechanism for calculating this tax is for a corporation or individual to add up all income from every source; subtract certain deductions, exemptions, and credits; and then to apply the tax rate to the difference.

There are two categories of sales taxes, general and excise. A general sales tax is levied against nearly all products and services. An excise tax is levied against specific products.

As the term *property tax* indicates, the tax base for this revenue source is property, and the tax is collected from the property owner. Land and buildings are commonly referred to as real property. There are also two categories of personal property, tangible and intangible. The valuation of real property is the central issue in relation to the property tax. The process for establishing the assessment of property is as varied as are the different states because each state legislature views this process differently.

The tax rate of a school district is levied against the assessed valuation of each taxpayer's property. Every state has a statute that sets forth the procedure for establishing the tax rate. Proposition 13 in California ushered in limitations on the property tax, which has spurred on the same type of action by legislatures in almost every other state. Among the most widely used methods of controlling taxes by legislatures are the *homestead* exemption and the *circuit breaker*. The property tax, however, is very suitable as a vehicle for financing public education because of its stability and ease of administration.

The first major court case dealing with the property tax and its appropriateness in relation to equity in educational opportunity was *San Antonio Independent School District* v. *Rodriguez*. Many other court cases are also concerned with similar property tax issues.

## Endnotes

1. Paul D. Travers and Ronald W. Rebore, *Foundations of Education: Becoming a Teacher* (Englewood Cliffs, New Jersey: Prentice Hall, Inc., 1987), p. 247.

2. Roe L. Johns, Edgar L. Morphet, and Kern Alexander, *The Economics & Finance of Education*, 4th ed. (Englewood Cliffs, New Jersey: Prentice Hall, Inc., 1983), pp. 80, 81.

3. Thomas H. Jones, "Taxation for Education," in *Principles of School Business Management*. R. Craig Wood, ed. (Reston, Virginia: ASBO International, 1986), pp. 77-79.

4. Johns, Morphet, and Alexander, pp. 102-104.

5. Jones, pp. 82, 83.

6. *Ibid.*, p. 88.

7. Johns, Morphet, and Alexander, p. 111.

8. Ronald C. Fisher, *State and Local Public Finance* (Glenview, Illinois: Scott, Foresman and Company, 1988), pp. 134-139.

9. *Ibid.*, p. 98.

10. Data Research, Inc., *1989 Deskbook Encyclopedia of American School Law* (Rosemount, Minnesota: Data Research, Inc., 1989), pp. 356-362.

## Selected Bibliography

Aaron, Henry J., *Who Pays the Property Tax? A New View* (Washington, D.C.: Brookings Institution, 1975).

Break, George F., *Financing Government in a Federal System* (Washington, D.C.: Brookings Institution, 1980).

Due, John F., and John L. Mikesell, *Sales Taxation, State and Local Structure and Administration* (Maryland, Baltimore: Johns Hopkins University Press, 1983).

Fisher, Ronald C., *State and Local Public Finance* (Glenview, Illinois: Scott, Foresman and Company, 1988).

Johns, Roe L., Edgar L. Morphet, and Kern Alexander, *The Economics and Financing of Education*, 4th ed. (Englewood Cliffs, New Jersey: Prentice-Hall, Inc., 1983).

Jones, Thomas H., "Taxation for Education," *Principles of School Business Management*, R. Craig Wood, ed. (Reston, Virginia: ASBO International, 1986).

Raphaelson, Arnold H., "The Property Tax," *Management Policies in Local Government Finance*, J.R. Aronson and E. Schwartz, eds. (Washington, D.C.: International City Management Association, 1987).

Rosen, Harvey S., *Public Finance*, 2nd ed. (Homewood, Illinois: Richard D. Irwin, 1988).

# 4

# Financing Capital Projects and Debt Management

The management of debt is now an integral part of school business management. Traditionally, public schools have used general obligation bond issues to obtain sufficient capital for the construction of new schools, purchases of land, furniture, equipment, and even school buses. However, during the last few years, districts have also used municipal leasehold financing for both the construction and renovation of facilities. Short-term debt offerings of one year or less have likewise been used to offset deficits in cash flow until tax, revenue, or bond proceeds are received.

## Short-Term Debt

Short-term notes presently amount to between 20 and 30 percent of the total municipal debt market.[1] Four different short-term financing instruments are available to all governmental bodies: tax anticipation notes (TANs), revenue anticipation notes (RANs), bond anticipation notes (BANs), and tax-exempt commercial paper (TECP). The first three represent the most common short-term debt offerings used by school districts. These notes are exempt from federal income tax, and, therefore, are sold at lower rates than taxable securities. The Tax Reform Act of 1986 dealt with the issue of short-term debt instruments regarding arbitrage restrictions and the possible loss of federal tax exemption for violation of the arbitrage regulations. With respect to short-term debt instruments, the act requires that the amount of funds borrowed cannot exceed 90 percent of the *cumulative cash flow deficit.* The cumulative cash flow deficit is equal to the maximum deficit in a fund during the fiscal year. This application of the regulation will be presented in the following section on tax anticipation notes.[2]

## Tax Anticipation Notes

TANs are utilized to offset cash flow deficits within a particular fund in anticipation of ad valorem tax payments. The proceeds from the notes are used by districts for operating expenses until tax collections are received, usually in January and February. Although specific state laws vary on the issuance of tax anticipation notes, most generally require the payment of the notes, from tax receipts, by the end of the fiscal year in which they were issued. However, since taxes are received shortly after the beginning of the calendar year, the funds to be used to retire the notes can be invested at market rates until the maturity date of the notes. Since tax anticipation notes are tax-exempt, interest cost will be lower than taxable notes. Therefore, the district, by investing the funds at market rates, can earn a higher interest rate than they are currently paying on the notes. An example may help to clarify this point. Exhibit 4-1 shows a cash flow forecast used as the basis for issuing tax anticipation notes in the amount of $1,054,000 in the General Fund.

The maximum cumulative deficit of $1,053,809 occurs in December. Therefore, the district, by rounding to the nearest thousand, could issue notes in the amount of $1,054,000. If the notes were sold at an interest rate of 6 percent per year to bear interest from September 1 through June 15, the total interest expense would be approximately $50,600. Since the district receives property taxes in January and the notes do not mature until June 15, the district could invest the $1,054,000 at market rates until the maturity date. Exhibit 4-2 demonstrates the calculation of the interest expense at 6 percent and the interest income to the district at 7 percent by reinvesting the funds from January through June.

EXHIBIT 4-1 • *General Fund Cash Flow—School Year 1988-89*

| Source | July | August | Sept. | October | Nov. | Dec. | January | February | March | April | May | June |
|---|---|---|---|---|---|---|---|---|---|---|---|---|
| Local income | 8,935 | 6,036 | 5,717 | 2,819 | 1,861 | 2,002 | 1,409,000 | 1,044,290 | 59,103 | 22,069 | 40,586 | 123,057 |
| Sales tax | 143,987 | 96,747 | 194,113 | 144,000 | 112,698 | 157,650 | 144,746 | 95,100 | 168,233 | 168,232 | 168,233 | 168,233 |
| State income | 268,474 | 268,474 | 155,936 | 300,165 | 299,720 | 387,718 | 280,687 | 501,583 | 290,687 | 290,687 | 290,687 | 303,973 |
| Federal income | 0 | 0 | 0 | 0 | 0 | 38,000 | 0 | 0 | 0 | 3,724 | 0 | 0 |
| Food service | 61,825 | 71,900 | 108,629 | 85,000 | 170,549 | 175,292 | 94,000 | 111,761 | 121,761 | 101,761 | 111,761 | 121,761 |
| Miscellaneous | 31,872 | 37,865 | 52,896 | 32,825 | 28,400 | 18,343 | 9,915 | 104,624 | 75,364 | 37,686 | 8,572 | 23,760 |
| Total | $515,093 | $521,572 | $524,812 | $620,271 | $620,919 | $879,005 | $1,938,348 | $1,857,358 | $705,148 | $624,159 | $619,839 | $740,784 |
| Salaries | 178,227 | 178,227 | 179,227 | 175,227 | 175,227 | 189,227 | 175,227 | 175,227 | 170,227 | 168,227 | 176,227 | 176,227 |
| Benefits | 112,993 | 182,286 | 202,286 | 203,976 | 203,976 | 203,976 | 203,976 | 203,976 | 203,976 | 203,976 | 203,976 | 339,286 |
| Transporation | 115,000 | 125,000 | 171,450 | 131,450 | 151,450 | 151,450 | 151,450 | 151,450 | 151,450 | 151,450 | 151,450 | 125,000 |
| Supplies | 80,000 | 40,000 | 20,000 | 46,720 | 90,000 | 119,655 | 27,750 | 49,802 | 7,425 | 22,870 | 22,870 | 2,267 |
| Utilities | 80,000 | 80,000 | 80,000 | 80,000 | 90,000 | 102,000 | 90,000 | 90,000 | 80,000 | 80,000 | 80,000 | 84,000 |
| Food service | 86,000 | 155,000 | 133,500 | 113,500 | 112,500 | 115,500 | 113,000 | 113,000 | 113,000 | 93,000 | 83,000 | 95,000 |
| Miscellaneous | 134,968 | 83,779 | 55,663 | 33,149 | 123,304 | 267,795 | 39,945 | 96,945 | 57,944 | 83,193 | 29,680 | 29,320 |
| Total expenditures | $787,188 | $844,292 | $842,126 | $784,022 | $946,457 | $1,149,603 | $801,348 | $880,400 | $784,022 | $802,716 | $747,203 | $851,100 |
| Surplus/(Deficit) | (272,095) | (322,720) | (317,314) | (163,751) | (325,538) | (270,598) | 1,137,000 | 976,958 | (78,874) | (178,557) | (127,364) | (110,316) |
| Beginning cash balance | 618,207 | 346,112 | 23,392 | (293,922) | (457,673) | (783,211) | (1,053,809) | 83,191 | 1,060,149 | 981,275 | 802,718 | 675,354 |
| Ending cash balance | $346,112 | $23,392 | ($293,922) | ($457,673) | ($783,211) | ($1,053,809) | $83,191 | $1,060,149 | $981,275 | $802,718 | $675,354 | $565,038 |
| Tax anticipation note proceeds | | | 1,054,000 | | | | | | | | | |
| Tax anticipation note redemption | | | | | | | | | | | | 1,054,000 |
| Cash balance with note proceeds | | | $760,078 | $596,327 | $270,789 | $191 | $1,137,191 | $2,114,149 | $2,035,275 | $1,856,718 | $1,729,354 | $565,038 |

EXHIBIT 4-2 • *Tax Anticipation Notes Net Interest Cost*

1. Sale of Tax Anticipation Notes of $1,054,000 at 6 percent per year from September 1 through June 15 (288 days).

$$\text{Interest Expense} = \frac{\$1,054,000 \cdot .06}{360 \text{ Days}} \cdot 288 \text{ Days}$$

$$\$50,592 = \frac{\$63,240}{360} \cdot 288 = \$175.66 \cdot 288$$

2. Investment of $1,054,000 at a rate of 7 percent in certificates of deposit from January 1 through June 15 (166 days).

$$\text{Interest Income} = \frac{\$1,054,000 \cdot .07}{360 \text{ Days}} \cdot 166 \text{ Days}$$

$$\$34,020 = \frac{\$73,780}{360} \cdot 166 = \$204.95 \cdot 166$$

3. Interest Expense    $50,592
   Interest Income    $34,020
   Net Difference    $16,572

4. At a 6 percent interest expense on $1,054,000 of 288 days, and a 7 percent income for 166, the net difference of $16,572 represents an actual interest cost to the district of 1.96 percent.

## Revenue Anticipation Notes

RANs are similar to tax anticipation notes. They are used for cash flow in anticipation of revenue due to the district at a later date.

## Bond Anticipation Notes

BANs provide needed capital to initiate construction, renovations, or major purchases before the district receives the proceeds from the sale of bonds. Many districts involved in new construction find it advantageous to begin the site work during the warmer, drier time of the year. Therefore, a bond anticipation note will allow the awarding and payment of contracts before the sale of the bonds.

## Tax-Exempt Commercial Paper

TECP refers to obligations issued with maturities of up to 270 days. Tax-exempt commercial paper is often used during construction to allow the municipality to wait for a more favorable time to market long-term debt offerings.

## Marketing Short-Term Notes

Although state laws vary regarding the sale of short-term notes, school districts, if allowed, may negotiate or competitively seek bids for the notes. Often, bank depository bids include a request for an interest rate on short-term loans. If acceptable to the district, the bank will purchase the notes for a specified period of time at the interest rate stipulated. The public sale of notes is usually more desirable and a better test of the market. However, the district may benefit from a fixed rate offered by the depository at an earlier date if the interest rates have increased. Even states that allow the district to choose between a negotiated and a competitive sale may establish a different interest ceiling based on the type of sale. For example, negotiated notes may not exceed an interest rate of 10 percent, while competitive bids may not exceed 14 percent.

For the past several years, both Standard and Poor's[3] and Moody's Investor Service[4] have provided ratings for short-term notes. The debt ratings are provided for the benefit of potential bidders and indicate the investment quality of the offering. For an application fee based on the size of the offering, the rating agencies look at the relative strength of the issue regarding the ability of the district to meet the principal and interest payments. The ratings have a direct effect on the interest rate bids. The higher the rating, the lower the interest rate. Exhibit 4-3 is a listing and explanation of the ratings.

If the issue is not rated, one or more of the following may be responsible.

1. The district did not apply for a rating. If the district feels that its present financial condition would not warrant a high rating, it may decide that an unrated issue would not be as harmful as one with a low rating.
2. There is a lack of essential data pertaining to the issue. The rating agencies did not have sufficient data to rate the issue before the bids were accepted.

EXHIBIT 4-3 • *Ratings of Short-Term Notes*

| *Standard & Poor's* | |
| --- | --- |
| SP-1 | Very strong or strong capacity to pay principal and interest. Those issues determined to possess overwhelming safety characteristics will be given a plus (+) designation. |
| SP-2 | Satisfactory capacity to pay principal and interest. |
| SP-3 | Speculative capacity to pay principal and interest. |

| *Moody's Investors Service* | |
| --- | --- |
| MIG 1/VMIG 1 | This designation denotes best quality. There is present strong protection by established cash flows, superior liquidity support or demonstrated broad-based access to the market for refinancing. |
| MIG 2/VMIG 2 | This designation denotes high quality. Margins of protection are amply although not so large as in the preceding group. |
| MIG 3/VMIG 3 | This designation denotes favorable quality. All security elements are accounted for, but there is lacking the undeniable strength of the preceding grades. Liquidity and cash flow protection may be narrow and market access for refinancing is likely to be less well established. |
| MIG 4/VMIG 4 | This designation denotes adequate quality. Protection commonly regarded as required of an investment security is present and although not distinctly or predominantly speculative, there is specific risk. |

EXHIBIT 4-4 • *Taxable Equivalent of a 7 Percent Municipal Bond*

$$\text{Taxable Equivalent} = \frac{\text{Tax - Free Yield \%}}{100\% - \text{Tax Bracket (\%)}}$$

$$\text{15 Percent Tax Bracket} = \frac{.07}{100 - 15} = 8.24\%$$

$$\text{28 Percent Tax Bracket} = \frac{.07}{100 - 28} = 9.72\%$$

$$\text{33 Percent Tax Bracket} = \frac{.07}{100 - 33} = 10.45\%$$

3. The district decided to negotiate the sale rather than seek competitive bids. Rating agencies do not rate private sales.
4. The agencies decided that the issue did not meet minimum standards for investment quality.[5]

## Financing Capital Projects

The general obligation bond issue has been the traditional vehicle used by school districts to finance the construction and renovation of school facilities. Also referred to as municipal bonds, these securities are exempt from federal income tax, and usually from state income tax if the purchaser lives in the state where the issue is offered. Since they are tax-exempt, districts can sell the bonds below the market rate for taxable or corporate bonds. Exhibit 4-4 demonstrates the equivalent yield of a 7 percent tax-exempt bond.

An investor in the 15 percent tax bracket would have to buy a corporate taxable bond at 8.24 percent to obtain the same after tax yield of a 7 percent municipal bond. Likewise, investors in the 28 percent and 33 percent tax brackets would have to purchase, respectively, a 9.72 percent and 10.45 percent taxable bond to obtain the same yield.

## Bond Issue Procedures

Although each state has slightly different requirements for bringing a bond issue to market, Exhibit 4-5 represents a general overall outline of the most significant requirements of a school district from inception through the sale of the bonds.

### Determination of Building Needs

The business administrator, at the direction of the superintendent, prepares a summary of the district facility needs over a specified period of time. Exhibit 4-6 is an example of a detailed facility needs assessment over a ten-year period. Each project is listed separately with an estimate of the architectural/engineering fees and the construction costs. In order to properly determine the applicable costs, estimates of labor, materials, and equipment are projected based on a reasonable assumption concerning the rate of inflation over the specified period of time.

EXHIBIT 4-5 • *Bond Issue Procedures*

1. Determine building needs
2. Determine bonding capacity
3. Select bond council
4. Resolution by board of education designating
   A. Election date and polling places
   B. Amount of bonds to be sold
   C. Purpose of bond sale
   D. Certification by treasurer of the board relative to outstanding bonds
5. Submission of the following items to election authority
   A. Board resolution authorizing bond election
   B. Sample ballot
   C. Notice of election
6. Election day
7. Resolution by the board of education to approve the results of the bond election
   A. Certification by the secretary of the board identifying the election authority's abstract of votes cast in the election.
   B. Certification by the secretary of the board relative to the publishing of election notices
8. Preparation of bond maturity schedule
9. Selection of paying agent, bond registrar, and transfer agent
10. Preparation of bond sale
11. Acceptance of bond bids by board of education
12. Resolution by board of education directing the issuance of the bonds
13. Registration by state auditor
14. Closing of sale and delivery of bonds
    A. Non-litigation certificate
    B. Receipt of funds signed by treasurer of the board
    C. Signature verification of the president and secretary of the board

## Determination of Bonding Capacity

The need for new or renovated physical facilities has to be coordinated with the bonding capacity available to the district. Thirty-five of the fifty states currently limit the amount of long-term debt (longer than one year) of school districts.[6] In every case, the limit is expressed as either a dollar amount, a percentage of the property values, or a percentage of revenue. Exhibit 4-7 is an example of a district with a long-term debt limitation of 10 percent.

EXHIBIT 4-6 • *Building Needs*

| Project | Year | Architect. Fees | Const. Cost | Total Cost |
|---|---|---|---|---|
| Renovation—elementary school | 1990 | $91,000 | $1,209,000 | $1,300,000 |
| Phase I—new high school | 1991 | $455,000 | $6,045,000 | $6,500,000 |
| New junior high school | 1992 | $581,000 | $7,719,000 | $8,300,000 |
| Phase II—new high school | 1993 | $588,000 | $7,812,000 | $8,400,000 |
| Renovation—present high school | 1994 | $336,000 | $4,464,000 | $4,800,000 |
| New elementary school | 1995 | $245,000 | $3,255,000 | $3,500,000 |
| Phase III—new high school | 1996 | $189,000 | $2,511,000 | $2,700,000 |
| Renovation—present junior high school | 1997 | $105,000 | $1,395,000 | $1,500,000 |
| Phase IV—new high school | 1998 | $161,000 | $2,139,000 | $2,300,000 |
| Present junior high school addition | 1999 | $168,000 | $2,232,000 | $2,400,000 |
| Phase V—new high school | 2000 | $175,000 | $2,325,000 | $2,500,000 |

EXHIBIT 4-7 • *Bonding Capacity*

| A | B | C | D | E | F | G | H |
|---|---|---|---|---|---|---|---|
| Year | Assessed Valuation | Debt % | Bonding Capacity (B x C) | Outstanding Bonds | Current Bonding Capacity (D -E) | Building Needs | Difference (F - G) |
| 1990 | 300,000,000 | 10% | 30,000,000 | 26,000,000 | 4,000,000 | 1,300,000 | 2,700,000 |
| 1991 | 315,000,000 | 10% | 31,500,000 | 25,000,000 | 6,500,000 | 6,500,000 | 0 |
| 1992 | 330,750,000 | 10% | 33,075,000 | 24,400,000 | 8,675,000 | 8,300,000 | 375,000 |
| 1993 | 347,287,500 | 10% | 34,728,750 | 25,400,000 | 9,328,750 | 8,400,000 | 928,750 |
| 1994 | 357,706,125 | 10% | 35,770,613 | 27,400,000 | 8,370,613 | 4,800,000 | 3,570,613 |
| 1995 | 368,437,309 | 10% | 36,843,731 | 29,400,000 | 7,443,731 | 3,500,000 | 3,943,731 |
| 1996 | 379,490,428 | 10% | 37,949,043 | 31,400,000 | 6,549,043 | 2,700,000 | 3,849,043 |
| 1997 | 390,875,141 | 10% | 39,087,514 | 33,400,000 | 5,687,514 | 1,500,000 | 4,187,514 |
| 1998 | 402,601,395 | 10% | 40,260,140 | 35,400,000 | 4,860,140 | 2,300,000 | 2,560,140 |
| 1999 | 414,679,437 | 10% | 41,467,944 | 37,400,000 | 4,067,944 | 2,400,000 | 1,667,944 |
| 2000 | 427,119,820 | 10% | 42,711,982 | 39,400,000 | 3,311,982 | 2,500,000 | 811,982 |

The current bonding capacity is determined by simply multiplying the assessed valuation by .10 (10 percent). The assessed valuation of the district represents one-third of the market value of all property located within the boundaries of the district. Projection of the assessed valuation over the period represented by the building needs assessment will provide the basis for determining the bonding capacity each year. In a growing district, the previous five-year's growth in assessed valuation provides an indication of the percentage of increase expected over the next ten-year period. While a recession may slow the residential and commercial growth of the district, it would also serve to perhaps reduce the need for a new facility at that time. Exhibit 4-7 has a column that lists the outstanding bonds previously sold by the district. This figure must be subtracted from the total bonding capacity to obtain the current bonding capacity. The specific costs of the building needs are then subtracted from the current bonding capacity. A negative figure in any year would indicate that there is an insufficient bonding capacity to cover the building costs.

### Selection of Bond Counsel

Within the legal profession, the practice of law regarding the issuance of general obligation bonds is a specialty. Law firms specializing in bond issues are listed in the *Directory of Municipal Bond Dealers*. The bond attorney provides counsel to the district regarding the following:

1. Determination of the district's legal authority to issue the bonds;
2. Preparation of all official minute entries and resolutions passed by the board of education authorizing the election, preparing the ballot, selling the bonds, issuing the bonds, and the final delivery and closing of the bond sale;
3. Review of all information contained in the prospectus sent to bidders;
4. Preparation of the official transcript for certification of the bonds by the state auditor; and
5. Issuance of a legal opinion, printed on each bond certifying that all legal requirements have been met by the district. Exhibit 4-8 is an example of a legal opinion written by a bond attorney which appears on the bonds.

EXHIBIT 4-8 • *Sample Legal Opinion*

---

TO WHOM IT MAY CONCERN

This is to certify that we have examined a transcript of the proceedings of the Board of Education Meeting of the _____ School District, in the County of _____ in the State of _____, and other documents relative to the issuance of One Million, Five Hundred Thousand Dollars ($1,500,000) of School Bonds of said District, dated October 1, 1986; said bonds bearing interest at the rates per annum, hereinafter designated and maturing, without option of prior payment, in the amounts and at the times following, to-wit:

| Rate of Interest | Amount | Maturity |
|---|---|---|
| 6.50% | $ 50,000 | March 1, 1990 |
| 6.50% | $ 50,000 | March 1, 1991 |
| 6.50% | $75,000 | March 1, 1992 |
| 6.50% | $75,000 | March 1, 1993 |
| 6.50% | $50,000 | March 1, 1994 |
| 5.80% | $50,000 | March 1, 1995 |
| 5.75% | $100,000 | March 1, 1996 |
| 5.75% | $100,000 | March 1, 1997 |
| 5.75% | $100,000 | March 1, 1998 |
| 5.75% | $100,000 | March 1, 1999 |
| 5.75% | $100,000 | March 1, 2000 |
| 5.75% | $100,000 | March 1, 2001 |
| 5.80% | $150,000 | March 1, 2002 |
| 5.80% | $150,000 | March 1, 2003 |
| 5.80% | $100,000 | March 1, 2004 |

We have also examined the law under authority of which said bonds are issued and executed bond numbered 1 of said issue prior to its completion and authentication.

From such examination we are of the opinion that the bonds of the aforesaid issue, when property completed and authenticated as provided on the face of each of said bonds, shall constitute valid and legally-binding general obligations of the _____ School District, payable both as to principal and interest, from the ad valorem taxes which may be levied without limit as to rate or amount, upon all taxable, tangible property within the territorial limits of said district.

In view of the provisions of the Tax Reform Act of 1986, the board of education of the said district has covenanted not to do and not to refrain from doing anything, within its lawful powers, in the course of issuing said bond or in the use or expenditure of the proceeds thereof which would result in the interest income derived or to be derived from said bond becoming taxable for Federal Income Tax purposes.

Very Truly Yours,

_____

Signature of Bond Attorney and Firm

---

EXHIBIT 4-9 • *Sample Bond Authorization Ballot*

---

Shall the board of education of the _____ School District borrow money in the amount of one million, five hundred thousand dollars ($1,500,000) for the purpose of purchasing a schoolhouse site; and erecting an elementary school; and issue bonds for the payments thereof.

---

## Election Date and Polling Places

Each state governs the election dates available to school districts and the percentage of votes necessary to pass a bond issue. While many require a simple majority of the voters to approve a bond issue, others require "super majorities" of 57 percent or even 66 2/3 percent for approval.

## Preparation of the Ballot

Exhibit 4-9 is a typical example of a ballot authorizing the district to issue bonds. Voter approval of a bond issue automatically allows the board of education to raise the property tax levy to a level sufficient to pay the principal and interest on the bonds.

## Preparation of the Bond Maturity Schedule

Bonds, unlike short-term debt offerings where the entire principal of the borrowing is payable on a specified date, have different maturity dates throughout the life of the issue. Therefore, each year, a specific number of bonds mature, and the principal of those bonds is payable at that time. Exhibit 4-10 is an example of a bond maturity schedule for an issue of $1.5 million.

During each of the years listed, the amount of bonds payable to the investors is indicated. It is to the advantage of the district to develop a maturity schedule that allows for the payment of bonds as soon as financially feasible. The longer the maturity schedule, the higher the interest rate will be. Higher rates will have to be offered to attract investors of a bond maturing in fifteen years versus a bond maturing in two or three years, because investors are taking a greater risk regarding the return on the investment. A fifteen-year bond purchased at 8 percent will not be an

EXHIBIT 4-10 • *Bond Maturity Schedule*

| Year | Amount |
|------|--------|
| 1981 | $ 50,000 |
| 1982 | $ 50,000 |
| 1983 | $75,000 |
| 1984 | $75,000 |
| 1985 | $50,000 |
| 1986 | $50,000 |
| 1987 | $100,000 |
| 1988 | $100,000 |
| 1989 | $100,000 |
| 1990 | $100,000 |
| 1991 | $100,000 |
| 1992 | $100,000 |
| 1993 | $150,000 |
| 1994 | $150,000 |
| 1995 | $150,000 |
| 1996 | $100,000 |

attractive investment if interest rates should rise during the term of the bond. The investor will be unable to sell the bond, except at a discount, in the secondary market. However, in the event that interest rates fall below the bond rate, the investor will have a higher current investment income than is available in the market. The investor also will be able to sell the bond in the secondary market at a premium. Since the future is always unknown, the higher interest rates on longer maturing bonds gives the investor a measure of safety and an incentive to purchase.

## Selection of a Paying Agent, Bond Registrar, and Transfer Agent

Prior to 1982, general obligation bonds were issued in bearer form. The owners of the bonds were literally the individuals who had them in their possession. No record of bond owners was maintained. Coupons were attached to the bonds and represented the interest payments. When interest was due, the appropriate coupon was detached and submitted to the paying agent. When the bond matured, the bond was submitted to the paying agent and the principal was paid.

Since January, 1983, all general obligation bonds must be issued in registered form to retain their tax-exempt status.[7] This federal law requires school districts, through a bond registrar, to maintain a current list of bond holders. Basically, the responsibilities of the paying agent, bond registrar, and transfer agent are:

1. To act as the district's agent when interest payments and bond principal are due to the investors. The paying agent receives the funds from the district and disburses them to the investors.
2. To be responsible for issuing the bonds, in registered form, to the investors in an amount no lower than stipulated by the district at the time of sale.
3. To maintain a record of ownership and to act as transfer agent each time the bonds are sold on the secondary market. The secondary market refers to the sale of bonds between investors subsequent to the original issue of the district.

Since designation of the paying agent, bond registrar, and transfer agent must precede the sale of the bonds, districts take bids for these services well in advance of the actual sale. The choice of the agent is based on the fees charged for the issue. As long as the bids are from reputable, professional agents, the district will select the bid representing the lowest fee structure. The agent's services will continue until the last bond of the issue has matured.

## Preparation for the Bond Sale

Several items must be accomplished prior to the actual acceptance of bids. The district is responsible for the preparation of the prospectus, the application for a bond rating, and the publication of the sale.

### *Prospectus*
The prospectus is the formal written offer to sell the bonds. This document contains financial, legal, and historical information concerning the district. From this information, prospective bidders will decide whether to bid for the bonds, and at what interest rate. The prospectuses of many districts are prepared by financial consultants and encompass several pages and many different formats. They all should include, at a minimum, the following information:

1. The date, time, and place where bids will be accepted, opened, and awarded.

2. The minimum denomination of each bond. Most general obligations bonds are issued in a minimum denomination of $5,000, or any whole multiple thereof.

3. The maximum interest rate allowed by state law, if applicable. Even when bonds are sold competitively, the state may regulate the maximum allowable rate.

4. The bond registrar, paying agent, and transfer agent.

5. The maturity schedule of the bonds.

6. The date each year that the applicable bonds will mature and the semi-annual dates for the payment of interest. For example, the issue may stipulate that the bonds will mature on March 1 of each calendar year, and interest will be paid annually on September 1 and March 1.

7. A legal opinion by the bond attorney attesting to the tax-exempt status of the bonds.

8. Specific requirements for bidding the bond rates. It is customary that all bonds of the same maturity bear the same interest rate. Also that proposed interest rates be stated in whole multiples of either 1/8 of 1 percent or 1/10 of 1 percent. The allowable spread of interest rates should be identified. For example, "any bid will be rejected which specifies interest rates the highest of which exceeds the lowest of which by more that 2 percent per year."

9. The specific amount of the "good faith check." Bond bids should require the submission of a "good faith check" equal to 2 percent of the total bond issue. If a bidder is awarded the sale and refuses to purchase the bonds at the bid price, the bidder forfeits the check to the district. After the bid is awarded by the board of education, the checks of the unsuccessful bidders are returned, and the successful bidder's check is retained until the delivery of the bonds and closing of the sale. The check is not cashed, but held by the district.

10. The anticipated delivery date of the bonds is identified. The customary delivery date is between thirty and forty-five days after the sale.

11. The following financial and demographic information is presented.

    A. The population growth of the district over the past twenty years.

    B. The assessed valuation of the district for the current year and previous five years.

    C. The total bonded indebtedness of the district and a listing of outstanding bonds.

    D. A cash flow analysis of the disctrict's funds for the current year and for the previous five years.

    E. The tax collections of the district for the current year and for the previous five years.

F.   A listing of the overlapping debt. Overlapping debt is the current indebtedness of other taxing jurisdictions within the boundaries of the school district. (e.g., fire district, library district, municipalities, etc.)

G.   A listing of the largest taxpayers within the district. It is important for investors to know if the district's commercial base is limited to one or two large companies. A loss of one of these large taxpayers could have a negative effect on the district's ability to meet the debt payments. Therefore, from the investors point of view, it is more desirable to have the tax base spread among a number of commercial and residential properties.

12.   The proposal form to be used by the bidders.

### Bond Ratings

Similar to the ratings assigned to short-term notes, Standard and Poor's and Moody's Investors Service rate general obligation bond issues. The process is initiated by an application prepared by the district and mailed to the rating service about one month before the sale. Exhibit 4-11 represents the procedure used by Moody's on receipt of the application.[8]

Exhibit 4-12 is an explanation of the ratings assigned by Standard and Poor's[9] and Moody's[10] to bond issues.

EXHIBIT 4-11 • *Mechanics of the Rating Process*

---

1.   Application
2.   Municipal calendar entry
3.   Assignment of issue to analyst
4.   Receipt of documentation
5.   Preliminary research
6.   Meeting and/or on-site visit (optional)
7.   Completion of analysis
8.   Analyst's rating recommendations
9.   Sign-off procedure with area manager
10.   Presentation to municipal department rating committee
11.   Committee decision
12.   Rating assignment
13.   Rating released to issuer
14.   Rating released to public
15.   Distribution of municipal credit report
16.   Annual request to issuer for debt

---

EXHIBIT 4-12 • *School Bond Rating Classifications*[9]

---

*Standard & Poor's*

*AAA*

Debt rated AAA has the highest rating assigned by Standard & Poor's to a debt obligation. Capacity to pay interest and repay principal is extremely strong.

*AA*

Debt rated AA has a very strong capacity to pay interest and repay principal and differs from the highest rated issues only in a small degree.

*A*

Debt rated A has a strong capacity to pay interest and repay principal although it is somewhat more suspectible to the adverse effects of changes in circumstances and economic conditions than debt in higher categories.

*BBB*

Debt rated BBB is regarded as having an adequate capacity to pay interest and repay principal. Whereas such debt normally exhibits adequate protection parameters, adverse economic conditions or changing circumstances are more likely to lead to a weakened capacity to pay interest and repay principal for debts in this category than for debts in higher rated categories.

*BB, B, CCC, CC*

Debt rated in any of the above categories is regarded, on balance, as predominantly speculative with respect to capacity to pay interest and repay principal.

*Moody's Investor Service*

*Aaa*

Bonds which are rated Aaa are judged to be of the best quality. They carry the smallest degree of investment risk and are generally referred to as "gilt-edge." Interest payments are protected by a large or by an exceptionally stable margin and principal is secure. While the various protective elements are likely to change, such changes as can be visualized are most unlikely to impair the fundamentally strong position of such issues.

*Aa*

Bonds which are rated Aa are judged to be of high quality by all standards. Together with the Aaa group they comprise what are generally known as high-grade bonds. They are rated lower than the best bonds because margins of protection may not be as large as in Aaa securities or fluctuation of protective elements may be of greater amplitude or there may be other elements present which make the term risks appear somewhat larger than in Aaa securities.

*A*

Bonds which are rated A possess many favorable instrument attributes and are to be considered as upper medium grade obligations. Factors giving security to principal and interest are considered adequate, but elements may be present which suggest a susceptibility to impairment sometime in the future.

*Baa*

Bonds which are rated Baa are considered as medium-grade obligations; i.e., they are neither highly protected nor poorly secured. Interest payments and principal security appear adequate for the present but certain protective elements may be lacking or may be characteristically unreliable over any great length of time. Such bonds lack outstanding investment characteristics and, in fact, have speculative characteristics as well.

*Ba*

Bonds which are rated Ba are judged to have speculative elements. Their future cannot be considered as well assured. Often the protection of interest and principal payments may be very moderate, and, thereby, not well safeguarded during both good and bad times over the future. Uncertainty of position characterizes bonds in this case.

*B*

Bonds which are rated B generally lack characteristics of a desirable investment. Assurance of interest and principal payments or of maintenance of other terms of the contract over any long period of time may be small.

*Caa, Ca, C*

These bonds are in poor standing with high degrees of default.

---

It is always to the school district's advantage to have the highest possible rating. Ratings impact the sale of bonds in two ways. First, the higher the rating, the lower the interest rate bid for the bonds. A higher rating reflects less risk to the investors and therefore a lower interest rate. Secondly, the rating has an impact on the number of bidders. Generally, higher rated issues attract more bidders because the issue reflects less risk and higher marketability. The rating agencies release their rating for the bond issue shortly before the bid date. Exhibit 4-13 demonstrates the relationship between interest rates and Moody's bond ratings of Aaa, A, and Baa on sales as of May 2, 1988.[11]

In order to maintain current information on the school district, the rating agencies request annual audit and budget information. If a district feels that its tax base has improved to the extent that a higher rating is warranted, an on-site visit should be requested. This gives the rating agencies the opportunity to do an in-depth analysis of the district's current and potential strength.

EXHIBIT 4-13 • *General Obligation Bond Issues*

| Maturity | Aaa | A | Baa |
|----------|-------|-------|-------|
| 1988 | 4.50% | 4.75% | 5.00% |
| 1989 | 4.75% | 5.00% | 5.25% |
| 1990 | 5.00% | 5.25% | 5.50% |
| 1991 | 5.20% | 5.50% | 5.75% |
| 1992 | 5.45% | 5.75% | 6.00% |
| 1993 | 5.70% | 6.00% | 6.25% |
| 1994 | 5.90% | 6.20% | 6.50% |
| 1995 | 6.00% | 6.35% | 6.70% |
| 1996 | 6.20% | 6.50% | 6.90% |
| 1997 | 6.30% | 6.60% | 7.00% |
| 1998 | 6.40% | 6.70% | 7.10% |
| 2008 | 7.50% | 7.75% | 8.00% |
| 2018 | 7.80% | 8.00% | 8.20% |

## Publication of the Sale

After the development of the prospectus and the application for the bond rating has been completed, the district begins the process of soliciting bids from bond underwriters. Districts in the bond market frequently maintain a current bid list based on previous bond issues. However, if the district has not sold bonds for several years, the bond attorney can identify commercial banks and brokerage firms with an interest in underwriting bond issues appropriate to the size and rating of the debt offering. A copy of the prospectus is also sent to the *Bond Buyer*, the daily newspaper of the bond market. For a fee, the bid announcement is listed along with other issues on the market at the same time.

The role of the underwriter is discussed in Coe's *Public Financial Management.*

> Regardless of whether publicly or privately issued, bonds are initially underwritten by banking firms or commercial banks. Underwriting is the intermediate service of transferring securities from governments to investors. Investment bankers provide three basic services: (1) origination, (2) distribution, and (3) risk bearing. Origination occurs in a negotiated sale when underwriters assist the government in designing and marketing the issue. Distribution and risk bearing happen when underwriters take possession of the bonds and price them for resale to investors.[12]

Unless specifically prohibited by state law, districts have the option of selling the bonds through a negotiated sale or competitive bidding. This discussion has centered on bringing the issue to market on a competitive basis. However, there are two occasions when a negotiated sale may be to the advantage of the district. First, if the bond issue is small and is unlikely to attract a lot of bidders, the district may find it beneficial to negotiate the sale with a local bank. Often, the district's bank depository will assist the district in finding a buyer, or will, at times, purchase the issue. Second, if the district feels that its present financial circumstances would not warrant at least a Baa through Moody's or a BBB through Standard & Poor's, a negotiated sale may be more beneficial. Private sales are not rated by the two agencies; therefore, the district does not risk a low rating. Without these two factors, a competitive sale is more favorable to the district.

### Sale of the Bonds

Bond bids are typically opened and awarded at a board of education meeting. The bond attorney should be present to review the bids for compliance with the specifications in the proposal form. General obligations bonds are normally sold at par (face value); however, market conditions at times require the underwriter to offer to purchase at a discount (below par) or at a premium (above par). Some states regulate the sale of bonds at a discount. Statutes may be present that disallow any sale of bonds below a certain percentage of par. For example, the state may require bonds to be sold at not lower than 95 percent of par.

Bond proposal forms require the bidder to list the interest rates by maturity dates and to calculate the gross interest cost, net interest cost, and average interest rate.

*Maturity Dates* The bidder lists each of the maturity dates identified in the prospectus with the interest rates proposed. As stipulated in the prospectus, all bonds maturing on the same date must bear the same interest rate. Exhibit 4-14 is an illustration of this section of the bid.

*Gross Interest Cost* This represents the total interest cost over the entire life of the issue. It identifies the total interest cost payable by the district based on the interest rates on each of the maturity dates.

*Net Interest Cost* This is a common method of calculating the total interest expense to the issuer of the bonds. The net interest cost reflects the gross interest expense plus the discount or minus the premium. A discounted sale increases the interest costs because the sale of the bonds will be at less than par. Likewise, a premium decreases the overall net interest because the bidder is paying above par for the bonds. If the bonds are sold at par, the gross interest expense and the net interest cost will be the same. The bidder with the lowest net interest cost is awarded the bid.

EXHIBIT 4-14 • *Interest Rates*

| Date of Maturity | Principal | Rate |
|---|---|---|
| March 1, 1981 | $ 50,000 | 6 1/2% |
| March 1, 1982 | 50,000 | 6 1/2% |
| March 1, 1983 | 75,000 | 6 1/2% |
| March 1, 1984 | 75,000 | 6 1/2% |
| March 1, 1985 | 50,000 | 6 1/2% |
| March 1, 1986 | 50,000 | 5 4/5% |
| March 1, 1987 | 100,000 | 5 3/4% |
| March 1, 1988 | 100,000 | 5 3/4% |
| March 1, 1989 | 100,000 | 5 3/4% |
| March 1, 1990 | 100,000 | 5 3/4% |
| March 1, 1991 | 100,000 | 5 3/4% |
| March 1, 1992 | 100,000 | 5 3/4% |
| March 1, 1993 | 150,000 | 5 3/4% |
| March 1, 1994 | 150,000 | 5 4/5% |
| March 1, 1995 | 150,000 | 5 7/8% |
| March 1, 1996 | 100,000 | 5 7/8% |

## Average Interest Rate

This represents the average rate paid by the district during the life of the issue.

In order to verify the net interest cost and average interest rates, the district can use the *Table of Bond Years* usually found in the prospectus. The following represents an explanation of the *Table of Bond Years* in Exhibit 4-15.

Column 1  Represents the calendar years that the principal of the issue is payable.

Column 2  Represents the time lapse between the issuing date of the bonds and the maturity date. The bonds maturing in 1981 represent bonds issued 1.4 years previously. Likewise, bonds maturing in 1996 represent bonds issued 16.4 years previously.

Column 3  Even though general obligations bonds are issued in $5,000 denominations, bond dealers use $1000 when referring to the issue. This is the result of a time when these bonds were issued in $1000 denominations. Therefore, it has become a tradition to refer to them in 1000's.

Column 4   Bonds years is the product of multiplying column two by column three. The year 1981 represents the maturity of $50,000 of bonds issued for 1.4 years each.

Column 5   Cumulative bond years is the accumulating effect of column four. Each of the bond years is added to the maturing bonds for the year.

Column 6   Interest rates represent the rates proposed by the successful bidder (Exhibit 4-12).

Column 7   This represents the product of multiplying the bonds years (column 4) by the interest rates (column 6). Therefore, the $50,000 of bonds maturing in year 1981 will earn approximately $4,600 (4.60 x 1000) of interest. The total of column 7 represents a total gross interest cost of approximately $902,434.67 (902,434.67 x 1000).

EXHIBIT 4-15 • *Table of Bond Years*

| Year (1) | Years Run (2) | x | Number of 1000's (3) | | Bond Years (4) | | Cumulative Bond Years (5) | Interest (6) | Total (7) |
|---|---|---|---|---|---|---|---|---|---|
| 1981 | 1.41667 | X | 50 | = | 70.8335 | = | | 6.5000% | 4.60417750 |
| 1982 | 2.41667 | X | 50 | = | 120.8335 | = | 191.6670 | 6.5000% | 7.85417750 |
| 1983 | 3.41667 | X | 75 | = | 256.2503 | = | 447.9173 | 6.5000% | 16.65626625 |
| 1984 | 4.41667 | X | 75 | = | 331.2503 | = | 779.1675 | 6.5000% | 21.5312625 |
| 1985 | 5.41667 | X | 50 | = | 270.8335 | = | 1050.0010 | 6.5000% | 17.60417750 |
| 1986 | 6.41667 | X | 50 | = | 320.8335 | = | 1370.8345 | 5.8000% | 18.60834300 |
| 1987 | 7.41667 | X | 100 | = | 741.6670 | = | 2112.5015 | 5.7500% | 42.64585250 |
| 1988 | 8.41667 | X | 100 | = | 841.6670 | = | 2954.1685 | 5.7500% | 48.39585250 |
| 1989 | 9.41667 | X | 100 | = | 941.6670 | = | 3895.8355 | 5.7500% | 54.14585250 |
| 1990 | 10.41667 | X | 100 | = | 1041.6670 | = | 4937.5025 | 5.7500% | 59.89585250 |
| 1991 | 11.41667 | X | 100 | = | 1141.6670 | = | 6079.1695 | 5.7500% | 65.64585250 |
| 1992 | 12.41667 | X | 100 | = | 1241.6670 | = | 7320.8365 | 5.7500% | 71.39585250 |
| 1993 | 13.41667 | X | 150 | = | 2012.5005 | = | 9333.3370 | 5.7500% | 115.71877875 |
| 1994 | 14.41667 | X | 150 | = | 2162.5005 | =11495.8375 | | 5.8000% | 125.42502900 |
| 1995 | 15.41667 | X | 150 | = | 2312.5005 | =13808.3380 | | 5.8750% | 135.85940438 |
| 1996 | 16.41667 | X | 100 | = | 1641.6670 | =15450 | | 5.8750% | 96.44793625 |
| Total | | | 1500 | | 15,450 | | | | 902.43467138 |

| | |
|---|---|
| Gross Interest Cost | $902,434.67 |
| Net Interest Cost | $902,434.67 |
| Average Interest Rate | 5.84099922% |
| Net Interest Cost Rate | 5.84099922% |

EXHIBIT 4-16 • *Differences in Net Interest Cost*

---

*Bonds Sold at Par*

| | |
|---|---|
| Gross Interest Cost | = $902,434.67 |
| Net Interest Cost | = $902,434.67 |

$$\text{Average Interest Rate} = \frac{\text{Total Interest Cost}}{\text{Total Bond Years} \cdot 1000}$$

$$= \frac{\$902,434.67}{15,450 \cdot 1000} = \frac{\$902,434.67}{15,450,000} = 5.84\%$$

Net Interest Cost Rate    = 5.84%

*Bonds Sold at a Discount of $30,000*

| | |
|---|---|
| Gross Interest Cost | = $902,434.67 |
| Net Interest Cost | = Gross Interest Cost + Discount |
| | = $902,434.67 + $30,000 |
| | = $932,434.67 |
| Average Interest Rate | = 5.84% |

$$\text{Net Interest Cost Rate} = \frac{\text{Total Interest Cost} + \text{Discount}}{\text{Total Bond Years} \cdot 1000}$$

$$= \frac{\$902,434.67 + \$30,000}{15,450 \cdot 1000}$$

$$= \frac{932,434.67}{15,450,000} = 6.04\%$$

*Bonds Sold at a Premium*

| | |
|---|---|
| Gross Interest Cost | = $902,434.67 |
| Net Interest Cost | = Gross Interest Cost - Premium |
| | = $902,434.67 - $30,000 |
| | = $872,434.67 |
| Average Interest Rate | = 5.84% |

$$\text{Net Interest Cost Rate} = \frac{\text{Total Interest Cost} - \text{Premium}}{\text{Total Bond Years} \cdot 1000}$$

$$= \frac{\$902,434.67 - \$30,000}{15,450 \cdot 1000}$$

$$= \frac{\$872,434.67}{15,450,000} = 5.65\%$$

---

If the bonds are sold at par (face value), the gross interest cost and the net interest cost would be the same amount. This would also be true for the average interest rate and the net interest rate. Exhibit 4-16 demonstrates the different results for bonds sold at par, discount, and premium.

### *Printing and Delivery of the Bonds*

After the award by the board of education, the bonds are printed and delivered to the underwriter. Specifications for printing are prepared by the bond attorney and competitive bids are received by professional printing firms. While the printing of the bonds and the acceptance of printing bids are a minor matter, the district should remember that the printed bonds are a reflection of the district. Therefore, printing quality should supercede price in this case.

The bond attorney inspects the bonds for accuracy and prepares the final transcript for delivery. Many states require certification of the bonds by a state official, usually the state treasurer or state auditor. The official reviews the transcripts to verify that the district is not exceeding the statutory debt limit and that proper resolutions were approved by the board of education throughout the bond process. A book entry of the bonds at the state level insures that the interest will be tax-exempt for state income taxes. The delivery of the bonds to the underwriter is accompanied by a non-litigation certificate and a signature guarantee certificate. The non-ligation certificate, usually signed by the clerk of the circuit court, stipulates that no lawsuits have been filed challenging the legitimacy of the bond election or issue. The signature guarantee, after it is signed by the president of the bank depository, attests to the validity of the board president's and secretary's signature appearing on the bonds. A final legal opinion by bond counsel is prepared and the bonds are exchanged for the purchase price minus the good faith check already in the district's possession. The funds are made available immediately for investment by the district.

## Arbitrage

Arbitrage refers to the investing of the proceeds of a security at a higher interest rate than the rate paid through the sale of the security. With respect to school district general obligation bonds, arbitrage is the investment of the cash received from the sale of the bonds at an interest rate higher than the interest rate paid on the bonds. As mentioned earlier, this is possible because tax-exempt bonds are sold at lower rates than taxable bonds.

The *Tax Reform Act of 1986* places severe restrictions on the arbitrage of school bond proceeds. It requires a rebate to the U.S. Government every five years. While the act took effect on January 1, 1986, the U.S. Treasury did not issue regulations governing the computation of the arbitrage until June, 1989. Essentially, an arbitrage rebate requires a mandatory payment to the U.S. Treasury whenever bond proceeds are invested at a higher yield than the tax-exempt borrowing rate. The act does provide for the following exception to the arbitrage restrictions.

1.  The rebate does not apply to school districts issuing $5 million or less each calendar year.
2.  The rebate does not apply if the bonds proceeds are expended with six months of the sale.
3.  The rebate does not apply if the proceeds are invested in qualified federally tax-exempt securities or mutual funds.
4.  The rebate does not apply if the invested proceeds earn income at a computed weighted average below the yield on the bonds.

Revisions to the act were passed by Congress in December, 1989. The most significant change for school districts is the exemption from the rebate if bond proceeds are expended within two years for construction projects. However, more revisions are anticipated and school districts should pay particular attention to further developments. To districts that do not qualify for one or more of the exemptions, tracking of the interest income on the bonds is necessary. The rebate requires a payment of 90 percent of the "excess" earnings at each five-year interval during the life of the bond issue, and a final payment within sixty days after the last bond is redeemed. Failure to comply with the rebate requirements can result in forfeiture of the tax-exempt status of the bonds to the investors.

## Refunding Bonds

When structuring a bond issue, the school district has the option of including a call provision. This allows the district to redeem outstanding bonds prior to their maturity date. The advantage of the call provision is the flexibility the district has to take advantage of a decrease in bond rates. The disadvantages are related to the effect of the call provision on both interest cost and marketability. Bonds issues with a call provision customarily sell at a higher interest rate than those without the provision. The higher interest rate acts as an incentive to encourage investors to purchase a bond with a call provision. Marketing bonds with a call provision usually requires the stipulation that, if the call provision is executed, the district will purchase the bonds at or above par.

The refunding process is accomplished through the issuance of bonds at a lower interest rate. The proceeds allow the district to exercise the call and to pay off the initial bonds. The debt service of the refunding bonds is handled in the same manner as the original issue.

Refunding can also occur if the district did not include a call provision. The proceeds from the refunding bonds are invested, usually in government securities, and timed to mature when the principal and interest on the original issue is payable each year. Essentially, the refunding bonds simply meet the debt service requirements of the original issue. The investor is not affected, and can retain ownership of the bonds until maturity. Depending on state statutes, the refunding bonds may not affect the district's debt limitation.

## Municipal Leasehold Revenue Financing

An alternative to the use of general obligation bond issues to finance capital projects is municipal leasehold revenue financing. The school district board of education creates a not-for-profit school building corporation which finances the construction or renovations of a school facility. The financing comes from the sale of tax-exempt bonds issued by the not-for-profit building corporation. The school district acquires ownership of the facility through lease payments equal to the principal and interest on the bonds. When the last bond matures, the not-for-profit building corporation is dissolved and the facility becomes the property of the school district.

The primary advantage of this type of financing for the school district is the method by which the lease payments are made. The lease payments are handled as normal operating costs in the general fund. Therefore, no bond election is required. If the district cannot afford the lease payments from current operating funds, a tax levy election would be required. However, in some states, operating levy elections require only a simple majority for passage, while bond elections require a higher majority for approval. Since these lease payments are expended from operating costs, the board must approve the payments through the annual budgeting process.

Since the school district cannot collateralize the lease payments through the automatic increase in ad valorem taxes, the bonds are essentially based on the "good faith" of the district to approve the lease payments each year. As a result, bond insurance guaranteeing the payment of principal and interest is necessary to attract investors for this type of bonds. The leasing agreement is not considered debt to the school district and has no effect on statutory debt limitation. With the exception of establishing a separate school building corporation, the procedure for this financing is similar to a bond issue.

## Summary

The issuance of debt by school districts has become a major responsibility of the business administrator. With the variety of both short-term and long-term financing instruments available, districts must choose the type of debt most beneficial to their current needs. Short-term notes are used to cover deficits in cash flow until tax, revenue, or bond proceeds are received. Long-term debt instruments provide the district with the opportunity to fund the construction or renovation of school facilities, or fund major purchases when operating capital is insufficient to cover the costs. The passage of the Tax Reform Act of 1986, and subsequent revisions, limit the district's ability to arbitrage the proceeds from both short- and long-term debt. Further revisions in the act are anticipated, and may have future consequences for the district. The recent use of municipal leasehold revenue financing has provided another alternative for districts to finance capital expenditures. Regardless of the methods used, school districts will continue to occupy a significant position in the debt market.

## Glossary of Terms[13]

**Accrued interest**   In the sale of a new issue of municipal bonds, the dollar amount, based on the stated rate or rates of interest, that has accrued on the bonds from the dated date, or other stated date, up to but not including the date of delivery. When a bond is purchased in the secondary market, the dollar amount, based on the stated rate of interest, that has accrued on the bond from the most recent interest payment date, up to but not including the date of settlement. Accrued interest is paid to the seller by the purchaser and is usually calculated on a 360-day-year basis.

$$\text{accrued interest} = \text{interest rate} \cdot \text{par value} \cdot \frac{\text{number of days}}{360}$$

**Ad valorem tax**   A direct tax based "according to value" of property. Counties and school districts and municipalities usually are, and special tax districts may be, authorized by law to levy ad valorem taxes on property other than intangible personal property. Local governmental bodies with taxing powers may issue bonds or short-term certificates payable from ad valorem taxation.

**Advanced refunding**   The refinancing of outstanding bonds by the issuance of a new issue of bonds prior to the date on which the outstanding bonds become due or callable. Accordingly, for a period of time, both the issue being refunded and the refunding issue are outstanding. Bonds are "escrowed to maturity" when the proceeds of the refunding bonds are deposited in escrow for investment in federal securities in an amount sufficient to pay, when due, the principal of and interest on the issue being refunded. Bonds are considered pre-refunded when the refunding bond proceeds are escrowed only until the call date of the refunded issue. The Internal Revenue Code restricts the yield which may be earned on investment of the proceeds of refunding bonds.

**Arbitrage**   Generally, transactions by which securities are bought and sold in different markets at the same time for the sake of the profit arising from a difference in prices in the two markets. With respect to the issuance of municipal bonds, arbitrage usually refers to the difference between the interest paid on the bonds issued and the interest earned by investing the bond proceeds in other securities. Arbitrage profits are permitted on bond proceeds for various temporary periods after issuance of municipal bonds.

**Assessed valuation**   An annual determination of the just or fair market value of property by the county property appraiser for purposes of ad valorem taxation. If a tax on property is imposed by virtue of the value of its use, the assessed valuation is its classified use value.

**Average maturity**   The number of years equal to the total bond years divided by the total number of bonds (1 bond = $1000 regardless of actual denomination). The average maturity reflects how rapidly the principal of an issue is expected to be paid and is important to underwriters in calculating bids for new issues of municipal securities.

$$\text{average maturity} = \frac{\text{total bond years}}{\text{number of bonds}}$$

**BAN**   Bond anticipation note.

**Bearer bond**   A bond which is presumed to be owned by the person who holds it. The Tax Equity and Fiscal Responsibility Act of 1982 requires the issuance of municipal bonds in fully registered form, with minor exceptions.

**Bid**   A proposal to purchase an issue of bonds offered for sale either in a competitive offering or on a negotiated basis, specifying the interest rate(s) for each maturity and the purchase price which is usually stated in terms of par, par plus a premium, or par minus a discount

**Bond**   Written evidence of the issuer's obligation to repay a specified principal amount on a certain date (maturity date), together with interest at a stated rate, or according to a formula for determining that rate. Bonds are distinguishable from notes, which mature in a much shorter period of time. Bonds may be classified according to maturity (serial vs. term), source of payment (general obligation vs. revenue), method of transfer (bearer vs. registered), issuer (state vs. municipality vs. special district), or price (discount vs. premium).

**Bond Buyer** A trade paper of the municipal bond industry published in New York City each business day. The paper contains advertisements for offerings of new issues of municipal bonds, notes of bond redemptions, statistical analyses of market activity, results of previous bond sales, and articles relating to financial markets and public finance.

**Bond counsel**  An attorney (or firm of attorneys) retained by the issuer to give a legal opinion that the issuer is authorized to issue proposed bonds, the issuer has met all legal requirements necessary for issuance, and interest on the proposed bonds will be exempt from federal income taxation and where applicable, from state and local taxation. Typically, bond counsel may prepare or review and advise the issuer regarding authorizing resolutions or ordinances, trust indentures, official statements, validation proceedings, and litigation.

**Bonded debt**  The portion of an issuer's total indebtedness represented by outstanding bonds.

**Bond election or bond referendum**  A process whereby the qualified voters of a governmental unit are given the opportunity to approve or disapprove a proposed issue of municipal securities. An election is most commonly required in connection with general obligation bonds. Requirements for voter approval may be imposed by constitution, statute, or local ordinance.

**Bondholder**  The owner of a municipal bond, to whom payments of principal and interest are made. The owner of a bearer bond is the person having possession of it, while the owner of a registered bond is the person whose name is noted on the bond register.

**Bond Investor's Guaranty Insurance Company (BIG)**  Recently formed company providing noncancellable insurance contracts that agree to pay a bondholder all, or any part, of a scheduled bond principal and interest payment as it becomes due and payable, in the event the issuer is unable to pay. Consists of American International Group, Bankers Trust New York Corporation, Government Employee Insurance Company (GEICO), Philbro-Salomon, Inc., and Xerox Credit Corporation.

**Bond proceeds**  The money paid to the issuer by the purchaser or underwriter for a new issue of municipal bonds. The money is used to finance the project or purpose for which the bonds were issued and to pay certain costs of issuance as may be provided in the bond contract.

**Bond years**  The product of the number of bonds (1 bond = $1000 regardless of actual denomination) and the period of time from issuance to the stated maturity. It is used in calculating the average life of an issue and the net interest cost. Computations often include bond years for each maturity or for each interest rate, as well as total bond years for the entire issue.

**Callable bond**  A bond which permits or requires the issuer to redeem the obligation before the stated maturity date at a special price, usually at or above par by giving notice of redemption in a manner specified in the bond contract.

**Closing**  The meeting of concerned parties on the date of delivery to sign bonds and requisite legal documents and to physically deliver the bonds in exchange for payment of the purchase price. The parties at closing usually include representatives of the issuer, bond counsel, and the purchasers (underwriters). Sometimes a preclosing meeting is held on the day before delivery to review the adequacy of the closing procedures and documents.

**Commercial paper (tax-exempt)**   Short-term unsecured promissory notes issued in either registered or bearer form, and usually backed by a line of credit with a bank. Maturities do not exceed 270 days and generally average 30-45 days.

**Competitive bid**   A method of submitting proposals to purchase a new issue of bonds by which the bonds are awarded to the underwriting syndicate presenting the best bid according to stipulated criteria set forth in the notice of sale.

**Debt limit**   The maximum amount of debt which an issuer of municipal securities is permitted to incur under constitutional, statutory, or charter provisions.

**Debt service**   The amount of money necessary to pay interest on an outstanding debt, the serial maturities of principal for serial bonds, and the required contributions to an amortization or sinking fund for term bonds. Debt service on bonds may be calculated on a calendar year, fiscal year, or bond fiscal year basis.

**Denomination**   The face amount or par value of a bond that the issuer promises to pay on the maturity date. Most municipal bonds are issued in the minimum denomination of $5000, although a few issues are available in smaller denominations. Registered bonds may be issued in larger denominations.

**Federal funds**   Refers to immediately available funds representing non-interest-bearing deposits at Federal Reserve banks. They are subsequently used to pay for new issues of municipal bonds.

**Fully registered**   A bond registered as to both principal and interest according to the bond contract. Such bonds are payable to the owner, or in order of the owner, whose name is noted on records of the issue.

**General obligation bonds (G.O. bonds)**   Bonds secured by the full faith and credit of the issuer. General obligation bonds issued by local units of government are secured by a pledge of the issuer's ad valorem taxing power. Ad valorem taxes necessary to pay debt service on general obligation bonds are typically not subject to the constitutional property tax mill rate limits. Such bonds constitute debts of the issuer and normally require approval by election prior to issuance. In the event of default, the holders of general obligation bonds have the rights to compel a tax levy or legislative appropriation, by mandamus or injunction, in order to satisfy the issuer's obligation on the defaulted bonds.

**Good faith deposit**   A sum of money enclosed with the bid in a competitive sale. It is usually in an amount from 1 to 5 percent of the par value of the bond issue, and is generally in the form of a certified or cashier's check. The check is returned to the bidder if the bid is not accepted. The check of the successful bidder is retained by the issuer and applied against the purchase price if the bonds are delivered. In the event the winning bidder fails to pay for the bonds on the delivery date, the check is usually retained by the issuer as full or partial liquidated damages.

**Investment banker**   A firm or an individual member of a firm that underwrites new issues of municipal securities.

**Lease rental bond** Bond usually issued by a non-profit authority and secured by lease payments made by the municipality leasing the project financed by bond proceeds. Source of lessee payments may vary from property taxes to general fund resources to revenues of an enterprise.

**Legal opinion** The written conclusions of bond counsel that the issuance of municipal securities and the proceedings taken connection therewith comply with applicable laws, and that interest on the bonds will be exempt from federal income taxation and, where applicable, from state and local taxation. The legal opinion is generally printed on the bonds.

**Liquidity** Usually refers to the ability to convert assets (such as investments) into cash.

**Market value** Price at which a security can be traded in the current market.

**Maturity** The date upon which the principal of a municipal bond becomes due and payable to the bondholder.

**Municipal bonds** A general term referring to bonds of local governmental subdivisions such as cities, towns, villages, counties, and special districts as well as states and subdivisions thereof, which are exempt from federal income taxation.

**Net interest cost (NIC)** A common method of computing the interest expense to the issuer of bonds. It usually serves as the basis of award in a competitive sale. NIC allows for premium and discount and represents the dollar amount of interest payable over the life of an issue, without taking into account the time value of money. While the net interest cost actually refers to the dollar amount of the issuer's interest cost, it is also used in reference to the average net interest cost rate, reflecting the overall rate of interest to be paid by the issuer over the life of the bonds.

**No litigation certificate** Document provided at the closing of a bond issue which certifies that there is no current litigation affecting issuer's offering in any materially adverse way.

**Notice of redemption** A publication of the issuer's intention to call outstanding bonds prior to their stated maturity dates, in accordance with the bond contract.

**Notice of sale** A publication by an issuer describing an anticipated new offering of municipal bonds. It generally contains the date, time and place of sale, amount of issue, type of bond, amount of good faith deposit, basis of award, name of bond counsel, maturity schedule, time and place of delivery, and bid form.

**Par value** In the case of bonds, the amount of principal which must be paid at maturity. Par value is also referred to as the face amount of a security.

**Paying agent** The entity responsible for the payment of interest and principal on municipal bonds on behalf of the issuer. The paying agent is usually a bank or trust company, but may be the treasurer or some other officer of the issuer. The paying agent may also provide other services for the issuer, such as reconciliation of the bonds and coupons paid with the sums of money paid to the paying agent by the issuer, destruction of paid bonds and coupons, indemnification of the issuer for wrongful payment, and registration of the bonds.

**Point**  One percent of par value. Because bond prices are quoted at a percentage of $1000, a point is worth $10 regardless of the actual denomination of a bond. A bond discounted 2 1/2 points, or $25, is quoted at 97 1/2 percent of its value, or $975 per $1000.

**Premium**  The amount by which the price paid for a security exceeds par value, generally representing the difference between the nominal interest and the actual or effective return to the investor.

**Premium call price**  The price over par value, expressed as a percentage of par, which the issuer agrees to pay upon redemption of the outstanding bonds prior to the stated maturity date as provided in the bond contract.

**RAN**  Revenue anticipation note.

**Ratings**  Evaluations of the credit quality of notes and bonds usually made by an independent rating service. Many financial institutions also rate bonds for their own purposes. Ratings generally measure the probability of the timely repayment of principal and interest on municipal bonds. Ratings are initially made before issuance and are continuously reviewed and may be amended to reflect changes in the issuer's credit position. The information required by the rating agencies varies with each bond issue, but generally includes demographics, debt burden, economic base, finances, and management structure. The information is evaluated and the issue is assigned a letter rating which reflects the credit-worthiness of the bonds. The higher the credit rating, the more favorable the effect on the marketability of the bond.

**Registered bond**  A bond listed with the registrar as to ownership, which cannot be sold or exchanged without a change of registration. The Tax Equity and Fiscal Responsibility Act of 1982 requires that all municipal securities with maturities in excess of one year be issued in fully registered form. Existing bearer bonds with attached coupons may provide for registration as to principal and interest in several ways, the most common being the exchange of said bond for a registered bond which has no coupons; the interest payments are then paid directly to the owner. Registration affords protection against payment being made to unauthorized holders of such bonds, as the owner's name is actually placed on the bond itself.

**Serial bonds**  Bonds of an issue in which some bonds mature in each year over a period of years.

**Structuring an issue**  The process of formulating a bond issue within the issuer's legal and financial constraints so the bonds are acceptable in the marketplace. In structuring a new issue of municipal securities, the issuer must determine such factors as maturities, the methods of repayment, redemption provisions, application of bond proceeds, and security provisions and covenants.

**TAN**  Tax anticipation note.

**Tax-exempt bonds**  Bonds whose interest is exempt from federal income taxation pursuant to Section 103 of the Internal Revenue Code, and may or may not be exempt from state income tax or personal property taxation in the jurisdiction where issued. If the bond is exempt from state income tax, it possesses *double exemption* status. *Triple exemption* bonds are exempt from municipal income tax, as well as federal and state income tax.

**Underwrite or underwriting** The process of purchasing all or any part of a new issue of municipal securities from the issuer and offering said securities for sale to the investors.

## Endnotes

1. Freda Stern Ackerman, *Moody's on Municipals: An Introduction to Issuing Debt* (New York: Moody's Investor's Service, Inc.), p. 18.

2. Internal Revenue Code of 1986 (New York: Commerce Clearing House, 1990), p. 4685.

3. Standard & Poor's Corporation, *S & P's Municipal Finance Criteria* (New York: Standard & Poor's Corporation, 1989) p. 85.

4. *Moody's on Municipals*, pp. 51-52.

5. *Ibid.*, p. 50.

6. Deborah A. Verstegen, *School Finance at a Glance* (Washington, D.C.: Education Commission of the States and National Conference of State Legislatures, 1988), pp. 27-32.

7. Internal Revenue Code of 1986, Section 149, p. 4690.

8. *Moody's on Municipals*, p. 42.

9. *S & P's Municipal Finance Criteria*, p. 119.

10. *Moody's on Municipals*, pp. 47-48.

11. "Public Finance," *Newsletter* (Kansas City, Missouri: George K. Baum & Company, June 1988), p. 1.

12. Charles K. Coe, *Public Financial Management* (Englewood Cliffs, New Jersey: Prentice Hall, 1989), p. 173.

13. *Moody's on Municipals*, pp. 54-86.

## Selected Bibliography

Ackerman, Freda, *Moody's on Municipals: An Introduction to Issuing Debt* (New York: Moody's Investor Service, 1987).

Holt, Robert L., *The Complete Book of Bonds* (New York: Harper & Row, 1985).

Standard & Poor's Corporation, *S & P's Municipal Finance Criteria* (New York: Standard & Poor's Corporation, 1989).

The New York Institute of Finance, *How the Bond Market Works* (New York: NYIF Corporation, 1988).

# 5

# Constructing the School District Budget

Budgeting is the most important task of the board of education and the administration. This statement may evoke a strong denial from some board members and administrators who have been conditioned to believe that developing the instructional program is their most important task. However, it is self-evident that *everything* undertaken by the school district costs money. There is no aspect of operations that does not have a price tag attached. This is not always apparent to the casual observer.[1]

For example, a teachers' union negotiating with the administration may take the position that payroll deduction of union dues is a no-cost item to the district. Someone, however, would have to be assigned by the central office administrator responsible for payroll to perform this function. That person receives a salary and would have a certain amount of work time dedicated to implementing the payroll deduction. If the school district has a large teaching staff, additional clerical help could be needed.

Of course, developing and improving the instructional program is the central objective, not only of the board of education but also of the administration. Budgeting is the process that brings this objective to fruition.

Also, there is no question about how necessary it is for the board of education to involve administrators, faculty, staff, high school students, parents, and concerned citizens in the process of developing goals and objectives for the school district. This is an ongoing need that is sometimes formalized by a master plan. The master plan is updated after a certain number of years, perhaps three or five.

Goals and objectives should be developed for every aspect of school-district operations from the maintenance of facilities to the instructional program. Once identified, these goals and objectives become the priorities that are used in developing the budget.

The process for involving the various public groups in developing goals and objectives is outside the scope and purpose of this text, but it is important to understand the relationship that exists between district goals and objectives and budget priorities.

There is another reason why budgeting is such an important task. The taxpayers of each school district are entitled to know how much of their tax monies are being spent for every aspect of school operations. Boards and administrators are the custodians of public monies and expenditures must hold up against all public scrutiny.

The public is constantly barraged by the news media with reports of misconduct and fraud not only in public organizations but also in private business and industry. This has created a sensitivity in taxpayers that requires school board members and administrators to develop budgeting and budget management processes that will ensure accountability.

## Budgeting Responsibility of the Board of Education

The budgetary process is essentially political. The governance of every school district in the United States is entrusted to a board of education consisting of members who are either elected or appointed. In those states where board members are appointed, those making the appointments are certainly elected officials. Nashville, Tennessee is a case in point.

The public should have a voice in budgeting because public schools are financed through local, state, and federal taxation.[2] The largest portion of this financing is generated through local property taxes, while state income and corporate taxes make up the bulk of state financing.

The federal government, particularly under the Bush administration, finances less than 10 percent of the cost of education in the United States. From the time of the American Revolution, education has been a responsibility of state government.

From this political perspective, it is no surprise that most states have statutory provisions designating the local board of education as having direct responsibility over preparing the budget. An integral part of this responsibility is setting the tax rate that will generate local property tax receipts.

Except in the smallest of school districts, it is impossible for the board of education as a whole or even a committee of the board to develop the budget without the assistance of the professional staff. Further, it would be inappropriate for the board or a committee of the board to undertake such a task without consultation with administrators, teachers, and staff members.

Therefore, in most school districts, the board of education requires the superintendent of schools to develop the budget and, then, reserves to itself the right to approve the budget. The superintendent, in turn, will usually call upon central office staff and upon the building principals and teachers to develop aspects of the budget to be consolidated into the district budget.

Because education is a state responsibility, most state legislatures have passed statutory requirements that boards of education must follow in approving the budget. To monitor these requirements, state legislatures have also created state departments of education. These agencies usually develop guidelines that local districts must follow in order to be in compliance with state statutes. State departments of education can usually withhold state aid if the local district is out of compliance.

One final point needs to be made. As political entities, board of education members are certainly influenced by the citizens who voted them into office or by the elected officials who appointed them to their respective boards. The challenge is for board members to resist this influence unless it is directed toward the growth and development of the educational program. The discernment of this motive requires continual vigilance.

## Budgeting Responsibility of the Administration

As the chief executive officer of the board of education, the superintendent is responsible for coordinating the budgeting tasks of the administration staff.[3]

In school districts of over 3000 students, the superintendent usually shares budgeting tasks with a business manager or assistant superintendent. The model used in this text is that of a school district with an assistant superintendent for business and financial services. Thus, this person would have the job responsibility of implementing the administrative budgeting process. For clarity, the budgeting process has been divided here into nine steps.

### Calculate an Enrollment Projection[4]

There are two aspects to projecting future enrollments—the first step in the budgeting process from an administrative perspective.

#### *Enrollment Protection Process*

This first aspect consists of developing an ongoing process of enrollment projection. All school districts should have a method of projecting enrollments for a five-year period. Each year, a new five-year projection can be made when the actual enrollment is verified during the first month of each academic year.

In addition, it is better to select a certain day on which the official enrollment will be taken. For example, the fourth Wednesday in September will allow enough time for the school year to settle in, and should yield an accurate indication of each school's enrollment.

A second date that also produces significant data is the fourth Wednesday in January. This gives the administration the opportunity to calculate the percent of increase or decrease in the pupil population from the first to the second semester.

It is timely for the enrollment projection to be calculated during October of each year because this gives the superintendent and staff an opportunity to study the implications of the new figures before the beginning of the budgeting cycle, December 1.

There are many methods for projecting enrollments, but the most popular is undoubtedly the *percentage of retention*, or *cohort-survival*, technique. This method is predicated on birth rates and the historical retention of students. Birth rates are usually available from state departments of vital statistics. The information provides the number of live births by zip code or census tract. Exhibit 5-1 demonstrates the essence of this technique.

#### *Demographic Data*[5]

There is additional data that can be useful when considering enrollment projection. This data should be weighed against the numerical data produced by the cohort-survival technique.

*Housing starts* are significant because this information shows the market for residential development. Such information is often available from county and/or municipal departments of planning and zoning. Real estate companies and agents also are good sources of information about housing stock turnover and the potential for new residential developments.

EXHIBIT 5-1 • *Cohort-Survival Technique*[6]

Instructions
- I. 1. Fill in birth rate
  2. Fill in first grade enrollment
  3. Do necessary calculations to find average ratio
- II. 1. Fill in enrollment data
  2. Multiply by average ratio
- III. 1. Fill in enrollment data
  2. Do necessary calculations to find retention ratio
  3. Fill in projected first grade enrollment from II into appropriate columns of III
  4. Multiply enrollment for a specific year and class by the retention ratio for the next class—result is the predicted enrollment for that year, next class
  5. Complete chart

I

|  | Birth Rate | 1st Grade Enrollment | | Enrollment Ratio of Birth Rate |
|---|---|---|---|---|
| 1974 | | 1980–1981 | | |
| 1975 | | 1981–1982 | | |
| 1976 | | 1982–1983 | | |
| 1977 | | 1983–1984 | | |
| 1978 | | 1984–1985 | | |
| | | Ratio Totals | | |
| | | Divide by 5 | | |
| | | Average ratio | | |

II

| Birth Rate | X Average Ratio | Projected 1st Grade Enrollment | For Years |
|---|---|---|---|
| 1979 | | | 1985–86 |
| 1980 | | | 1986–87 |
| 1981 | | | 1987–88 |
| 1982 | | | 1988–89 |
| 1983 | | | 1989–90 |

III

| Year | Enrollment by Grade | | | | | | | | | | | |
|---|---|---|---|---|---|---|---|---|---|---|---|---|
| | 1 | 2 | 3 | 4 | 5 | 6 | 7 | 8 | 9 | 10 | 11 | 12 |
| 1974–75 | | | | | | | | | | | | |
| 1975–76 | | | | | | | | | | | | |
| 1976–77 | | | | | | | | | | | | |
| 1977–78 | | | | | | | | | | | | |
| 1978–79 | | | | | | | | | | | | |
| Total by grade | | | | | | | | | | | | |
| Divide by 5 | | | | | | | | | | | | |
| Divide grades | | $\frac{2}{1}$ | $\frac{3}{2}$ | $\frac{4}{3}$ | $\frac{5}{4}$ | $\frac{6}{5}$ | $\frac{7}{6}$ | $\frac{8}{7}$ | $\frac{9}{8}$ | $\frac{10}{9}$ | $\frac{11}{10}$ | $\frac{12}{11}$ |
| Retention ratio | | | | | | | | | | | | |
| P r o j e c t e d   1985 –86 | | | | | | | | | | | | |
| 1986 –87 | | | | | | | | | | | | |
| 1987 –88 | | | | | | | | | | | | |
| 1988 –89 | | | | | | | | | | | | |
| 1989 –90 | | | | | | | | | | | | |
| E n r o l l m e n t   1990 –91 | | | | | | | | | | | | |
| 1991 –92 | | | | | | | | | | | | |
| 1992 –93 | | | | | | | | | | | | |
| 1993 –94 | | | | | | | | | | | | |
| 1994 –95 | | | | | | | | | | | | |

It is very helpful to have a school-district zoning map that highlights the zoning of the various regions of the district—residential, multiple family, business, commercial, recreational, and so on. This information will enhance the data received from a department of planning and zoning and from real estate companies. Such maps can be purchased from companies specializing in real estate development and, in some areas, from government agencies.

The most important message about zoning is that it is usually very difficult to get a tract of land rezoned when there is a strong and well-organized county or municipal government.

Utility companies are another source of information about the potential development of residential and multiple family areas.

Finally, a very important source of information is, of course, a school-district census. It is a good idea to take a census at least every five years. This will provide the administration with good comparative data from the last census and also can be used to verify the accuracy of all other sources of information.

## Calculate Staffing Needs[7]

The second step is to calculate the staffing needed as a consequence of the educational goals and objectives of the school board and as a consequence of the enrollment projection for the forthcoming academic year. Staffing includes not only the professional staff, teachers and administrators, but also support personnel such as teacher assistants, secretaries, custodians, cafeteria workers, bus drivers, and so on. In fact, it is safe to say that for every two teachers there is usually one support person. The overall objective of this second step is the development of a *human resource forecast*. The process for reaching this objective begins with a profile that indicates the status of current human resources. Such a profile will include not only the name of every employee but also his or her age, sex, job title, date of employment, education, special skills, job assignment, and certification for professional personnel.

From this profile, it will be possible to estimate the number of people and the kinds of education and skills that they should have to meet not only the goals and objective of the school district but also the demands imposed by the enrollment projection.

This profile will also help identify a school district's supply of human resources. An increase in this supply can come from two situations—newly hired employees and individuals returning from absences such as maternity, military, and sabbatical leaves. Both types of increases are easily incorporated into a human resource forecast because hiring is controlled and leaves are usually for set periods of time.

Decreases, however, are more difficult to predict. Deaths, voluntary resignations, and dismissals are unpredictable except in the broadest sense, as by statistical averaging.

The available labor force also has a significant effect on the human resource forecast. In recent years, there has been a decrease in the number of applicants for certain types of teaching positions, such as mathematics and science.

The final activity in human resource forecasting is matching the school district's future human resource needs with the current supply. This will pinpoint shortages, highlight areas of potential overstaffing, and identify the number of individuals who must be recruited to satisfy these needs.

A dollar figure can then be applied to the forecast. Teachers expecting to retire will probably be replaced by younger teachers who will receive less money in salary. A younger staff also could affect the premium for medical and hospital insurance paid on behalf of employees by the district because younger people tend to be healthier.

If the goals and objectives of the school district call for the development of new programs, more money must be budgeted for additional staff, equipment, and supplies. Likewise, an anticipated increase in enrollment will require an increase in these same areas. Further, in those districts experiencing a significant increase in enrollment, it may be necessary to plan for a bond issue election as a source of additional funds to build classrooms or even new schools.

The other side of this coin, decreasing enrollment, will obviously affect the budget because teachers and other staff members will probably be placed on involuntary leave. Some districts have developed *early retirement incentive programs* designed to encourage employees to retire when they become eligible to receive retirement benefits.

This has the effect of reducing the amount of money needed for salaries because these individuals will be replaced by people who are not on advanced steps of the salary schedule. The incentive payments plus the salaries paid to replacements is usually a lesser dollar amount than that paid to the early retirees when they were active employees.

## Project End-of-the-Year Balance

Although it might seem unnecessary, the third step is projecting the end-of-year balance for the current fiscal year.[8]

The budget is a *plan* for implementing the goals and objectives of the school district. It is never chiseled in stone! Emergencies may arise requiring the expenditure of monies that were not budgeted.

For example, a fire in a school could cause such extensive damage that it is necessary to rebuild almost the entire structure. Typically, insurance companies will not insure a building at 100 percent replacement value. Rather, insurance companies will co-insurance a building at 90 percent or 80 percent of replacement value because this approach requires the respective school board, as an entity, to share in the risk and thus, be responsible for developing life-safety and risk-management procedures.

Supplies, equipment, and purchased services may end up costing more than was budgeted. Many districts where caught off-guard in the early and mid-eighties when insurance companies significantly increased their premiums. In fact, many school districts were required to pay as much as a 100 percent or greater increase in premiums. Loss experience coupled with formerly low premiums and the decrease in investment interest have been identified as the reasons insurance premiums increased so dramatically. Thus, in a real-life situation, a school district experiencing a fire that severely damaged a school building probably would have been unable to get reinsurance when the policy expired.

Many more examples could be given, but it should be sufficient to state that staying within the approved budget for any given year will require continual monitoring. Therefore, it is very important to develop a formal procedure for analyzing revenues and expenditures on a monthly basis and for presenting this analysis to the board of education for consideration at the regular monthly board meeting.

This will give the board the opportunity to modify the budget if need be. Because the board of education is required by state statute in most states to formally approve the school district's budget, it is necessary for the board to take official action if the members wish to modify the budget. This topic will be discussed in greater detail in Chapter 6.

## Project Revenues

The most difficult task in the entire budgeting process is the projection of revenues. During this fourth step, the board of education and the administration can definitely control expenditures. Revenues, however, are affected by many variables which makes projection nothing more than an educated guess. The experience and education of the person making that *educated* guess is the major concern of the superintendent of schools and the board of education.[9]

A talented and insightful assistant superintendent for business and financial services can literally make the difference in the effectiveness of the budgeting process. In small school districts, this statement applies to the superintendent because he or she will probably be responsible for projecting revenues.

All revenue projections begin with an estimation of the basis upon which local property taxes are levied. The property tax has come under considerable attack beginning with the 1970 decision of the California supreme court in the *Serrano v. Priest* case. The court ruled that the state's system for financing schools was unconstitutional on the grounds that it discriminated against the poor because it made the quality of a child's education a function of the wealth of his parents and neighbors. In other words, property value was the basis for the system that discriminated.

However, in almost every state, the property tax is still the primary source of local revenue. That revenue is generated through a tax rate which is applied against some measure of the aggregate value of the property in a given district. The measure, assessed valuation, is usually a percent of the fair market value of the property.

For example, if a house has a fair market value of $100,000 and the percent of assessed valuation is 20 percent, the tax rate is applied against $20,000. A detailed discussion of this topic is contained in Chapter 6.

Projecting the assessed valuation is difficult because of the fluctuations that occur on a regular basis in all assessments. These fluctuations may occur because of commercial or residential growth in the district, because of reassessment, or because property has been taken off the tax rolls.

In addition, some municipalities are permitted by some states to give a tax abatement for a certain number of years as a means of attracting business and commercial enterprises. This, of course, affects school district revenues from those abated properties.

An experienced assistant superintendent for business and financial services will be able to analyze the trends in assessment and will understand the governmental mechanism used in making assessments. Further, the assistant superintendent often has an open channel of communication with the local assessor.

Exhibit 5-2 is a listing of typical revenues derived from local, state, and federal sources. Of course, there are some differences in sources of revenue not only between school districts in a given state but also from state to state.

EXHIBIT 5-2 • *Categories of Revenues by Source*

| *Local Sources* |
| --- |
| Current real estate and personal property taxes |
| Delinquent taxes |
| Surcharge taxes |
| Intangible taxes |
| Sales taxes |
| Tuition from out-of-district students |
| Interest on checking account |
| Interest on investments |
| Fees and rentals from district property |
| Gate receipts from athletic events |

| *State Sources* |
| --- |
| State foundation formula grant |
| Pupil transportation grant |
| Handicapped children grant |
| Vocational program grant |

| *Federal Sources* |
| --- |
| Chapter I grant |
| Chapter II grant |
| Vocational program grant |
| Public Law 94-142 |
| Public Law 874 |

The other major source of revenue for school districts is the state grant-in-aid. The methods used by the states to fund education are numerous and varied. The foundation program, flat grants, percentage equalization, and power equalization are the primary methods used. However, each state proves its individuality by the types and number of provisions peculiar to its method.

Almost all these state grants-in-aid operate on the reimbursement principle. Thus, the base data used by a school district to request reimbursement is readily available. The level of funding by the various state legislatures is also usually available before the statutory budget setting deadlines.

Nevertheless, new legislation and the state budgeting process may present funding problems for individual school districts. When this occurs, the revenue projection process may be delayed until the ramifications of such situations are fully analyzed.

## Identify Expenditures

The most involved step in the budgeting process is developing the procedure used to identify appropriate expenditures. This is the fifth step. The most effective procedure provides the opportunity for input from those who are affected by the expenditures. In addition, the philosophy of expenditure development will dictate the type of budget that will be used.

### Budget Formats

There are basically four types of budgets: the zero-based budget, the line-item budget, the performance budget, and the program budget.[10]

Zero-based budgeting was developed in 1969 for businesses by Peter A. Pyhrr, a manager for Texas Instruments. This format has subsequently been utilized by many state governments and by the federal government since 1976.

The basic concept of zero-based budgeting is that all administrators will annually reassess their programs from the foundation up. As part of this analysis, each administrator will provide justification for the financial resources requested in order to meet the program goals. Thus, major changes may occur in the scope of a program and in the allocation of financial resources from one budget period to another.

A line-item budget will show each employee, each piece of equipment, each category of supply, and each purchased service on individual lines of a list. This is the oldest format of budgeting and the one that is the easiest to construct.

While the line-item format provides detailed information, it usually does not relate programs to spending. Thus, objectives and priorities are not tied to the expenditure plan.

The performance budget format ties expenditures to accomplishments. The *excellence in education* movement, if not directly, then by implication, promotes this type of budget format. It is especially suited for pilot programs but does not account for the intangibles that are present in ongoing programming.

The program budget is the most popular type of format and is the most suited to public school districts. It is known by various names but the most recognizable is *PPBS*, which means planning, programing, budgeting system.

This format was originally developed for the U.S. Department of Defense in the 1960s. Because of his desire for long-term planning, Secretary of Defense Robert McNamara was instrumental in the introduction of this method. He was assisted by Charles J. Hitch, a former Rand Corporation executive, who had experience in relating costs to output.

EXHIBIT 5-3 • *Statement of Goals for a PPBS Budget*[11]

---

*Goal Statements*

---

To work with each child to help him learn the basic intellectual skills of linguistic flexibility in thought and tongue through a foreign language.

To develop fluency in a foreign language to such a degree that an eighth grade student could visit a foreign county and understand and converse with a native speaker on an elementary level, comprehend partially a publication in that language, and write clearly in the language.

---

*Objective Statement and Evaluative Criteria*

---

At the end of the eighth grade:

That 75 percent of the students be able to communicate in the language of instruction at an elementary level with a native speaker of that language as evaluated by the teacher.

That 50 percent of the students should be able to read a magazine or newspaper article in the language of instruction and state briefly, in that language, a summary of the article as measured by the teacher.

That 80 percent of the students will be able to write with ease a dictation exercise in the language of instruction based on previously studied material from the text based on a teacher-prepared dictation test.

That 75 percent of the students will give a five-minute oral report in the language of instruction on a topic of the student's choice to the teacher's satisfaction.

That 70 percent of the students will pass the vocabulary test provided in the text with 85 percent accuracy.

---

*Program Description*

---

The foreign language program covers the four years of fifth, sixth, seventh, and eighth grades in the subjects of Spanish and French. There are six teachers in the program, three in each subject. The fifth and sixth grade students receive 150 minutes of instruction weekly, the seventh grade students 135 minutes of instruction weekly, and the eighth grade students 110 minutes of instruction weekly. Instruction is provided in a classroom environment using textbooks. It includes both written and oral work. Teachers may use other instructional materials such as songs, plays, magazines, newspapers, flashcards, etc. A language laboratory is available containing records, tape recorders and filmstrips.

---

This author believes that the PPBS budget format is the most effective for public school districts, and it is the basis upon which other aspects of this chapter are built. Exhibit 5-3 is an example of program goals which would become the basis for a PPBS approach to budgeting. Exhibit 5-4 sets forth how programs can be broken down in order to identify total costs.

EXHIBIT 5-4 • Categories of Expenditures [12]

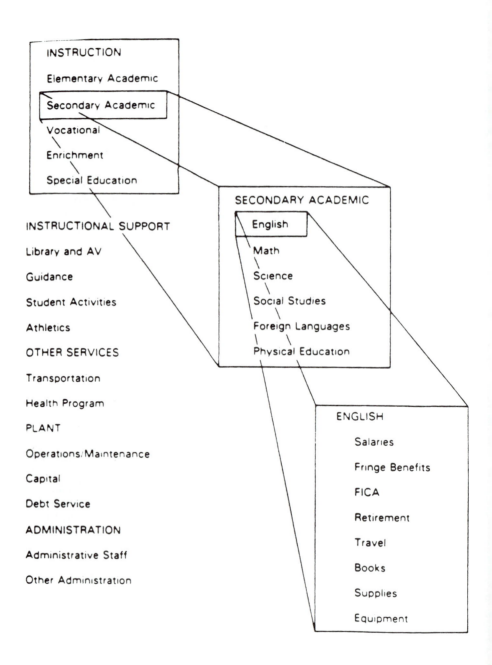

### Staff Involvement in Developing the Budget

Essential to developing the expenditure portion of the budget is the involvement of staff members who will be affected by the budget. Of course, not every single employee can be directly involved, but it certainly is possible to consult with representatives of the various employee groups.

The PPBS format presupposes that building principals and certain central office administrators have budget management responsibilities.[13] This means that they are responsible for identifying expenditures for their buildings and programs which will be incorporated into the *district* budget.

Upon approval of the board of education, these administrators are then responsible for overseeing the expending of that portion of the district budget that they helped to develop.

Usually, the chief fiscal administrator, the assistant superintendent for business and financial services, develops *budget guidelines* and a *decision package* that provide direction to the principals and program administrators as they develop their budgets.

It is sound administrative practice to allow the principals and program administrators the opportunity to establish their own method for involving their respective staff members. An elementary principal might appoint a teacher from each grade level to serve on a budget committee, while a high school principal might require department chairpersons to participate in the budgeting process. Another principal might prefer the election of teachers at-large to serve on the budget committee. The emphasis is not on the method of selection but rather on representative participation.[14]

At the central office, one administrator has the responsibility for identifying expenditures necessary to the operation of the central office. This person serves in a capacity similar to that of a building principal. This administrator budgets for supplies, equipment, furniture, and site-specific purchased services. In this context, purchased services could refer to maintenance agreements on copy machines and word processing equipment.

This central office administrator might hold the title of office manager or, more likely, is an assistant superintendent who acts as the office manager in addition to having other program responsibilities.

*Program administrators* usually refer to assistant superintendents. For example, the assistant superintendent for business and financial services is probably responsible for food service, pupil transportation, property and casualty insurance, and legal service budgeting in addition to other administrative components.

The assistant superintendent for human resources is responsible for costing out the staffing and fringe benefit expenditure budgets. The assistant superintendent for instructional services would be responsible for budgeting district-wide new textbook adoptions.

Each of these program administrators would involve other staff members in determining expenditures. For example, the assistant superintendent for business and financial services would consult the food service manager who, in turn, would consult the cooks on what kitchen equipment needs to be replaced and what new equipment needs to be purchased.

The assistant superintendent for human resources consults building principals in determining staffing, and consults the director of employee relations when budgeting for new fringe benefits that were approved in the collective bargaining process.

The assistant superintendent for instructional services would probably have developed the new textbook adoption list with input from a district committee composed of teachers who would be using the textbooks.

Thus, every building and department is involved in the expenditure development process. The organizational chart in Chapter 1 sets forth the line responsibilities of the various staff members. This is a good guide as to the categories of employees involved in this process.

### Budget Guidelines

The basic economic principle of *scarcity* is always operational in the budgeting process. There is never enough money to support the desires and aspirations of employees. This is as it should be! In fact, working within a budget sometimes spurs creativity. Staff members who are content to operate with the same level of expenditures from year to year are also generally content with the *status quo*. On the other hand, financing is limited, and it is a responsibility of the school district's administration to incorporate this concept of limitation within the district's long-range planning.

Developing budget guidelines is a practical way to handle this situation.[15] The principals and program administrators should be required by such guidelines to identify three levels of expenditures. First, that level which is necessary to carry out the basic mission of the district. For example, teachers have a right to expect that their students will be provided with necessary supplies, materials, and textbooks.

In addition, teaching can be ineffective if the classrooms are uncomfortably cold in the winter or too hot in the spring. Therefore, essentials constitute the first level of expenditures.

The second level of expenditures should represent the *growth and development* that is to be expected in every aspect of the school district. No program ever remains static. First, it would cease to be effective and then it would become counterproductive.

The building maintenance program is a good example. Facilities will deteriorate if *preventive* maintenance is not practiced. Therefore, it is necessary to replace roofs before leaks cause water damage to the contents and structure of a school building.

The counseling and guidance program might constitute another example. In the last ten years, there has been an increase in the number of violent acts committed by students upon other students and upon themselves. A school community that has experienced a number of student suicides will certainly be in need of counselors specially trained to handle the aftermath of such situations.

Growth and development is a characteristic of a good school district because the needs of students are constantly changing. Those who have lived their adult lives through the 1960s, 1970s, and into the 1980s certainly appreciate the phenomenon of change.

The third level of expenditures can be reserved for *special requests*. A principal or program administrator may wish to pilot a project that would seriously impact their budget if it were financed from the building allocation. For example, a principal might pilot an after-school tutorial program for low-achieving students.

Thus, the budget guidelines should instruct principals and program administrators as to the development of three levels of expenditures. The guidelines should also cover the following:

1. A per pupil or per teacher financial allocation
2. An amount that should be retained as a contingency in case of an emergency
3. The expectation that staff members should be involved in developing the budget
4. A time line for completing the budget
5. A date when the principal or program administrator will be required to make a presentation of his or her budget to certain central office administrators
6. A statement concerning economy of operation

Two of these guidelines require further explanation. The formula allocations mentioned in number one above is an arbitrary amount. An elementary school could receive $65 per pupil to be used for the purchase of supplies, instructional materials, and instructional equipment.

A middle school might receive $75 per pupil and a high school, $115 per pupil. The amounts will vary depending upon the economic situation in the local community, the per pupil allocations of surrounding school districts, and the economic situation of the school district itself.

Certainly, a school district with little growth in revenues and a higher growth in expenditures must adjust the per pupil allocation to prevent the district from going bankrupt. It may not be possible to use formula allocations for every aspect of the district's operations.

The personnel department, as an example, would not have a formula, but rather a benchmark above which the personnel administrator must not climb in filling job vacancies. Thus, if a school district's present budget for salaries is $20 million, the assistant superintendent for human resources could be instructed to carry out the personnel function by not exceeding a 5 percent increase in salaries. Of course, this is intricately related to the calculation of staffing needs.

As mentioned earlier, the assistant superintendent for instructional services would probably have the responsibility for district-wide textbook adoptions. Because the selection of textbooks is best accomplished with input from a committee of teachers who will use a given textbook, it is possible to know the exact amount of money needed to purchase the recommended textbooks. Thus, the textbook adoption allocation is the actual cost of the books.

Guideline number six is extremely important. All school districts and, for that matter, all businesses must practice *economy of operation*. This refers to the concept that every aspect of the school district's operations must be continually reviewed for the purpose of identifying areas where resources are being wasted.

Energy consumption is an obvious example. In the 1970s, citizens of the United States learned first hand the pitfalls of wasting energy. Long lines at the gas pump prompted auto manufacturers to rethink the design of automobiles in order to build a more efficient vehicle. At that time, it was also popular in schools to post a small sign next to the light fixture switch commanding, "Turn off the lights when leaving the room."

This urgency has subsided somewhat but the potential for wasting materials and supplies is ever present. Further, the abuse of equipment and the purchasing of unnecessary supplies, materials, and equipment often occurs without notice.

The same concern also applies to personnel. Once a position is created, it is very difficult to cut it from the budget, even if it is not needed. However, economy of operation is absolutely necessary, and it must be the responsibility of every principal and program administrator to justify the number and types of positions that are allocated to their building or program. This justification can become a part of the budget presentation that each principal and program administrator must make before certain central office administrators.[16]

Seeking a tax levy increase will often test the effectiveness of *economy of operation*. In the past ten years, taxpayers have become more vigilant about the expenditures of their school districts. If they believe that the school board and administration are mismanaging or wasting their tax dollars, they will not vote to raise taxes.

The budgeting process provides the superintendent and his or her staff with the opportunity to analyze the efficiency of operations. The next chapter gives a detailed explanation of those management techniques that can be used to accomplish economy of operation.

### Decision Packet

Because the central office business division is responsible for constructing the actual budget document, it is necessary to establish a procedure which will provide uniformity in the collection of data. A proven way to accomplish this is to give each principal and program administrator a listing of all the line item accounts for which they budget.

This listing of line-item accounts should also contain historical data such as: (1) the previous year's expenditures in each account; (2) the current year's budget in each account; and (3) the expenditures year-to-date in each account. Of course, this document should have a space next to each line item account on which the proposed expenditures can be entered.

Enclosed in the packet should also be a current price listing of all supplies, materials, and equipment. It is true that prices may change before the budgeting process is completed. However, the contingency that was mentioned in the budget guidelines can be used for this purpose.

Also, it is important to establish a method by which principals and program administrators can move dollar amounts from one line-item account to another if the need arises. This will give administrators the necessary flexibility to handle emergency situations and to have money available if prices change. The superintendent or assistant superintendent for business and financial services, however, should make it perfectly clear to all principals and program administrators that under no circumstances may they exceed the total dollars allocated for their building or program![17]

The final items in the decision packet should be a sufficient number of *purchase orders* that can be used in the purchase of supplies, materials, and equipment. It is common to prenumber the purchase orders so as to identify the building or program for which the purchases are being made.

In addition, the purchase orders should have a space for the signature of the principal or program administrator and a place for a countersignature by a central office administrator responsible for the district's purchasing function.

This entire process should be handled through computerization.[18] There is available both hardware and software that can accommodate the budgeting process at a reasonable price. Only the very smallest or poorest of school districts might find it necessary to perform this function without the aid of a computer.

## Internal Review of the Budget

After budget requests have been submitted to central office by the building principals and program administrators, the assistant superintendent for business and financial services should schedule a conference with each of these administrators. The purpose of these conferences is the sixth step, or internal review of the budget requests by the superintendent of schools, his or her cabinet, and the assistant superintendents.

The principals and program administrators should be required to explain the process each used to involve staff, and must be prepared to explain why the formula appropriation was distributed, as such, to the various line-item accounts. In addition, each administrator must be prepared to explain how the school or program will exhibit growth and development as a consequence of the budget requests. Finally, this is the time for the administrators to justify special requests.

The superintendent and cabinet members may request additional information, or may make suggestions to the administrator as to what changes might be considered. However, the atmosphere should be informal and more of a work session than a judicial review.

This process will provide the superintendent and the assistant superintendents with the valuable information and insight needed to construct the district budget. While the assistant superintendent for business and financial services has the responsibility for the construction of the budget document, its content becomes the responsibility of the superintendent and the cabinet.

It should be remembered that the superintendent and the assistant superintendents each have budget requests of their own because they are also program administrators. For example, the superintendent usually has the responsibility of developing the budget for the district's audit services and for miscellaneous expenses incurred by the board of education, such as travel and membership dues in the National School Boards Association.

These budget reviews have the potential for revealing costs that could have been overlooked without face-to-face discussion. If a building principal had made a special request to pilot an environmental education program that incorporates visits on school district buses to wildlife reservations, he or she may not have been aware of all the costs that could be involved. The assistant superintendent for human resources would know, for example, that current negotiations with the union representing bus drivers might result in a 6 percent increase in wages and an 8 percent increase in fringe benefits. While this might seem like a minuscule cost differential for such a minor program, the cumulative effects of all such exceptions could amount to a substantial sum of money.

After all the budget reviews and accompanying discussions are completed, the assistant superintendent for business and financial services will be directed by the superintendent to proceed with the construction of the *preliminary budget*. Modifications to the building and/or program budgets may have been made by the superintendent in consultation with the assistant superintendents or the superintendent may retain the budgets as they are until step seven has been completed.

## Construction of the Preliminary Budget

The seventh step is the construction of the preliminary budget document. This document incorporates all of the materials generated by the preceding six steps. The document format is usually an outgrowth of trial and error over many years. Each board of education will probably decide on a format that best meets the expectations of their unique school community. Of course, the format may change from time to time because every community is continually changing and because membership on boards of education will also change.

However, there are items that must be incorporated into every budget document if it is to fairly represent the fiscal requirements of a school district and meet the customary design for such a document. Exhibit 5-5 outlines these basic requirements.

## External Review and Approval of the Budget[19]

It is essential to provide the opportunity for citizens to express their opinions concerning the proposed budget. Step eight is to provide this external review. Without this opportunity, it is almost certain that

FIGURE 5-5 • *The Formal Budget Document*[20]

---

Cover or title page
Contents or index
Letter of transmittal from the board president
Budget message from the superintendent
The educational plan
    School system goals, objectives, and priorities
    School system organization
    Educational program including proposed changes
    Administration and supervision program
    Instructional staff (qualifications, experience, tenure, and salary schedule)
    Noncertificated staff
    Student enrollment
    Teacher-student ratio
    Supplies and equipment
Estimated expenditures
    Summary of estimates
    Detailed estimate for each budget classification
    Data supporting detailed estimates
Estimated revenue
    Summary of estimates
    Analysis of revenue from all sources
        Federal
        State
        County
        Local (valuation of property, percent of taxes collected and so on)
Comparison of estimated expenditures and receipts (of revenue) including per
    student expenditure and the proportion of federal, state, and local
    expenditure that contributes to it
Long-range plans for the school system

---

dissatisfaction will arise in the community and the board of education will lose the confidence of the taxpayers. In fact, many states have statutory provisions that require a public hearing before budget approval.

A very effective approach to receiving taxpayer input is the public hearing. Experience teaches that such a hearing must be well publicized if it is to be well attended. Therefore, the administration should publish a notice in a newspaper of general circulation that lists the date, time, and place of the hearing.

It would be appropriate to extend a personal invitation to community leaders, elected officials, business leaders, officers of parent organizations, and all employees of the school district. The news media also should be notified, and it is extremely effective to hold a pre-hearing briefing for the representatives of newspapers and television stations.

A summary of the budget document should be prepared and presented to those attending the hearing. The president of the board of education is the most appropriate person to chair the hearing. Of course, it is important for all board members to be in attendance along with the superintendent of schools and his or her cabinet.

The atmosphere at the hearing should be relaxed but orderly. An agenda will help to achieve this end. The hearing should begin with opening remarks by the president followed by a budget overview presented by the superintendent and appropriate cabinet members.

A common practice is to hand out cards to those wishing to address the school board about the budget. On the card, each person would write their own name and address. These cards would be collected by a staff member and presented to the president of the board who calls on each individual at the appropriate time during the hearing. Also, it is helpful to provide a microphone for people who wish to make a statement.

The opinions and information received at the public hearing can then be analyzed and evaluated to determine their effect on the budget. This is a task that will require a certain amount of time before a subsequent meeting can take place at which the modified budget will be approved by the board of education. Of course, the superintendent and his or her staff are responsible for performing the task of analysis and evaluation with direction from the board of education.

### Public Relations and the Budget

The public hearing often reveals the concerns of those in attendance, not only about the budget but also about other issues. Thus, a secondary effect of the public hearing is public relations.[21] Further, the entire budgeting process can become a significant public relations tool if properly executed.

After the adoption of the formal budget, communicating information about the budget is of primary importance. It is a mistake to assume that those who are interested in the contents of the budget document have attended the public hearing or the board meeting at which the formal budget was adopted. It is also wrong to assume that an ordinary citizen or a staff member will be able to accurately interpret all of the data contained in the budget document. Therefore, a condensed and understandable "popular budget" should be constructed. It is important, however, to make the entire approved budget document available in the central office and in each school building for those who wish to review the complete document.

FIGURE 5-1 • *Where The School Dollar is Spent* [22]

---

WHERE THE SCHOOL DOLLAR IS SPENT

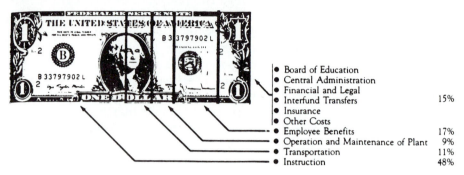

|  |  |
|---|---|
| ● Board of Education |  |
| ● Central Administration |  |
| ● Financial and Legal |  |
| ● Interfund Transfers | 15% |
| ● Insurance |  |
| ● Other Costs |  |
| ● Employee Benefits | 17% |
| ● Operation and Maintenance of Plant | 9% |
| ● Transportation | 11% |
| ● Instruction | 48% |

School books, pencils, school houses

| Sources of Income | Amount | Percentage |
|---|---|---|
| Local Tax Sources | $14,368,968 | 59.6% |
| State Tax Sources | 8,149,221 | 33.8% |
| Other Sources | 1,600,716 | 6.6% |
|  | $24,118,905 | 100.0% |

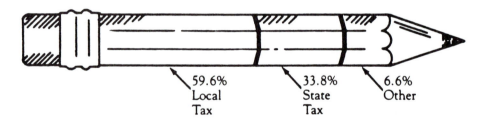

59.6%
Local
Tax

33.8%
State
Tax

6.6%
Other

---

The "popular budget" should be both informative and attractive. The use of graphics helps to make the figures understandable. Some of the most widely used are the dollar bill and circle divided according to the percent of revenue received by each source and these same symbols divided according to the percent expended by each category. Figure 5-1 is a good example of the use of graphics for this purpose.

Other aspects to include in the popular budget are: summaries of major categories of revenues and expenditures, brief descriptions of all instructional and non-instructional programs, comparisons of current and past yearly expenditures on a formula basis such as per pupil costs, and comparisons with other school districts in the surrounding communities.

By way of introduction, the president of the school board should write a cover letter to the "popular budget" that describes the current successes and needs of the district. This is an opportunity for the board to address issues that have been revealed through the public hearing and to present other school data such as the school calendar for the forthcoming academic year.

### Staff Relations and the Budget

Equally important is the manner in which the approved budget is communicated to the faculty and staff of the school district. First, several copies of the approved budget and "popular budget" documents should be available in every school. A thorough briefing of the budget should be conducted for all the administrators in the district to such an extent that they, in turn, will be able to explain the budget to their faculties and staff members and to parents.

It should then be the responsibility of each principal and supervisor to hold a meeting for their personnel in order to discuss and answer questions about the budget. Feedback about these meetings should be communicated back to the superintendent and cabinet members.

### Revising the Budget

There is no one point in time when it can be said that budgeting is complete. It is an ongoing process that calls for a well-developed procedure to monitor the status of the budget over the entire fiscal year. Monitoring the budget will be thoroughly discussed in the following chapter.

Most school districts are mandated by state statutes to follow a fiscal year that usually begins the first of July and ends June 30. This, of course, supports the academic year which, by tradition, begins in late August or early September and terminates in late May or early June. The period of time when the budget is developed for the following year is between December and June. Exhibit 5-6 illustrates the overlapping of the fiscal year, academic year, and the budget preparation period. Exhibit 5-7 is an example of a budget planning calendar. Most other private and public companies and agencies follow the calendar year.[23] This presents a timing problem which can have a tremendous effect on the school district's budget.

EXHIBIT 5-6 • *School Calendars*

| July 1 | (Fiscal Year) | | June 30 |
|---|---|---|---|
| Sept. 1 | (School Year) | June 1 | |
| Dec. 1 | (Budget Prep) | | June 30 |

EXHIBIT 5-7 • *Budget Planning Calendar*

| | |
|---|---|
| July 1 | Beginning of fiscal year |
| December 1 | Beginning of the budgeting cycle for the next fiscal year which will begin on the forthcoming July 1 and deadline for completing budgeting guidelines and budget preparation documents |
| January 1 | Deadline for building principals and program administrators to submit budget requests to the assistant superintendent for business and financial services |
| February 1 | Commencing of collective negotiations process with the teacher union and other employee unions |
| March 1 | The beginning of budget presentations by building principals and program administrators to the superintendent and his or her cabinet |
| April 1 | Ratification of the collectively negotiated teacher and other employee master contracts by the board of education |
| May 1 | Deadline for development of the preliminary budget, board of education meeting, the preliminary budget is presented. At a time and date in late May set by the board of education, a public hearing is held at which citizens and employees may address the board on issues related to the preliminary budget |
| June 30 | Date before which the board of education must approve the proposed budget and set the tax rate for the new fiscal year commencing on July 1 |

For example, in states where local revenue is generated through a tax on real estate and personal property, tax bills are mailed to taxpayers during the fall months and payment is due in December before the end of the calendar year. The amount of taxes owed depends on the assessed valuation of the personal and real estate property. The assistant superintendent for business and financial services will have projected the total amount of revenue due from property taxes based on historical data and other information available from the government agency responsible for assessing property. This projection must be completed before the budget approval which, in this example, would be required in June.

However, changes to the assessed valuation could occur after the budget is approved in June. These changes would affect the revenue actually received.

Another situation that occurs frequently in school districts is the return of teachers from the summer recess toting newly acquired graduate degrees. The board and superintendent, along with other administrators, have traditionally seen this as a positive situation because this helps to increase the competency of the teaching staff. Most school districts have policies that reward this achievement with an increase in salary. Thus, the expenditures noted in the budget for salaries might not be sufficient, if more teachers received graduate degrees than anticipated .

There are many more examples that could be cited, but the point at hand is that the budgeting process must include a procedure for amending the budget when, due to unforseen circumstances, anticipated revenues and expenditures differ significantly from original projections.

Finally, there is one other situation that occurs in many suburban and urban school districts that can have a tremendous effect on an approved budget. This is the process of collective negotiations. Most school districts are required by state law to approve a budget by a given date even if an agreement has not been reached with representatives of employees over salaries and fringe benefits.

Approximately 80 percent of the expenditures in most school-district budgets are for salaries and fringe benefits. Therefore, it is absolutely impossible to finalize the expenditure part of the budget unless negotiations have been completed. Obviously, an agreement after a budget approval deadline will require revising the budget. When such a revision is required, the board of education must take formal action for the revision to be legal.

## Summary

Budgeting is the most important task of the board of education and administration. There is no aspect of operations that does not have a price tag attached. Of course, developing and improving the instructional program is the central objective not only of the board of education but also of the administration. Budgeting, however, is the process which brings this objective to fruition.

The board of education has the overall responsibility for the budgeting process. Thus, budgeting is essentially a political process because the governance of every school district in the United States is entrusted to a board of education consisting of members who were either elected or appointed by elected officials.

Except in the smallest of school districts, it is impossible for the board of education as a whole or even a committee of the board to develop the budget without the assistance of the professional staff. Therefore, in most school districts, the board requires the superintendent of schools to develop the budget, and reserves to itself the right to approve the budget.

The superintendent, in turn, will usually call upon central office staff and building principals and teachers to develop aspects of the budget to be consolidated into the district budget.

In order to enhance and clarify this presentation, the budgeting process has been divided into nine steps.

1. *Calculate an Enrollment Projection* All school districts should have a method of projecting enrollments for a five-year period. Each year a new five-year projection can be made when the actual enrollment is verified. There are many methods for projecting enrollments, but the most popular is undoubtedly the *percentage of retention* or *cohort-survival* technique.

Other data that can be useful when considering enrollment projections include: housing starts, information about zoning, information from utility companies, and data received from a district census.

2. *Calculate Staffing Needs* Calculating the staffing needed as a consequence of the educational goals and objectives of the school board and as a consequence of the enrollment projection for the forthcoming academic year is the second step. Staffing includes not only the professional staff, teachers and administrators, but also support personnel such as teacher assistants, secretaries, custodians, cafeteria workers, bus drivers, etc. The overall objective of the second step is the development of a human resource forecast. A dollar figure can then be applied to the forecast.

3. *Project the End-of-the-Year Balance* The budget is a plan for implementing the goals and objectives of the school district. It is never chiseled in stone. Emergencies may arise requiring the expenditure of monies that were not budgeted.

Because the board of education is required by state statute in most states to formally approve the school district's budget, it is necessary for the board to take official action if the members wish to modify the budget.

4. *Project Revenues* The most difficult task in the entire budgeting process is the projection of revenues. The board of education and the administration can definitely control expenditures. Revenues, however, are affected by many variables that make projection nothing more than an educated guess.

Local revenue projections are dependent upon the assessed valuation of local property in most states. An experienced assistant superintendent for business and financial services will be able to analyze the trends in assessment and will understand the governmental mechanism that is employed in making assessments.

A second major source of revenue is the state grant-in-aid. Almost all grant-in-aid programs operate on the reimbursement principle. The basic data used to request reimbursement is readily available and, thus, projecting this revenue is not as difficult as projecting local tax revenue.

5. *Identify Expenditures* The most involved step in the budgeting process is developing the procedure used to identify appropriate expenditures. The most effective procedure provides the opportunity for input from those who are affected by the expenditures.

The program budget is the most popular type of format, and it is the most suited to public school districts. It is known by various names but the most recognizable is PPBS, planning, programing, budgeting system.

Usually the chief fiscal administrator, the assistant superintendent for business and financial services, develops budget guidelines and a decision package to provide direction to the principals and the program administrators as they develop their budgets.

The basic economic principle of scarcity is always operational in the budgeting process. Thus, principals and program administrators should develop a three-level budget. First, that level which is necessary to carry out the basic mission of the district. The second level of expenditures should represent the growth and development that is to be expected in every aspect of the school district. The third level can be reserved for special requests.

Budget guidelines should also cover the following: a per pupil or per teacher financial allocation; an amount to be retained as a contingency in case of an emergency; the expectation that staff members be involved in developing the budget; a time line for completing the budget; a date when the principal or program administrator is required to make a presentation of a budget to certain central office administrators; and a statement concerning economy of operation.

The decision package should include a listing of all the line-item accounts and historical data such as: the previous year's expenditures in each account; the current year's budget in each account; and the expenditures year-to-date in each account.

6. *Internal Review of the Budget* After budget requests have been submitted to central office by the building principals and program administrators, the assistant superintendent for business and financial services should schedule a conference with each of these administrators.

The purpose of these conferences is the review of the budget requests by the superintendent and his or her cabinet, the assistant superintendents.

These budget reviews have the potential for revealing costs that could be overlooked without face-to-face discussion.

7. *Construction of the Preliminary Budget* The preliminary budget document incorporates all of the materials generated by the preceding six steps. The document format is usually an outgrowth of trial and error over many years. Each board of education will probably decide on a format that best meets the expectations of their unique school community. However, there are items that must be incorporated into every budget document such as a description of the educational plan, estimated expenditures, and estimated revenue.

8. *External Review and Approval of the Budget* It is essential to provide an opportunity for citizens to express their opinions concerning the proposed budget. Without this opportunity, it is almost certain that dissatisfaction will arise in the community, and the board of education will lose the confidence of the taxpayers. In fact, many states have statutory provisions that require a public hearing before budget approval. A very effective approach for getting taxpayer input is the public hearing.

After the adoption of the formal budget, communicating information about the budget to the community is of primary importance. Equally important is the manner in which the approved budget is communicated to the faculty and the staff of the school district.

9. *Revising the Budget* There is no point in time when it can he said that budgeting is complete. If, due to unforseen circumstances, anticipated revenues and expenditures differ significantly from original projections, the budgeting process must include a procedure for amending the budget. In modifying the budget, the board of education must take formal action for the revision to be legal.


## Appendix A

This appendix contains an example of revenue and expenditure summary pages from a budget document. The revenue sheet layout sets forth the sources of revenue (local, county, state, and federal). There is a description of each line account and a comparison of revenues beginning with actual receipts in 1986-87; a revised estimate of receipts for the current fiscal year in which the budget was developed; and the proposed budget along with an indication of the percent of increase or decrease from the current year's budget.

APPENDIX TABLE A-1 • *Proposed Budget 1988–89 (June 14, 1988) Operating Fund Revenues and Comparisons*

| Source | Description | Actual Revenue 1986–87 | Revised Estimate 1987–88 | Proposed Budget 1988–89 | 1987–88/1988–89 % Increase/Decrease |
|--------|-------------|-----------------------|--------------------------|-------------------------|--------------------------------------|
| Local | Current taxes, real estate & personal property, merch. mfg. | 8,460,626 | 8,628,210 | 9,187,681 | 6.48 |
| | Delinquent tax | 780,132 | 400,000 | 650,000 | 62.50 |
| | Surcharge tax | 578,592 | 780,912 | 800,000 | 2.44 |
| | Intangible tax | 42,914 | 365,575 | 43,000 | <88.24> |
| | Sales tax | 2,274,413 | 2,391,356 | 2,455,892 | 2.70 |
| | Tuition—patrons | 16,338 | 11,000 | 10,000 | <9.09> |
| | Tuition—summer school | 6,394 | 3,000 | 3,000 | 0.00 |
| | Interest—savings | 66,701 | 60,000 | 25,000 | <58.33> |
| | Interest—investments | 293,321 | 175,000 | 175,000 | 0.00 |
| | Athletics | 37,101 | 35,000 | 25,000 | <28.57> |
| | Fees & rentals | 148,067 | 150,000 | 110,000 | <26.67> |
| | Leases | 124,614 | 109,000 | 120,000 | 10.09 |
| | *Total Local Sources* | 12,829,213 | 13,109,053 | 13,604,573 | 3.78 |
| County | Fines, forfeitures | 28,261 | 29,911 | 30,000 | .30 |
| | Utility taxes | 357,054 | 421,795 | 350,000 | <17.02> |
| | Other county | 246,377 | 199,871 | 200,000 | .06 |
| | *Total County Sources* | 631,692 | 651,577 | 580,000 | <10.98> |

APPENDIX TABLE A-1 • *Proposed Budget 1988–89 (June 14, 1988) Operating Fund Revenues and Comparisons (Continued)*

| Source | Description | Actual Revenue 1986–87 | Revised Estimate 1987–88 | Proposed Budget 1988–89 | 1987–88/1988–89 % Increase/Decrease |
|---|---|---|---|---|---|
| State | Minimum guarantee | 2,477,299 | 2,375,425 | 2,454,380 | 3.32 |
| | Transportation | 541,276 | 551,506 | 551,000 | <.09> |
| | Exceptional pupil | 33,647 | 34,693 | 36,428 | 5.00 |
| | Handicapped pupil | 674 | 706 | 700 | <.85> |
| | Gifted & talented | 48,680 | 51,964 | 52,000 | .07 |
| | Insurance tax | 311,602 | 352,629 | 378,708 | 7.40 |
| | Vocational aid | 10,126 | 7,000 | 7,000 | 0.00 |
| | Fair share fund | 168,958 | 165,600 | 165,780 | .11 |
| | Voluntary student transfer program | 1,776,751 | 2,300,000 | 2,300,000 | 0.00 |
| | Incentives/tuition reimbursement | 8,468 | 39,505 | 39,000 | <1.28> |
| | ECDA—Senate Bill 658 | 12,945 | 48,920 | 38,000 | <22.32> |
| | *Total State Sources* | 5,380,145 | 5,927,948 | 6,022,996 | 1.60 |
| Federal | PL 874 | 8,381 | 1,203 | 1,000 | <16.87> |
| | Vocational aid | 1,738 | 600 | 600 | 0.00 |
| | Chapter I | 36,938 | 30,562 | 31,621 | 3.47 |
| | Drug-free program | 0 | 20,634 | 21,000 | 1.77 |
| | Block grant | 33,417 | 39,329 | 40,230 | 2.29 |
| | *Total Federal Sources* | 80,474 | 92,328 | 94,451 | .29 |
| | *Total Operating Revenue* | 18,921,524 | 19,780,906 | 20,302,020 | 2.63 |

APPENDIX TABLE A-2 • Proposed Budget 1988–89 (June 14, 1988) Comparison of
Operating Fund Expenditures

| Description | Actual 1986-87 | Estimated 1987–88 | Proposed 1988–89 | % of Increase/ Decrease |
|---|---|---|---|---|
| Certificated salaries | 11,461,171 | 12,239,844 | 13,016,325 | 6.34 |
| Classified salaries | 2,141,207 | 2,245,721 | 2,365,041 | 5.31 |
| Benefits | 2,070,725 | 2,402,298 | 2,677,874 | 11.47 |
| Purchased services | 2,469,290 | 2,822,576 | 2,811,706 | <.39> |
| Supplies | 708,105 | 878,650 | 874,010 | <.53> |
| Capital outlay | 568,626 | 435,521 | 255,044 | <41.44> |
| *Total Operating Expenditures* | 19,419,124 | 21,024,610 | 22,000,000 | 4.64 |

The expenditures are categorized by the items that the revenues purchase. In this example, the revenues are being used to pay for: the salaries of certificated employees, the salaries of classified employees, fringe benefits, contracted services (purchased services), supplies, and capital outlay. There is a comparison between the actual expenditures from 1986–87 with the estimated expenditures for the current fiscal year. The proposed expenditures are presented along with an indication of the percent of increase or decrease from the current year's budget.

# Appendix B

Appendix B also contains an example of revenue and expenditure summary pages from a budget document. In this example, however, the revenues are set forth by source (local, county, state, and federal), revenue account number, description of the account, and fund (operations, teachers, and building). Also, there is a total column.

The assessed valuation of the school district is indicated at the top of the revenue page and the tax rate (total of $1.86) is indicated by fund; $0.88, operations; $0.87 teachers; $0.11, building. This means, for example, that $4,346,858 is generated by the tax rate of $0.88 for account number 5111 of the operations fund. In other words, for every $100 of the assessed valuation ($514,543,068), $4,346,068 is generated by the $0.88 tax rate. Please note that this amount was also calculated at a 96 percent collection rate because not everyone will pay their taxes on time which is the reason for having a delinquent tax account (number 5112).

The receipts for all the other accounts are placed in the various funds based on each state's rules and regulations governing school district accounting. For example, 80 percent of the revenue received from this state's grant-in-aid (minimum guarantee) is placed in the teachers fund and 20 percent is placed in the operations fund.

APPENDIX TABLE B-1 • *Approved Budget 1988–89 (June 14, 1988) Operating Revenues by Fund, Source, and Account*

*Assessed Valuation $514,543,068*

| Source | Account | Description | Operations .88 | Teachers .87 | Building .11 | Total 1.86 |
|---|---|---|---|---|---|---|
| | | Tax Rate: | | | | |
| Local | 5111 | Current taxes, real estate & personal property, merch. mfg. | 4,346,858 | 4,297,464 | 543,359 | 9,187,681 |
| | 5112 | Delinquent tax | 307,528 | 304,031 | 38,441 | 650,000 |
| | 5113 | Surcharge tax | 378,494 | 374,194 | 47,312 | 800,000 |
| | 5114 | Intangible tax | 20,344 | 20,113 | 2,534 | 43,000 |
| | 5115 | Sales tax | 1,227,946 | 1,227,946 | | 2,455,892 |
| | 5121 | Tuition—patrons | | 10,000 | | 10,000 |
| | 5122 | Tuition—summer school | | 3,000 | | 3,000 |
| | 5141 | Interest—savings | 12,000 | 11,500 | 1,500 | 25,000 |
| | 5142 | Interest—investments | 51,000 | 119,000 | 5,000 | 175,000 |
| | 5180 | Athletics | 25,000 | | | 25,000 |
| | 5191 | Fees & rentals | | | 110,000 | 110,000 |
| | 5192 | Leases | | | 120,000 | 120,000 |
| | | *Total Local Sources* | 6,369,170 | 6,367,248 | 868,155 | 13,604,573 |
| County | 5211 | Fines, forfeitures | | 30,000 | | 30,000 |
| | 5221 | Utility taxes | 62,000 | 270,000 | 18,000 | 350,000 |
| | 5231 | Other county | 94,624 | 93,548 | 11,828 | 200,000 |
| | | *Total County Sources* | 156,624 | 393,548 | 29,828 | 580,000 |
| State | 5311 | Minimum guarantee | 490,876 | 1,963,504 | | 2,454,380 |
| | 5312 | Transportation | 551,000 | | | 551,000 |
| | 5313 | Exceptional pupil | | 36,428 | | 36,428 |
| | 5314 | Handicapped pupil | 700 | | | 700 |
| | 5315 | Gifted & talented | 1,560 | 50,440 | | 52,000 |
| | 5351 | Insurance tax | 378,708 | | | 378,708 |
| | 5361 | Vocational aid | 4,000 | 3,000 | | 7,000 |

APPENDIX TABLE B-1 • *Approved Budget 1988–89 (June 14, 1988) Operating Revenues by Fund, Source, and Account (Continued)*

Assessed Valuation $514,543,068

| Source | Account | Description | Operations .88 | Teachers .87 | Building .11 | Total 1.86 |
|--------|---------|-------------|-----------|----------|----------|-------|
| | | Tax Rate: | | | | |
| | 5391 | Fair share fund | | 165,780 | | 165,780 |
| | 5392 | Voluntary student transfer program | 575,000 | 1,725,000 | | 2,300,000 |
| | 5393 | Incentives—step up & tuition reimbursement | 21,000 | 18,000 | | 39,000 |
| | 5394 | ECDA—Senate Bill 658 (Parents as first teachers) | 38,000 | | | 38,000 |
| | | *Total State Sources* | 2,060,844 | 3,962,152 | | 6,022,996 |
| Federal | 5411 | PL 874 | 1,000 | | | 1,000 |
| | 5432 | Vocational aid | 600 | | | 600 |
| | 5433 | Chapter I | 10,621 | 21,000 | | 31,621 |
| | 5440 | Drug-free program | 21,000 | | | 21,000 |
| | 5437 | Block grant | 20,800 | 19,430 | | 40,230 |
| | | *Total Federal Sources* | 54,021 | 40,430 | 0 | 94,451 |
| | | *Total Operating Revenue* | 8,640,659 | 10,763,378 | 897,983 | 20,302,020 |

APPENDIX TABLE B-2 • *Approved Budget 1988–89 (June 14, 1988)*
*Operating Fund Balances*

|  | Operations | Teachers | Building | Total |
|---|---|---|---|---|
|  | *1987-88* | | | |
| Begin 7/1/87 | 3,443,916 | 280,935 | 0 | 3,724,851 |
| Revenue | 8,376,215 | 10,510,226 | 935,947 | 19,780,906 |
| Revenue & balance | 11,820,131 | 10,791,161 | 935,947 | 23,505,757 |
| Expenditures | 7,696,191 | 12,892,898 | 435,521 | 21,024,610 |
| Balance 6/30/88 | 4,123,940 | <2,101,737> | 500,426 | 2,481,147 |
| Transfers | <2,101,737> | 2,101,737 | 0 | 0 |
| Balances after transfer | 2,022,203 | 0 | 500,426 | 2,481,147 |
|  | *1988-89* | | | |
| Begin 7/1/88 | 2,022,203 | 0 | 500,426 | 2,481,147 |
| Revenue | 8,655,659 | 10,763,378 | 897,983 | 20,302,020 |
| Revenue & balance | 10,677,862 | 10,763,378 | 1,398,409 | 22,783,167 |
| Expenditures | 7,964,041 | 13,780,915 | 255,044 | 22,000,000 |
| Balance 6/30/89 | 2,713,821 | <3,017,537> | 1,143,365 | 783,167 |

This appendix contains a summary page showing the beginning balance, revenue, revenue plus balance, expenditures, balance after expenditures, transfers, and final balance for the current fiscal year. The beginning balance, revenue, revenue plus balance, and expenditures for the approved budget is indicated on the lower half of the page.

On the same sheet, expenditures are also indicated according to the fund from which they were expended. In this example, there was a deficit in the teachers fund as of June 30, 1988. This state's regulations require the district to transfer monies from other funds in order to offset the deficit. it is obvious from the decreasing end-of-the-year balances that this district is deficit spending which means that expenditures are greater than revenues. Once again, as of June 30, 1989, this district must transfer monies from the two other funds in order to offset the deficit in the teachers fund.

This school district must bring expenditures in line with revenues or it will be bankrupt. In almost every state, school districts are prohibited by law from allowing such a situation to occur. This district must be guilty of poor planning to be so close to bankruptcy.

It is also common practice to strive toward having an overall fund balance of no less than 10 percent of expenditures. This is to ensure that the district will not have to borrow money for cash flow reasons. Most school districts do not receive revenues on a regular monthly basis. For example, local tax money will reach the school district beginning in November with the bulk being received in January.

APPENDIX TABLE C-1 • Budget Crosswalk by Programs and Objects*

In this example, by reading from left to right, you can see what objects make up the total expense for each program. By reading down the columns, you can see the total expense for various objects of expenditure.

| Code | Program | Salary & Benefits | Textbooks | Supplies & Workbooks | Replaced Equipment | New Equipment | Other Expenses | Total |
|------|---------|-------------------|-----------|----------------------|--------------------|---------------|----------------|-------|
| 001 | Art | 438,099 | 640 | 51,613 | 227 | 6,415 | 2,695 | 499,689 |
| 002 | Business | 193,930 | 5,806 | 8,917 | 14,290 | 1,311 | 13,000 | 237,254 |
| 003 | Driver education | 11,440 | | 6 | 45 | 1,060 | 2,800 | 15,351 |
| 004 | Education of the handicapped | 204,676 | 2,899 | 5,614 | 220 | 2,104 | 105,205 | 320,718 |
| 005 | English | 367,180 | 15,974 | 1,209 | | 836 | 1,369 | 386,568 |
| 006 | Foreign language | 166,380 | 2,596 | 1,711 | | 586 | 75 | 171,348 |
| 008 | Home economics | 125,500 | 1,025 | 6,818 | 3,349 | 566 | 252 | 137,510 |
| 009 | Industrial arts | 257,720 | 204 | 18,261 | 59,991 | 21,800 | 1,190 | 305,166 |
| 010 | Language arts | 1,428,477 | 29,415 | 60,792 | 47 | 2,925 | 350 | 1,522,006 |
| 011 | Mathematics | 787,877 | 20,484 | 6,496 | 81 | 8,577 | 1,039 | 824,554 |
| 012 | Music | 394,114 | 4,683 | 10,077 | 12,279 | 18,834 | 3,470 | 443,457 |
| 013 | Unassigned expenses | | | | | | 5,400 | 5,400 |
| 014 | Physical education/health | 473,891 | 5,139 | 12,538 | 10,028 | 4,942 | 640 | 507,178 |
| 015 | Science | 546,935 | 16,698 | 18,993 | 425 | 37,710 | 4,360 | 625,121 |
| 016 | Social studies | 578,589 | 27,407 | 10,271 | 2,046 | 10,120 | 3,805 | 632,238 |
| 017 | Vocational education | 46,120 | 762 | 1,190 | | 1,137 | 36,840 | 86,049 |
| 030 | Continuing education | 52,600 | 1,663 | 136 | | | | 54,389 |
| 033 | Remedial reading | 110,750 | 3,472 | 2,717 | 220 | 1,856 | 300 | 119,315 |
| 034 | Special education programs | 294,600 | 1,404 | 8,006 | 515 | 12,099 | 4,975 | 321,599 |
| 035 | Student activities | 101,100 | | | | | 5,800 | 106,900 |

*Wagner and Sniderman, Budgeting School Dollars, p. 5.

APPENDIX TABLE C-1 • *Budget Crosswalk by Programs and Objects (Continued)*

| Code | Program | Salary & Benefits | Textbooks | Supplies & Workbooks | Replaced Equipment | New Equipment | Other Expenses | Total |
|---|---|---|---|---|---|---|---|---|
| 040 | Guidance | 364,702 | | 1,312 | 142 | 1,323 | | 367,479 |
| 041 | Improvement of instruction | | 240 | 2,300 | | | 12,190 | 14,730 |
| 042 | Learning resources | 172,748 | 51,710 | 20,736 | 20,401 | 44,218 | 20,180 | 329,993 |
| 043 | Student welfare services | 80,550 | 157 | 319 | | 24 | | 81,050 |
| 044 | Testing | 57,800 | | 8,836 | | 301 | | 66,937 |
| 046 | Other instructional support | 94,000 | | 50,900 | | | | 144,900 |
| 050 | Board of education | | | | | | 2,700 | 2,700 |
| 051 | Building leadership | 763,433 | | 11,712 | 3,333 | 4,366 | 9,800 | 792,644 |
| 052 | Central direction | 202,315 | | 6,000 | 2,223 | | 6,631 | 217,169 |
| 061 | Maintenance | 148,330 | | 52,344 | 65,669 | 16,993 | 152,251 | 435,857 |
| 062 | Plant operation | 676,422 | | 54,920 | | | 368,300 | 1,099,642 |
| 063 | Prof. & tech. services | | | | | | 1,500 | 1,500 |
| 064 | Transportation | 22,600 | | | | | 347,500 | 370,100 |
| | *Grand total* | $9,162,878 | $192,378 | $434,744 | $141,531 | $200,103 | $1,114,887 | $11,246,521 |

## Appendix C

This appendix contains an exhibit of a budget crosswalk by programs and objects. It could be an exhibit in a school district budget because it displays the total cost for each program. For example, the first line gives the code number (001) for the art program. Reading from left to right, the dollars that are budgeted for salaries and benefits, textbooks, supplies and workbooks, replaced equipment, new equipment, and miscellaneous expenses are given. The last column gives the total for the art program. By this crosswalk exhibit, it is also possible to obtain the total expense for all the programs by object. Thus, the total expense for salaries and benefits is $9,162,878.

## Endnotes

1. William T. Hartman, *School District Budgeting* (Englewood Cliffs, New Jersey: Prentice-Hall, Inc., 1988), p. 1.

2. Glen E. Robinson and Nancy Protheroe, "School District Budget Profiles," *School Business Affairs*, Vol. 53, no. 9 (September 1987), pp. 14–20.

3. Sam B. Tidwell, *Financial and Managerial Accounting for Elementary and Secondary School Systems*, 3rd ed. (Reston, Virginia: Association of School Business Officials, 1985), pp. 142–144.

4. William J. Holly, "Developing, Managing, and Gaining Public Support for the School District Budget", *OSSC Bulletin*, Vol. 30, no. 6 (February 1987), pp. 4, 5.

5. R. Craig Wood, ed., *Principles of School Business Management* (Reston, Virginia: Association of School Business Officials, 1986), pp. 156, 157.

6. American Association of School Administrators, *Declining Enrollment: What to Do*, Vol. II, AASA Executive Handbook Series (Arlington, Virginia: The Association, 1974), pp. 8,9.

7. Hartman, *School District Budgeting*, pp. 91–95.

8. Hartman, *School District Budgeting*, pp. 95, 96.

9. Hartman, *School District Budgeting*, pp. 121, 122.

10. Hartman, *School District Budgeting*, pp. 25–30.

11. National School Public Relations Association, *PPBS and the School: New System Promotes Efficiency, Accountability* (Arlington, Virginia: The Association, 1972), p. 21.

12. NSPRA, *PPBS and the School*, p. 18.

13. Leonard L. Gregory and Roger R. Farr, "Involving the Principal in the Budget Making Process," *School Business Affairs*, Vol. 54, no. 7 (July 1988), pp. 18, 19.

14. David S. Honeyman and Rich Jensen, "School-Site Budgeting," *School Business Affairs*, Vol. 54, no. 2 (February 1988), pp. 12–14.

15. Hartman, *School District Budgeting*, pp. 8, 9

16. Robert Lowe and Robert Gervais, "How to Handle Desperation Budget Cuts Without Despair," *The Executive Educator*, Vol. 9, no. 1 (January 1987), pp. 18, 19.

17. A.G. Womble, Jr., "Predict Expenses, and Nip Budget Overruns in the Bud," *The Executive Educator*, Vol. 9, no. 10 (October 1987), pp. 30, 31.

18. Clark J. Godshall, "Online Budget: Use Your PC to Create a Budget Document that Tracks Spending from Year to Year," *American School and University*, Vol. 59, no. 2 (October 1986), pp. 18–20.

19. Ivan D. Wagner and Sam M. Sniderman, *Budgeting School Dollars: A Guide to Spending and Saving* (Washington, DC: The National School Boards Association, 1984), p. 2.

20. Wagner and Sniderman, *Budgeting School Dollars*, pp. 217, 218.

21. Nancy W. Sindelar, "Building Confidence in Your Budget," *School Business Affairs*, Vol. 54, no. 1 (January 1988), p. 21.

22. Wagner and Sniderman, *Budgeting School Dollars*, p. 219.

23. Hartman, *School District Budgeting*, pp. 30, 31.


## Selected Bibliography

Augenblick, John, *Public School: Issues in Budgeting and Financial Management* (New Brunswick, New Jersey: Transaction books, Rutgers–the State University, 1986).

Goldstein, William, *Selling School Budgets in Hard Times* (Bloomington, Indiana: Phi Delta Kappa Educational Foundation, 1984).

Greenhalgh, John, *School Site Budgeting: Decentralized School Management* (Lanham, Maryland: University Press of America, 1985).

Hartman, William T., *School District Budgeting* (New Jersey: Prentice-Hall, Inc., 1988).

Hartman, William T. and Jon Rivenburg, "Budget Allocation Patterns: School District Choices for Available Resources," *Journal of Educational Finance*, Vol. 11 (Fall, 1985), pp. 219–235.

Honeyman, David S., and Rick Jensen, "School-Site Budgeting," *School Business Affairs*, Vol. 54, no. 2 (February 1988), pp. 12–14.

Kehoe, Ellen, "Education Budget Preparation: Fiscal and Political Considerations," in *Principles of Business Management*, R. Craig Woods, ed. (Reston, Virginia: Association of School Business Officials, 1986).

Lowe, Robert, and Robert Gervais, "Cut the Budget Without Despair," *The Executive Educator*, Vol. 9, no. 1 (January 1987), pp. 18–20.

Robinson, Glen E., and Nancy Protheroe, "School District Budget Profiles," *School Business Affairs*, Vol. 53, no. 9 (September 1987), pp. 11–21.

Sindelar, Nancy W., "Building Confidence in Your Budget," *School Business Affairs*, Vol. 54, no. 1 (January 1988), pp. 19–21.

Tidwell, Sam B., "Budgetary Accounting: Managing Revenues and Expenditures," in *Financial and Managerial Accounting for Elementary and Secondary School Systems*, (3rd ed.) (Reston, Virginia: Association of School Business Officials, 1985).

Wagner, Ivan D., and Sam M. Sniderman, *Budgeting School Dollars: A Guide to Spending and Saving* (Washington, DC: National School Boards Association, 1984).

Womble Jr., A. G., "Nip Budget Woes in the Bud," *The Executive Educator*, Vol. 9, no. 10 (October 1987), pp. 30–32.

# 6

# Managing the Budget

In a real sense, this chapter is a continuation of Chapter 5 because what is encountered while constructing the approved budget becomes the basis upon which the forthcoming budget is managed. A shortfall in the budgeted amount of state revenue could change future revenue projections. In like manner, significant increases in expenditures could affect future cost estimates. It is imperative for both the superintendent of schools and assistant superintendent for business and financial services and other administrators to always keep in mind that, as they project revenues and expenditures in the budget construction process, such projections are partially based on *estimates* and not actual figures. Thus, as the budget is being developed for any given year, the current year's budget will not have been completely implemented.

It is common practice in medium to large school districts to appoint a staff member from the business office, and more specifically from the accounting department, to assume the responsibilities of *budget management*. This person is usually given the title of either *budget director* or *budget manager*. In school districts with fewer than 5000 students, either the superintendent or the assistant superintendent for business and financial services will fulfill these responsibilities.

The budget director reports either directly to the superintendent of schools or to the appropriate assistant superintendent who, in turn, reports directly to the superintendent. It is the responsibility of the superintendent to establish channels of communication with the board of education concerning the implementation of the budget. The usual manner of communicating the implementation process is through financial reports

**139**

that are presented to the board during a regular board meeting. The common designation for such reporting is *budget operating summary*, which will be explained in detail later in this chapter.

Occasions may arise when a budget operating summary becomes the main topic of a special board meeting, such as when there is a significant shortfall in revenue or when there is a need to heighten community awareness concerning a tax levy increase.

The building principals and central office administrators who are responsible for program administration must also receive ongoing information about the status of the budget. These staff members were charged with developing the budget, and should be charged with implementing the budget under the direction of the superintendent. In order to effectively discharge this responsibility, they must receive regular reports setting forth the amount of funds that have been expended, the amount encumbered, and the balance in every account that they manage. This type of report is usually prepared on a monthly basis.

Throughout the entire budget implementation process, it is important to demonstrate that dollars are being spent only according to the educational plan that was the basis for budget development and in accordance with board of education policies such as the policy dealing with purchasing and the taking of bids.

At the end of the fiscal year, the final budget operating report is the annual audit report which should be performed by an independent certified public accounting firm. This chapter will now elucidate, from an operational perspective, each of the aspects just presented.

## Purchasing and Procurement

The first responsibility in implementing the approved budget is the establishment of effective purchasing and procurement procedures. The purchasing and procurement department of a school district is charged with a very specialized function that goes far beyond the mere "buying" of supplies, materials, and equipment. This function also includes the purchasing of services as is indicated in the title of this section by the term *procurement*. In addition, when supplies, materials, and equipment are purchased, they must be received, stored, inventoried, and distributed. This is properly referred to as *materials management*.

The objective of purchasing and procurement, of course, is to provide the material and purchase of services necessary to implementing the

EXHIBIT 6-1 • *Purchasing and Procurement Policy*

The board of education declares its intention to purchase supplies, materials, equipment, and services in a competitive manner. Through such a process, the school district will be responsive in maximizing the value of every budgeted dollar.

In addition, the board of education sets forth that the objective of the purchasing and procurement function is to serve the needs of the instructional program. The acquisition of supplies, materials, equipment, and services will be centralized in the business and financial services division which functions under the supervision of the assistant superintendent for business and financial services. The assistant superintendent, under the supervision of the superintendent of schools, is responsible for the quality and quantity of purchases and the quality of services procured. Such purchases and procurements must fall within the framework of budgetary limitations and must be consistent with the approved educational goals and programs of the district.

The administration is authorized to make individual purchases of budgeted items up to a maximum of $5000 without prior board of education approval. This limitation shall apply to all supplies, materials, equipment, and services except as otherwise provided in the following waiver when the estimated cost thereof exceeds $5000.

The limitation of $5000 is waived in the following situation:

> *In the event of emergency, disaster, or conditions imposing upon the general welfare, health, or safety of school children, the superintendent shall be authorized to make purchases and procurements necessary to alleviate the condition. The superintendent is to apprise the board of these actions at the next regular board meeting.*

Recognizing that the school district is supported primarily by tax monies paid by individuals and businesses of the state and local community, it shall be the policy of the district to purchase and procure services available locally or in this state when quality and price are competitive with companies not located in these areas.

Purchases shall be timed to provide the necessary goods and services without undue delay in delivery and with reasonable cost. The quantity of items purchased shall depend upon the need, the storage facilities available, and the effect on unit prices for volume purchases.

---

instructional program. In addition, the purchasing and procurement department must be committed to maximizing the value of every budgeted dollar as it carries out this vital function.

## Purchasing and Procurement Policy

The purchasing and procurement function will fail in its major objective unless there is a clearly articulated board of education policy, and unless there are well defined administrative procedures.[1] Exhibit 6-1 is a sample board of education purchasing and procurement policy.

Purchasing and procuring on a "competitive basis" can be accomplished in a number of ways. There are givens, however, which should be maintained by all school districts. The administration should always reserve the right to reject any or all bids or any part of any bid and to accept that bid which appears to be in the best interest of the district. In like manner, the administration should reserve the right to waive any informalities in the bidding process. Companies should be given the right to withdraw a bid prior to the scheduled time for the opening of bids. All bids received after the time and date for receiving bids, as stated in the specifications for bidding, should not be considered.[2]

The purchasing and procurement department should maintain a list of prospective bidders for all supplies, materials, equipment, and services. These companies can be contacted when the need arises. However, it is also important to advertise for bids for expensive items and, definitely, for all services. As suggested in the policy for purchasing and procurement, items costing over $5000 should be bid. This can also serve as the dollar amount above which the purchasing and procurement department will advertise for bids.

The phrase used to indicate that bids are being requested is *request for proposals* which is commonly referred to as an *RFP*. School districts that, by size or circumstance, are bidding a large number of items or services will usually number the requests. A number such as *RFP-205-91* indicates that this is request number 205 and that this request is for the 1991 fiscal year. Appendix A contains a sample RFP for auditing services.

This RFP for auditing services indicates that there will be a pre-proposal conference, which is a common practice. At such a conference, prospective bidders can receive clarifications and answers to their questions. It is a technique that helps to eliminate controversy after a bid opening. All interested parties are given the same information and can hear the questions of competitors.

In addition, the RFP for auditing services indicates a requirement that is common practice when procuring professional services. The companies are asked to submit two packages: package one consists of the company's qualifications, background information about the firm, the resumes of key individuals, and the work plan; package two contains the company's detailed cost proposal.

Because the objective is to secure the services of the firm that best meets the auditing needs of the school district, the first task is to analyze package one from all the bidding companies. In this way, the most technically qualified firm can be identified without regard to the cost. The cost proposals can then be considered from a financial perspective. If the most technically qualified firm also has the most cost-effective proposal, there is no problem in making a choice. However, if the most technically qualified firm does not have the lowest cost proposal, the administration must weigh the potential effect of accepting a lesser qualified firm with a lower cost proposal. It is obvious that all the firms should be ranked starting from the most technically qualified to the least technically qualified, and the cost proposals should be ranked in like manner. The administration, of course, must make a recommendation to the board of education. The board should study the analysis that the administration conducted regarding each firm's expertise when considering the administration's recommendation.

This process is not needed when securing bids for supplies, materials, and equipment. However, the major problem that is encountered when taking these types of bids is whether or not to accept alternate bids for items that do not meet the specifications exactly, but which a company presents as a good alternative. This, too, is a judgment call. The overriding principle is to purchase or procure the best items and services at the lowest cost without compromising the integrity of the school district. Obviously, purchasing and procurement is not an exact science.

The time and place to open bids will depend on the wishes of the administration and board of education. Most often, it will be sufficient to invite bidders to a bid opening that is conducted at the central office. At that time, an administrator from the purchasing department opens the bids.

Once again, using the figure in the proposed purchasing and procurement policy, items costing less than $5000 may be purchased by the taking of quotations. At all times, an attempt should be made to secure quotations from at least two or more vendors. Written quotations are more defensible than oral quotations, and written quotations should be required except in emergency situations. The purchasing administrator should determine the best quotation depending upon the price, quality of product, delivery time, and other factors considered important in a given situation. Records of all quotations should be kept on file for at least one year after delivery of the item.

Another situation that occurs in purchasing must be noted here. There are some supplies, materials, and equipment that can be purchased from only one vendor. For example, the instructional staff should be consulted when choosing a textbook, which, of course, is published by only one company. Also, parts for specialized equipment may be available from only one company.

It is important to note that most states have statutes pertaining to purchasing and bidding by school districts. Thus, it is critical for all purchasing administrators to become familiar with these laws. They must be certain that the assistant superintendent for business and financial services and, subsequently, the superintendent of schools are informed about such laws when reviewing and updating school board policies dealing with purchasing and procurement.

Many school districts have discovered the benefits of purchasing on a volume basis. Larger orders sometimes bring about greater dollar savings. For this reason, two or more school districts may join together in cooperative purchasing. This cooperative venture should not affect competitive bidding as described above.

## Receiving, Warehousing, and Distribution

It is important to reflect on the steps in the purchasing and procurement process in order to understand how the receiving, warehousing, and distribution tasks are implemented.

First, central office program administrators and building principals begin by processing a *requisition* form and sending it to the appropriate budget administrator.

Second, the budget administrator sends the requisition to the accounting department where the proper accounting code is entered or verified if this is the responsibility of the initiating administrator in a given district.

Third, the requisition is sent to the purchasing and procurement department which, in turn, initiates the purchasing or procurement process. Certain items such as supplies should be kept *in stock* in the warehouse in order that the requested item or items can be immediately sent to the originator of the requisition.

Fourth, the purchasing and procurement department issues a purchase order or contract after the bidding or procurement process. It is imperative that a purchasing agent be given the responsibility for following up on the order or contract in order to expedite delivery of an item or the receiving of a service. The administrator who initiated the requisition should be kept advised as to the status of the purchase or procurement.

Fifth, upon arrival of the item in the warehouse, the invoice or receipt is checked against the packing slip and the item is inspected in order to ensure that the proper item has been received and that it has not been damaged during shipping. The purchasing and procurement department must verify that the price on the invoice agrees with the bid or quotation price and that the terms of the order include f.o.b. shipping or delivery point.

Sixth, the received item must be inventoried. If it is an item that will be repaired rather than replaced and that costs over two hundred dollars, an asset inventory number should be attached. This procedure is arbitrary, but it is a reasonable guide. Supplies, of course, must also be inventoried but are not tagged with an asset inventory number because they are consumables.

The seventh and final step is the approval of the invoice or contract for payment. A "warrant list" is then presented for approval to the board of education at the next meeting. This list usually contains the number of the check, the name of the vendor or contractor, a short description of the item or service, the amount of the check, and the fund from which payment will be made.

An important decision that every school district must make is whether to centralize or decentralize the warehousing of supplies and materials. A centralized approach requires a facility for the receiving and storing of all goods purchased by the district. A decentralized approach allows for the receiving and storing, in each school, the materials needed by that school.

There are advantages and disadvantages to each approach. The decision will be affected by two main factors: the annual consumption of various supplies and the extent of standardization of supplies.

After items are received and inventoried at a centralized warehouse, provisions must be made to distribute the items to the location that requisitioned them. A catalogue of supplies is useful for requisitioning items from a central warehouse. In order to control the inventory, the catalogue can be broken down by categories with a coding system. With the computer programs now readily available, a perpetual inventory system should be maintained which provides an up-to-date continuous accounting of materials in the warehouse or school.[3]

## Accounting Policy and Procedures

Financial recordkeeping is one of those functions that is really necessary in all business organizations. Because school districts are financed through tax revenues, the level and scope of financial accounting must be such that it is readily evident that all tax monies are being spent for the purposes for which they were collected. The records of the financial transactions of the school district form the basis upon which sound financial decisions can be made by the administration and the board of education.

Systematic recordkeeping of financial transactions allows for the tracing of each transaction and identifies what was expended, for what purpose, and by whom. In addition, financial transaction recordkeeping identifies the source of the money used for the expenditure. That source will usually be local tax revenue, state revenue, or federal revenue. Such data is necessary in the construction of reports that are used for financial analysis of the budget, and these reports form the basis upon which financial decisions are made. The format for these reports will be covered in the following section.

Sometimes financial recordkeeping is referred to as bookkeeping. However, this is only one phase of a complete system that involves the recording, classifying, summarizing, interpreting, and reporting of results of the school district's financial activities. This system is commonly known as *accounting.*[4]

Education, of course, is a big business. It involves numerous financial transactions on a daily basis. Therefore, a sound accounting system must provide the administration with the following:

1. An accurate record of the details involved in business transactions
2. Safeguards assuring that the fiscal resources of the school district are used for their designated purpose
3. Data that can be used by the administration in planning
4. Information for local, state, and federal governmental agencies about the financial operations of the school district
5. An analysis of how the administration expended the school district's revenues in relation to the educational goals inherent in the approved budget

An adequate accounting system must also meet certain minimal criteria commonly accepted by those in the accounting profession. First, it must have a reasonable degree of internal controls that continuously insure the accuracy of transactions recorded. Second, the accounting system should be consistent with generally accepted governmental accounting principles, incorporating uniformity of procedures and the use of standard terminology and definitions. Third, it should be simple and flexible, not only to accommodate new programs with minimal disruption but also to help in the administration of the school district. Fourth, it should be a double-entry, accrual, and encumbrance system. Fifth, as a governmental accounting system, transactions should be recorded in the following dimensions in order to answer certain critical questions: what was purchased? (object); from what financial source? (fund); for what purpose? (function); for which school? (operational unit); and to provide what specific service? (program).

An accrual and encumbrance accounting system provides a school district with a truly realistic appraisal of its fiscal position. Under this type of system, revenues are recorded when earned and expenditures are recorded at the time the school district incurs financial liability, although receipt of the revenue or payment of an invoice may occur in another accounting period. Thus, in terms of expenditures, the following procedures will take place. The financial books are opened by recording the approved budget. When purchase orders are signed and contracts approved, the dollar amount is entered into an encumbrance column. When payments are made, the dollar amount is charged to a payment column, and the original amount encumbered is credited to encumbrances. This procedure gives a continual analysis of the progress in expending the budget because the budget balance is the difference between the appropriations on the one hand and the expenditures and encumbrances on the other.

Not only can the accounting system provide the administration with a summary of revenues and budget balances on a continual basis but such data can be formalized into a *budget operating summary* and presented to the board of education at its regular monthly business meeting. As a final note, it should be understood that the microcomputer and readily available software make it easy for even the smallest of school districts to have a computerized accounting system.

## Auditing School District Accounts and Programs

Auditing accounts and programs is a standard operating practice in school districts, in all governmental agencies, and in private business and industry. Most large corporations and large school districts have internal auditing procedures for the purpose of identifying ineffective and improper practices that could result in legal and/or financial problems. Internal auditing will be addressed later in this chapter. External audits are conducted by a certified public accounting firm at the end of each fiscal year. The audit should cover the entire scope of school-district operations and should attempt to analyze the accuracy of financial transactions and to verify financial records.

There is another significant service that the certified public accounting firm can perform for school districts. The firm can analyze the policies, procedures, and practices employed in conducting the business activities of the school district. This is extremely important because such an analysis can point out inefficiencies that may be costing the district a considerable amount of money.

In performing an audit, the certified public accountants must have access to certain records that will provide them with necessary data. The following is a partial list of those items that are usually examined: the minutes of the school board meetings, the budget document, all contracts, accounting records such as ledgers and journals, the record of revenue and nonrevenue receipts, bank account records, investment records, insurance policies, surety bonds, deeds to property, inventory lists, and original documents relating to the authorization of expenditures and the making of payments.[5]

While the auditing reports of accounting firms vary somewhat, they usually include the following: a letter of transmittal, a description of the scope and the limitations of the audit, a summary of the examination findings, financial statements and schedules, and recommendations for improving the accounting procedures and/or the business operations of the school district.

From time to time, the assistant superintendent for business and financial services should seek proposals from auditing firms in order to ascertain if the fee the school district is paying for auditing services is competitive with the fee structure of other firms. It is important for the school district to employ a firm based not only on its fee but also on the experience and qualifications of its accountants. School districts are required to take the lowest *and* best bid, not merely the lowest. A multiple-year contract with an auditing firm will give that firm sufficient time to assess accurately and in detail the business operations of the district. Appendix A contains a request for proposal document for securing auditing services.

The auditing report is usually presented directly to the board of education by the auditing firm. Of course, copies are made available to the superintendent and the assistant superintendent for business and financial services. An effective audit report will provide the board of education and the public with the assurance that the administration is conducting the business activities of the district in an honest, appropriate, and effective manner. Thus, the audit also becomes a method of protecting those charged with managing the fiscal resources of the district.

School districts seeking proposals from auditing firms will receive responses from various size firms. The six largest firms are probably the following: Peat, Marwick, Mitchell; Coopers & Lybrand; Price Waterhouse; Arthur Andersen; Deloitte, Touch; Ernst, Young.

A final note is in order concerning the Single Audit Act of 1984. Historically, the Office of Management and Budget (OMB) had required federal grants to be audited individually. This proved to be very costly and somewhat inefficient. In October 1979, the OMB adopted the single audit approach which was a shift in emphasis. The new emphasis was on the recipient, school districts receiving over $25,000 in federal assistance per year, rather than on the individual grant. Congress passed the Single Audit

Act in 1984 in order to reinforce this new approach in auditing. Thus, federal programs are a part of the regular school audit conducted by a CPA firm.

## Internal Auditing

The role and function of the internal auditor has grown in status over the last ten years primarily because of the accountability concerns of the public. The person occupying this position should be a valued resource member of the management team. As school districts continue to become more complex and diverse, and, as technology changes the way school districts educate students and perform administrative tasks, the role and function of the internal auditor will become even more necessary. Internal auditing can ensure the effective and efficient use of resources and can provide an independent view of all activities conducted by the school district. In order to maintain independence, the internal auditor should report directly to the superintendent of schools.

The internal auditing function should be concerned with the following areas. The first area is *financial fraud* which usually occurs when internal controls are weak. The public trust that tax dollars are being properly used is shaken by reports of fraud. This loss of confidence may not become obvious until a school district asks the taxpayers to increase the tax levy or to pass a bond issue. At this point, the taxpayers may send a message to the board of education and the administration by voting against the tax levy increase or bond issue. Second, *construction* or *remodeling projects* present a special challenge to the internal auditor because of the complexity of such projects. It is rather easy to overpay for materials and labor or even to pay for materials not used and for labor not rendered. Third, *program audits* are perhaps the most obvious internal auditing responsibility. Not only financial review but also procedures and systems review are an ongoing task of the internal auditor. Fourth, *new technology* review is becoming more critical for the internal auditing function. Computer system design now permits the networking of many data files. Unauthorized employees may have ready access to these files. Once again the internal auditor must assess new system controls in order to identify weaknesses and to propose solutions.

It should be obvious from this discussion that the internal auditor should be a person who has an appreciation for the complexity of the school district and has the capability of understanding the internal structure of the district. Thus, the internal auditor should be educated as an administrator and should have administrative experience at the building level as well as at the central office. It is not necessary for this person to have formal education and experience as an auditor or accountant although this would be highly desirable. The emphasis is on understanding and appreciating the systematic approach to school-district organization which always demands internal controls.[6]

## Financial Reporting

Perhaps the most important responsibility of the school district's administration to the board of education is the reporting of the financial condition of the district. There are primarily two reasons why this is so important. First, the members of the board of education are ultimately responsible to the taxpayers, whom they represent, for the cost-effective governance of the district. In our present socioeconomic society, quality education is very dependent upon the wealth of the district. Please understand that this statement does not refer to the individual performance of teachers and administrators. Rather, quality education, in this context, refers to the financial ability of the district to purchase appropriate materials, supplies, and equipment in addition to attracting quality teachers and administrators. Further, this refers to the financial ability of the district to properly maintain the facilities of the district which are so critical to effective instruction.[7]

Second, financial reporting allows the administration, under the leadership of the superintendent of schools, to demonstrate that the budget approved by the board is being properly implemented. Financial reporting should be a regular part of the monthly school board meeting. Appendix B contains a series of financial reports, which constitute the minimum amount of data that should be prepared for each board meeting. This type of reporting is also a good public relations vehicle because it sets forth the ongoing financial condition of the district for all interested parties to review. Also, it has become common practice during the last decade for members of the news media to be interested in receiving this data.

The first chart, entitled "Summary of Expenditures," provides information concerning the following expenditure categories, commonly termed *objects* in financial accounting: the salaries for certificated employees; the salaries for all other employees; employee fringe benefits; and purchase of service, supplies, and capital outlay. It should be noted that the only effective way to understand financial data is in comparison with other financial data. Thus, this chart is divided in half and compares expenditures in fiscal year 1988–89 with fiscal year 1989–90. This comparison is carried out in four ways. The first column on the left side of the chart is the budget for the 1988–89 fiscal year which is compared with the budget for the 1989–90 fiscal year. Further, each category or object is compared.

The second column from the left constitutes the expenditures by category for the month of January 1989 with the month of January 1990. The third column contains the year-to-date expenditures by category for the 1988–89 fiscal year which, in turn, is compared with the year-to-date expenditures for the 1989–90 fiscal year. The fourth column shows the percentage expended from the budget by category for the period ending January 31, 1989. This should be compared with the percentage expended for the period ending January 31, 1990. Perhaps the most important comparative figures are the percentages. Overall, in fiscal year 1988–89 the district expended 2.34 percent more of the budgeted amount than in fiscal year 1989–90. This is not a significant difference. The most significant difference occurs in the capital outlay category. There is a 26.14 percent difference between the two fiscal years. The budgeted amounts of $7,227,143 and $6,502,332 could not account for this significant difference. Even though the figures are significantly different in the two fiscal years, the answer to this concern lies in the category "year-to-date." In fiscal year 1988–89, the district expended considerably more money for this category by January 31 than in fiscal year 1989–90. There could be many reasons for this. For example, there might have been a delay in the delivery of large equipment or in the completion of major maintenance projects such as roofing for several buildings. Inclement weather would have an effect on the completion of such projects. The point is that financial reports point out discrepancies that need to be investigated and explained to the board of education. This acts as a check on the administration.

The second chart, "Summary of Revenues," is constructed in a similar fashion to the "Summary of Expenditures." The chart is divided in half with the left side containing data for the 1988–89 fiscal year and the right side containing data for the 1989–90 fiscal year. The revenues are set forth by source. The four largest sources are local, county, state, and federal. The column on the far left contains the account code for each line item of revenue. There are three columns for fiscal year 1988-89. The first is the budget column, the second is the column listing year-to-date revenue, and the final column shows the percentage of the budgeted amount received through January. There are six columns on the right side of the report. The first lists the original budget estimates for 1989–90. The next two columns have no direct comparisons with the previous year. The column entitled "adjustments to original estimates" contains revised figures because the administration received some information which alters the original budget revenues. It is prudent to make this known as soon as possible to the board of education, and this is why it is a part of the monthly financial report. The board and all interested parties can go to the monthly financial reports in order to identify when further information was available. This is extremely important if the administration and board are to maintain credibility with the public and with the employees of the district. During collective negotiations this kind of data will dispel accusations that the district has more money than is being reported. The amount in this column is either added or subtracted from the original budget estimate and is recorded in the column entitled "Revised Estimates as of 1/90." At the end of the current fiscal year, this column will become the "revised budget" for the financial report of the next fiscal year.

The last two columns on the right contain respectively the actual revenue received through January, 1990 and the percentage of revenue received through January, 1990. Once again this type of comparative data can be used to investigate and explain any questionable items.

The third financial chart is entitled, "Comparison of Period Ending January 31, 1990." This report is constructed from data contained in the previous two reports. However, the difference in this report is the direct implication of *budget calendarization*. The report begins on the extreme left side by setting forth the amount of revenue received during the month of January, 1990. The next column contains the actual revenue received for the first seven months of the fiscal year 1988–89. The next column, in like manner, contains the amount of revenue received for the first seven months of the current fiscal year. The next column contains the expected revenue for the first seven months of operation in fiscal year 1989–90, commonly referred to as the *revenue budget calendar*. This calendar is developed by analyzing past fiscal years in order to determine when revenue is usually received. The "adjustments to original estimates" column on the "Summary of Revenues" report should be used in this process in order to identify aberrations concerning the receiving of revenues.

The next portion of this report deals with expenditures and follows the same pattern as revenues. Once again, the expenditure budget calendar is developed from past experience. The last portion presents the surplus <deficit> comparisons which are calculated by subtracting the expenditures from the revenues contained in the three columns setting forth the actual 1988–89, actual 1989–90, and budget 1989–90 year-to-date figures.

The final column on the far right provides the figure that is the difference between the actual 1989–90 figures and the budget calendar figures which could be either a plus or a minus. For example, the figure $2,701,354 is the amount actually received in revenue over the amount that was originally estimated (budgeted). In like manner, the figure $13,805,337 represents the amount of money that was not expended year-to-date in comparison with the budget calendar expenditures for the first seven months. Finally, under the surplus <deficit> section of this report, the implication is that the district has $16,506,691 more in cash than was estimated for the period ending January 31, 1990.

The final chart, "Consolidated Schedule of Invested Funds," presents a schedule of investment which contains the following: type of security purchased, the broker for the transaction, the purchase date, the maturity date, the yield, the cost of the investment, the net interest expected, and the balance due at maturity. This is a fairly typical report which is, nonetheless, a very important report because it demonstrates that the school district's surplus cash is being properly invested.

## Summary

In a sense this chapter is a continuation of Chapter 5, because what is encountered while constructing the budget will become the basis upon which the forthcoming budget will be managed. It is a common practice in medium to large school districts to appoint a staff member from the business office and, more specifically, from the accounting department to assume the responsibilities of budget director.

The first responsibility in implementing the approved budget is the establishment of effective purchasing and procurement procedures. The objective of purchasing and procurement is to purchase the material and the services that are necessary to implementing the instructional program. In addition, the purchasing and procurement department must be committed to maximizing the value of every budgeted dollar as it carries out this vital function. The objectives of this department will not be achieved unless there is a clearly articulated board of education policy setting forth the mission of the purchasing and procurement department.

Purchasing and procurement should be carried out on a competitive bidding basis. However, the school-district administration should always reserve the right to reject any or all bids or any part of any bid, and to accept the bid that appears to be in the best interest of the district.

There are seven steps in the purchasing and procurement process: (1) a requisition is initiated; (2) verification is carried out by the accounting department; (3) the purchasing and procurement department initiates the purchasing or procurement process; (4) a purchase order or contract is executed; (5) received items are inspected and verified; (6) the received items are inventoried; and (7) the invoice or contract is approved for payment. After items are received and inventoried at a central warehouse, provisions must be made to distribute the items to the location that requisitioned them.

Financial recordkeeping is one of those functions that is a given in all organizations. Because school districts are financed through tax revenues, the level and scope of financial accounting must show that all tax monies are being spent for the purposes for which they were collected. The records of the financial transactions of the school district form the basis upon which sound financial decisions can be made by the administration and the board of education.

The accounting system must allow for a reasonable degree of internal control and be consistent with generally accepted governmental accounting principles. The accounting system should be a double-entry, accrual, and encumbrance system. The accounting system should provide the administration with a summary of revenues and budget balances on a continual basis. In addition, this data can be formalized into a budget operating summary and presented to the board of education at its regular monthly business meeting.

The external auditing of accounts and programs is a common business practice not only in school districts but also in private business and industry. The audit should cover the entire scope of school district operations and should attempt to analyze the accuracy of financial transactions and to verify financial records. The audit firm can also analyze the policies, procedures, and practices employed in conducting the business activities of the school district. The audit report is usually presented directly to the board of education by the audit firm.

The role and function of the internal auditor has grown in status over the last ten years primarily because of the accountability concerns of the public. Internal auditing can ensure the effective and efficient use of resources, and can provide an independent view of all activities conducted by the school district. Thus, the internal auditor should report directly to the superintendent of schools. The role and function of the internal auditor should be the reviewing of records and documents in order to ascertain if the district is in compliance with its own policies, procedures, and contracts, in addition to being in compliance with the rules and regulations of other governmental agencies that have jurisdiction over the district. The internal auditor can and should be a resource person to other administrators as they develop new programs.

One of the most important responsibilities of the administration is the reporting to the board of education concerning the financial condition of the district. The board is ultimately responsible to the taxpayers for the cost-effective governance of the district. The financial reports can also allow the administration to demonstrate that the budget approved by the board is being properly implemented. Financial reporting should be a regular part of the monthly school board meeting.

The budget operating summary should contain, as a minimum, a comparative summary of expenditures and revenues and a schedule of invested monies.

# Appendix A  An RFP for Auditing Services

## Desired Services

The annual audit will entail an audit of the district's financial, transportation, attendance, food service, and federal and state program records. The annual audit will review and test the district's system of internal accounting control and the system of administrative control over compliance with federal laws and regulations to the extent considered necessary by the auditor as required by the *GAO Standards for Audit of Governmental Organizations, Programs, Activities, and Functions: the GAO Guidelines for Financial and Compliance Audits of Federally Assisted Programs,* supplements approved by OMB, and generally accepted auditing standards established by AICPA. The annual audit shall conform to all state statutes.

The interim (preliminary) annual audit work is to be scheduled during the month of May. The final portion of the annual audit work will take place between July 1 and August 30. Twenty-four copies of the completed audit, management letter, and comprehensive annual financial report shall be submitted prior to October 1 to the Superintendent of Schools or a designated representative. A presentation to the board of education will be required.

The district will provide work area, records, and help in the preparation of audit schedules as requested by the auditor. Clerical assistance and supplies will be the responsibility of the auditing firm.

The comprehensive annual financial report (CAFR) will be in conformance with financial reporting requirements promulgated by the Association of School Business Officials (ASBO), the Government Finance Officers Association (GFOA), and the Single Audit Act of 1984. The CAFR should go beyond the requirements of generally accepted accounting principles (GAAP) and beyond the requirements of applicable statutes and regulations in an effort to provide all of the information necessary to meet the information needs of the many persons and groups with legitimate interests in the financial affairs of the district.

Financial statements should include, but not be limited to, a statement of:

1. Accountants' report
2. Combined balance—all governmental fund types
3. Combined statement of revenues, expenditures, and changes in fund balances—budget and actual—all governmental fund types
4. Notes on financial statements
5. Schedules:
   A. Revenues and other financing sources (uses)
   B. Expenditures by object

## Proposal Requirements

*A. Desired structure* All proposals should be responsive to the following instructions for ease of comparison and evaluation.

Paragraph layout and identification should permit easy reading and referencing. Multiple sections, paragraphs, and subparagraphs should be numbered or otherwise identified to assure proper identification of subordinated topic relationships and qualifying statement or phrases.

Proposers must submit all data required herein in order for their proposal to be evaluated and considered for award. Failure to provide such data may be deemed sufficient cause to disqualify the proposal from award consideration.

*B. Required content* Proposals should be responsive to the following instructions in the same order as presented.

1. *Cover sheet* Proposer must supply the information requested and sign the proposal cover sheet.
2. *Resume* Proposer must provide the requested information related to its history, qualifications, and experience. If you are a national firm, the information must be specific to the branch that will be providing the service.
3. *Personnel commitment* Proposer must provide the requested information regarding the personnel that it is proposing for this engagement. Please note that it is required that the manager and supervisor be committed to the project for the base year and the option years, if exercised.
4. *Use of consultants* Proposer will identify all consultants, experts, or subcontractors which would be engaged by your firm for this engagement.
5. *Proposed time and price* Proposer must complete and submit, as Package 2, time and price, its proposed worker hours, hourly rate (both by position and classification), travel, and administrative costs.

## Evaluation Process/Criteria

Proposals must be submitted in two packages. Package 1 (technical proposal) will consist of qualifications and background information on your firm, resumes of key individuals, and your work plan for providing the services. Package 2 (cost proposal) will consist of your firm's detailed cost proposal.

All technical proposals will be reviewed by the district's evaluation committee and points will be assigned for the non-cost evaluation elements listed below. For those proposals deemed to be qualified, the cost proposals will be opened and points assigned. The district may, at its sole discretion, elect to award this contract based on the initial evaluation/reading and without benefit of oral interviews. However, personal interviews may be conducted with short-listed firms. You will be contacted regarding the timing of your interview, if required. If oral interviews/discussions are held, a final evaluation will be done based on the original submittal plus the information (technical and cost) presented at that time.

Maximum Evaluation Points are as follows:

| | |
|---|---|
| Qualifications of firm | 30 |
| Personnel qualifications | 30 |
| Approach | 15 |
| Proposal responsiveness/quality | 5 |
| Cost | <u>20</u> |
| Total Points | 100 |

## General Instructions/Terms and Conditions

*A.* You are invited to submit five (5) copies of a proposal consisting of representation and certification materials and a statement of work (program narrative). The selected firm will be requested to provide the district with a projected cost budget.

*B.* You are requested to submit the proposal, typewritten on plain white bond paper, 8 1/2" x 11" in dimension, in booklet form. It is generally preferred that typewritten material be single-spaced, except where there is a reason for double-spacing, and that both margins be relatively wide.

*C.* You shall not, under penalty of law, offer any gratuities, favors, or anything of monetary value to any officer, employee, or agent of the district for the purpose of influencing favorable disposition toward either your, or any other, proposal submitted hereunder.

*D.* You shall not engage, in any manner, in any practices with any other contractor(s) which may restrict or eliminate competition or otherwise restrain trade. Violation of this instruction will cause your proposal to be rejected by the district.

*E.* All proposals submitted must be an original work product of an offerer. The copying, paraphrasing, or other use of substantial portions of the work product of another party in presenting a proposal to the district hereunder is not permitted. Failure to adhere to this instruction will cause proposal(s) to be rejected.

*F. Award/withdrawal* The district reserves the right to make an award within ninety (90) calendar days from the date proposals are opened, unless otherwise specified in the proposal, during which period proposals shall not be withdrawn. Should award in whole or in part be delayed beyond the period of ninety (90) days, or an earlier date specified by an offerer in his/her proposal, such award shall be conditioned upon offerer's acceptance.

*G.* The information presented in the request is not to be construed as a commitment of any kind.

*H.* Any written explanation desired by an offerer regarding the meaning or interpretation of the RFP or its related documents must be requested in writing and received by the director of purchasing and materials management. There will be no oral explanation or instructions given. Any information given to a prospective offerer concerning the RFP will be furnished to all prospective offerers as an addendum to the RFP, if such information is necessary to offerers in submitting offers on the RFP, or if the lack of such information would be prejudicial to uninformed offerers. No technical assistance or aid will be given by the district in the preparation of your proposal. Receipt of an addendum to the RFP by an offerer must be acknowledged by signing and returning the addendum with the proposal. Such acknowledgement must be received prior to the hour and date specified for final receipt of offers.

I. Telegraphic offers will not be considered in response to this RFP; nor will modifications by telegraphic notice be accepted.

J. If no offer is to be submitted, do not return the RFP. A letter or postcard should be sent to the issuing office advising whether future RFPs for the type of services covered by this solicitation are desired. Failure of the recipient to offer, or to notify the issuing office that future solicitations are desired, may result in removal of the name of such recipient from the mailing list for the type of services covered by the RFP.

K. Offers may be modified or withdrawn by written notice received prior to the exact hour and date specified for receipt of offers. An offer must be withdrawn in person by an officer or his/her authorized representative, provided his/her identity is made known and he/she signs a receipt for the offer, but only if the withdrawal is made prior to the exact hour and date set for receipt of offers. Offers and modifications thereof shall be enclosed in sealed envelopes and addressed to the office specified in the RFP for receipt, the RFP number, and the name and address of the offerer on the face of the envelope.

L. Any proposal received at the office designated in the RFP after the exact time specified for receipt will not be considered unless it is received before award is made, and under any of the following conditions:

1. It was sent by *registered* or *certified* mail not later than the fifth calendar day prior to the date specified for receipt of offers (e.g., the offer submitted in response to RFP requiring receipt of offers by the *29th* of the month must have been mailed by the *24th* or earlier).

2. It was sent by mail and it is determined by the district that the late receipt was due solely to mishandling by the district after receipt at the district's installation.

3. It is the only proposal received.

4. The only acceptable evidence for the establishment of the date of mailing and the time of receipt is as follows:

   a. The date of mailing of a late proposal or modification sent either by *registered* or *certified* mail is the U.S. Postal Service postmark on the wrapper or on the original receipt from the U.S. Postal Service. If neither postmark shows a legible date, the proposal or modification shall be deemed to have been mailed late. (The term *postmark* means a printed, stamped, or otherwise placed impression that is readily identifiable without further action as having been supplied and affixed on the date of mailing by employees of the U.S. Postal Service.)

    b.    The time of receipt at the district's installation is the time-date stamp of such installation on the proposal wrapper or other documentary evidence of receipt maintained by the district.

M. *Specific district rights*

1. The contract will be awarded to that responsible proposer whose offer, while conforming to the RFP, will be most advantageous to the district, price and other factors considered.
2. The right is reserved to accept other than the lowest cost proposed if an alternate offer is considered to be more advantageous to the district, cost and other factors considered.
3. The district reserves the right to reject any or all offers and to waive informalities and minor irregularities in offers received.
4. A contract or purchase order will be subject to the approval of the board of education.
5. The district may accept, within the time specified therein, any offer whether or not there are negotiations subsequent to this receipt, unless the offer is withdrawn by written notice received by the district prior to award. If subsequent negotiations are conducted, they shall not constitute a rejection or counteroffer on the part of the district.
6. The district may award a contract and/or issue a purchase order based on initial offers received, without discussion of such offers. Accordingly, each initial offer should be submitted on the most favorable terms, from a cost and technical standpoint, which the offerer can submit to the district.
7. In the event of tie proposals, the district is the sole determiner of the recipient of the final award.
8. The district reserves the right to negotiate with the second and/or third highest rated proposer(s) in the event the contract initially let under this proposal is terminated for noncompliance.
9. The district reserves the right to hold discussions and/or negotiate with each proposer in an attempt to clarify and qualify the proposer's intent to meet the district's requirements.

N. *Inspection and audit of data and records* Authorized representatives of the district and federal or state funding agencies will be permitted to inspect and audit all data and records of offer relating to contractor's performance under the contract.

O. *Indemnity* The contractor shall indemnify and hold harmless the district and its agents from any and all claims of damage to property and/or injuries to or deaths of employees, business invitees, or students of the district arising from any acts of the contractor and its employees.

P. *Non-responsible proposals* The district reserves the right to remove from mailing lists for future proposals and bids for an indeterminate period the name of any proposer for failure to accept a contract and/or purchase order, or the name of any contractor for unsatisfactory performance of contract, or the name of any contractor who engages in unlawful practices. This action will apply to the principals/officers of the firms as well.

*Q. Disputes* In the event of a conflict between any of the contract documents, the director of purchasing and materials management shall resolve any inconsistency and provide written notice to the supplier/contractor. Additionally, the director of purchasing and materials management shall, in good faith, decide all inconsistencies and/or disputes pertaining to the performance of the work required hereunder and of the administration provisions of the proposal and contract. The suppier/contractor will agree to proceed in a manner consistent with the decisions of the director of purchasing and materials management.

*R. Termination for convenience* The district may terminate the contract if it determines that the continuation of the project would not produce results commensurate with the future expenditure of funds. The district will notify the contractor, in writing, sixty (60) days prior to the effective termination date and the contractor will not incur new obligations after the effective date and shall cancel as many outstanding obligations as possible.

*S. Termination for default* The district, in its discretion, may terminate the contract in whole or part, at any time, whenever it is determined that the contractor has failed to comply with one or more of the terms and conditions of the contract or mechanical specifications incorporated therein, and the contractor has failed to correct such failure to the district's satisfaction within a period of ten (10) days after receiving written notice thereof from the district. In the event of the partial or total termination of the contract hereunder, it is hereby agreed that the district shall only be obligated to pay in accordance with the terms of the contract for material which has been accepted for payment by the district, and it is, hereby, further agreed that any termination of this contract shall comply with all of the provisions of this contract with obligation to any item which has been accepted by the district for payment.

*T. Taxes* The district is exempt from the payment of city, state, and federal taxes. Such taxes must not be included in the proposal price.

# Appendix B

APPENDIX TABLE B-1 • Summary of Expenditures as of January 31, 1990

| | FY89 | | | | FY90 | | | |
| --- | --- | --- | --- | --- | --- | --- | --- | --- |
| | Budget 1988–89 | January 1989 | Year-to-Date January '89 | Percent Expended | Budget 1989–90 | January 1990 | Year-to-Date January '90 | Percent Expended |
| Certified salaries | 52,663,498 | 4,998,739 | 26,255,667 | 49.86% | 58,083,909 | 4,715,791 | 27,524,985 | 47.39% |
| Non-certified salaries | 20,599,889 | 1,622,066 | 9,887,530 | 48.00% | 22,212,781 | 1,759,900 | 11,106,592 | 50.00% |
| Fringe benefits | 12,237,573 | 1,161,331 | 6,097,638 | 49.83% | 15,368,542 | 2,144,734 | 7,744,570 | 50.39% |
| Purchased services | 9,825,535 | 477,020 | 4,659,156 | 47.42% | 9,753,321 | 611,262 | 4,121,389 | 42.26% |
| Supplies | 3,677,033 | 144,973 | 1,762,778 | 47.94% | 3,974,896 | 186,859 | 2,083,415 | 52.41% |
| Capital outlay | 7,227,143 | 400,000 | 2,658,285 | 36.78% | 6,502,332 | 53,827 | 691,529 | 10.64% |
| *Total expenditures* | 106,230,671 | 8,804,129 | 51,321,054 | 48.31% | 115,895,781 | 9,472,373 | 53,272,480 | 45.97% |

APPENDIX TABLE B-2 • *Summary of Revenues as of January 31, 1990*

| Acct # | Source | FY89 | | | FY90 | | | | |
|---|---|---|---|---|---|---|---|---|---|
| | | Revised Budget 1988–89 | Actual Received Thru 1/89 | Percent Realized Thru 1/89 | Original Estimates 1989–90 | Adjustments to Original Estimates | Revised Estimates as of 1/90 | Actual Received Thru 1/90 | Percent Realized Thru 1/90 |
| | *Local Sources* | | | | | | | | |
| 5111 | Property taxes—current year | 50,254,747 | 44,324,544 | 88.20% | 51,248,795 | 2,800,000 | 54,048,795 | 48,818,178 | 90.32% |
| 5112 | Delinquent property taxes | 1,175,000 | 715,585 | 60.90% | 500,000 | 757,467 | 1,257,467 | 681,762 | 54.22% |
| 5113 | Sales tax | 2,505,100 | 1,456,691 | 58.15% | 2,600,000 | 0 | 2,600,000 | 1,652,856 | 63.57% |
| 5114 | Intangible tax | 320,573 | 0 | 0.00% | 300,000 | 35,765 | 335,765 | 335,765 | 100.00% |
| 5115 | Merchants & manufact. surtax | 5,553,500 | 4,601,087 | 82.85% | 5,653,500 | 210,000 | 5,863,500 | 5,004,739 | 85.35% |
| 5123 | Tuition—adult education | 288,000 | 160,801 | 55.83% | 280,000 | 0 | 280,000 | 211,432 | 75.51% |
| 5124 | Instructional matl.—adult ed | 2,500 | 392 | 15.68% | 1,000 | 0 | 1,000 | 291 | 29.10% |
| 5125 | Textbooks—adult ed. | 41,000 | 20,043 | 48.89% | 34,000 | 0 | 34,000 | 23,654 | 69.57% |
| 5141 | Investment earnings | 3,900,000 | 1,202,686 | 30.84% | 4,000,000 | 586,200 | 4,586,200 | 2,220,944 | 48.43% |
| 5142 | Intangible interest | 0 | 0 | 0.00% | 12,000 | 16,578 | 28,578 | 28,578 | 100.00% |
| 5151 | Food service—miscellaneous | 274,200 | 132,276 | 48.24% | 270,000 | 650 | 270,650 | 101,040 | 37.33% |
| 5161 | Food service—adult | 22,900 | 10,747 | 46.93% | 21,000 | 0 | 21,000 | 12,002 | 57.15% |
| 5162 | Food service—a la carte | 64,700 | 35,597 | 55.02% | 66,000 | 0 | 66,000 | 41,085 | 62.25% |
| 5177 | Tools | 4,500 | 2,164 | 48.09% | 0 | 1,850 | 1,850 | 1,013 | 54.76% |
| 5190 | Other local revenue | 49,700 | 15,865 | 31.92% | 40,000 | 64,959 | 104,959 | 80,606 | 76.80% |
| 5191 | Building rents | 134,747 | 51,515 | 38.23% | 115,000 | 0 | 115,000 | 44,254 | 38.48% |
| 5192 | Gifts and donations | 3,000 | 0 | 0.00% | 0 | 0 | 0 | 0 | 0.00% |
| | *Total local revenue* | 64,594,167 | 52,729,993 | 81.63% | 65,141,295 | 4,473,469 | 69,614,764 | 59,258,199 | 85.12% |
| | *County Sources* | | | | | | | | |
| 5221 | State assessed utility tax | 2,381,530 | 2,381,483 | 100.00% | 2,223,121 | 32,766 | 2,255,887 | 2,255,886 | 100.00% |
| | *State Sources* | | | | | | | | |
| 5311 | Minimum guarantee | 3,565,750 | 2,075,597 | 58.21% | 3,600,000 | 350,853 | 3,950,853 | 2,312,039 | 58.52% |
| 5312 | Transportation | 5,627,072 | 3,273,830 | 58.18% | 5,700,000 | 505,958 | 6,205,958 | 3,631,726 | 58.52% |
| 5313 | Exceptional pupil aid | 22,383,220 | 13,657,754 | 61.02% | 23,473,837 | (194,477) | 23,279,360 | 13,901,825 | 59.72% |
| 5351 | Foreign insurance tax | 344,318 | 344,318 | 100.00% | 347,900 | 24,910 | 372,810 | 372,810 | 100.00% |
| 5361 | Vocational/technical aid | 1,969,897 | 1,176,680 | 59.73% | 1,900,000 | 0 | 1,900,000 | 937,365 | 49.34% |
| 5371 | Food service—sch. lunch prog. | 9,000 | 0 | 0.00% | 9,000 | 0 | 9,000 | 2,786 | 30.96% |
| 5390 | Other state revenue | 14,976 | 0 | 0.00% | 10,000 | 25,949 | 35,949 | 19,440 | 54.08% |
| 5391 | Fair share—cigarette tax | 163,000 | 99,922 | 61.30% | 176,400 | 0 | 176,400 | 105,112 | 59.59% |
| 5392 | Desegregation aid | 859,726 | 656,850 | 76.40% | 900,000 | 767,937 | 1,667,937 | 1,439,262 | 86.29% |
| 5393 | Excell. act—tuition reimb. | 51,525 | 50,403 | 97.82% | 60,000 | 35,000 | 95,000 | 31,085 | 32.72% |
| | *Total state sources* | 34,988,484 | 21,335,354 | 60.98% | 36,177,137 | 1,516,130 | 37,693,267 | 22,753,450 | 60.36% |

APPENDIX TABLE B-2 • *Summary of Revenues as of January 31, 1990 (Continued)*

| Acct # | Source | FY89 | | | FY90 | | | | |
|---|---|---|---|---|---|---|---|---|---|
| | | Revised Budget 1988–89 | Actual Received Thru 1/89 | Percent Realized Thru 1/89 | Original Estimates 1989–90 | Adjustments to Original Estimates | Revised Estimates as of 1/90 | Actual Received Thru 1/90 | Percent Realized Thru 1/90 |
| | *Federal Sources* | | | | | | | | |
| 5421 | Title II-A Handicapped | 467,827 | 187,302 | 40.04% | 219,793 | 0 | 219,793 | (14,271) | -6.49% |
| 5422 | Title II-A Disadvantaged | 342,371 | 187,302 | 54.71% | 249,348 | 0 | 249,348 | (14,226) | -5.71% |
| 5423 | Title II-A Adult training | 44,703 | 0 | 0.00% | 0 | 0 | 0 | 0 | 0.00% |
| 5441 | Disabilities Act—B | 5,596,668 | 2,666,036 | 47.64% | 5,700,000 | (148,906) | 5,551,094 | 3,286,380 | 59.20% |
| 5445 | School lunch program | 252,032 | 83,611 | 33.17% | 205,000 | 0 | 205,000 | 99,225 | 48.40% |
| 5451 | ECIA, Chapter 1 | 865,124 | 210,796 | 24.37% | 500,000 | (3,161) | 496,839 | 248,420 | 50.00% |
| 5455 | ECIA, Chapter 2 Formula | 25,293 | 23,137 | 91.48% | 25,000 | (1,119) | 23,881 | 11,940 | 50.00% |
| 5461 | Drug free schools | 10,834 | 0 | 0.00% | 0 | 15,568 | 15,568 | 7,785 | 50.01% |
| 5465 | EESA Title II | 2,307 | 0 | 0.00% | 0 | 0 | 0 | 0 | 0.00% |
| 5466 | EESA Math/science training | 0 | 0 | 0.00% | 0 | 3,700 | 3,700 | 1,850 | 50.00% |
| 5481 | J.T.P.A. | 218,261 | 54,064 | 24.77% | 180,000 | (38,322) | 141,678 | 39,891 | 28.16% |
| | *Total federal sources* | 7,825,420 | 3,412,248 | 43.60% | 7,079,141 | (172,240) | 6,906,901 | 3,666,994 | 53.09% |
| | *Non-Current Sources* | | | | | | | | |
| 5631 | Net insurance recovery | 20,000 | 8,736 | 43.68% | 20,000 | 0 | 20,000 | 15,896 | 79.48% |
| | *Contracted Education Services* | | | | | | | | |
| 5811 | Tuition—other districts | 86,000 | 2,268 | 2.64% | 90,000 | (6,355) | 83,645 | 2,511 | 3.00% |
| 5831 | Contracted ed. services—DMH | 105,000 | (1,750) | -1.67% | 105,000 | 0 | 105,000 | 39,699 | 37.81% |
| 5832 | Cont. ed. serv.—hm. teaching | 7,500 | 7,231 | 96.41% | 7,300 | 0 | 7,300 | 7000 | 95.89% |
| 5841 | Trans. from other districts | 8,084 | 0 | 0.00% | 0 | 0 | 0 | 0 | 0.00% |
| | *Total contracted services* | 206,584 | 7,749 | 3.75% | 202,300 | (6,355) | 195,945 | 49,210 | 25.11% |
| | *Total revenue* | 110,016,185 | 79,875,563 | 72.60% | 110,842,994 | 5,843,770 | 116,686,764 | 87,999,635 | 75.42% |

APPENDIX TABLE B-3 • *Comparison of Period Ending January 31, 1990*

| Month of January '90 | 1988–89 Actual as of January '89 (7 Months) | 1989–90 Actual as of January '90 (7 Months) | 1989–90 Budget as of January '90 (7 Months) | Budget + (-) |
|---|---|---|---|---|
| | | *Revenue* | | |
| 45,366,203 | 79,875,563 | 87,998,643 | 85,297,289 | 2,701,354 |
| | | *Expenditures* | | |
| 9,472,373 | 51,321,054 | 53,272,480 | 67,077,817 | 13,805,337 |
| | | *Surplus (Deficit)* | | |
| | 28,554,509 | 34,726,163 | 18,219,472 | 16,506,691 |

APPENDIX TABLE B-4 • *Consolidated Schedule of Invested Funds for the Month Ended January 30, 1990*

| Type of Security | Broker | Purchase Date | Maturity Date | Yield | Cost of Investment | Net Interest Expected | Balance Due at Maturity |
|---|---|---|---|---|---|---|---|
| Daily Repro/Cash Balance | Mercantile Bank | | | 7.43 | | | 3,053,458.00 |
| Federal Farm Credit disc. note | Mark Twain Bank | 11/27/89 | 02/01/90 | 8.08 | 443,523.75 | 6,476.25 | 450,000.00 |
| Federal Home Loan disc. note | Mark Twain Bank | 11/27/89 | 02/01/90 | 8.11 | 606,115.30 | 8,884.70 | 615,000.00 |
| Freddie Mac disc. note | Southwest Bank | 01/04/90 | 02/12/90 | 8.16 | 1,596,081.55 | 13,918.45 | 1,610,000.00 |
| Fannie Mae disc. note | Merrill Lynch | 10/24/89 | 02/15/90 | 8.22 | 974,983.33 | 25,016.67 | 1,000,000.00 |
| Federal Home Loan disc. note | Southwest Bank | 12/27/89 | 02/16/90 | 8.29 | 998,438.87 | 11,561.13 | 1,010,000.00 |
| Federal Home Loan disc. note | Southwest Bank | 11/27/89 | 02/21/90 | 8.07 | 981,342.78 | 18,657.22 | 1,000,000.00 |
| Federal Home Loan debenture | Commerce Bank | 04/21/89 | 02/26/90 | 9.97 | 1,8%,487.14 | 94,712.86 | 1,991,200.00 |
| Federal Farm Credit disc. note | Southwest Bank | 11/01/89 | 02/27/90 | 8.37 | 584,188.00 | 15,812.00 | 600,000.00 |
| Federal Farm Credit debenture | Southwest Bank | 05/24/89 | 03/01/90 | 9.20 | 1,502,966.45 | 69,433.55 | 1,572,000.00 |
| Federal Home Loan disc. note | Merrill Lynch | 11/10/89 | 03/09/90 | 8.28 | 1,557,953.33 | 42,046.67 | 1,600,000.00 |
| Federal Home Loan disc. note | Southwest Bank | 12/22/89 | 03/12/90 | 8.15 | 599,291.11 | 10,708.89 | 610,000.00 |
| Federal Home Loan disc. note | Southwest Bank | 10/16/89 | 03/15/90 | 7.88 | 1,297,957.50 | 42,042.50 | 1,340,000.00 |
| Fannie Mae disc. note | Mark Twain Bank | 11/01/89 | 03/19/90 | 8.35 | 969,410.00 | 30,590.00 | 1,000,000.00 |
| Federal Home Loan debenture | Mark Twain Bank | 06/23/89 | 03/26/90 | 8.97 | 2,412,296.20 | 108,903.80 | 2,521,200.00 |
| Federal Home Loan disc. note | Southwest Bank | 12/27/89 | 03/28/90 | 8.22 | 499,764.02 | 10,235.98 | 510,000.00 |
| Federal Farm Credit disc. note | Mark Twain Bank | 11/21/89 | 04/05/90 | 8.13 | 970,825.00 | 29,175.00 | 1,000,000.00 |
| Freddie Mac disc. note | Mark Twain Bank | 01/02/90 | 04/12/90 | 8.15 | 1,041,747.50 | 23,252.50 | 1,065,000.00 |
| Federal Home Loan disc. note | Southwest Bank | 12/27/89 | 04/13/90 | 8.09 | 1,602,028.08 | 37,971.92 | 1,640,000.00 |
| Federal Farm Credit debenture | Mark Twain Bank | 01/04/90 | 04/20/90 | 8.14 | 2,017,368.68 | 96,131.32 | 2,113,500.00 |
| Federal Home Loan debenture | Mark Twain Bank | 08/22/90 | 04/25/90 | 8.59 | 1,508,323.17 | 65,176.83 | 1,573,500.00 |
| Federal Farm Credit disc. note | Southwest Bank | 12/27/89 | 04/26/90 | 8.14 | 598,979.25 | 16,020.75 | 615,000.00 |
| Federal Home Loan disc. note | A.G. Edwards | 08/17/89 | 05/03/90 | 8.42 | 942,940.00 | 57,060.00 | 1,000,000.00 |
| Fannie Mae debenture | Merrill Lynch | 09/21/89 | 05/10/90 | 8.44 | 1,008,692.51 | 42,807.49 | 1,051,500.00 |
| Federal Farm Credit disc. note | Commerce Bank | 01/10/90 | 05/11/90 | 8.00 | 974,153.06 | 25,846.94 | 1,000,000.00 |
| World Bank Discount note | A.G. Edwards | 01/18/90 | 05/15/90 | 8.08 | 584,848.50 | 15,151.50 | 600,000.00 |
| Fannie Mae disc. note | Mark Twain Bank | 01/02/90 | 05/16/90 | 8.13 | 1,942,007.78 | 57,992.22 | 2,000,000.00 |
| Federal Home Loan disc. note | Southwest Bank | 01/04/90 | 05/18/90 | 8.10 | 1,597,485.09 | 47,514.91 | 1,645,000.00 |

## Endnotes

1. Joseph L. Natale, "School District Purchasing," *Principles of School Business Management*, R. Craig Wood, ed. (Reston, Virginia: Association of School Business Officials International, 1986), pp. 501, 502.
2. Jim Tindell, "Specification Development," *School Business Affairs*, Vol. 53, no. 12 (December 1987), p. 37.
3. Ronald W. Rebore, *Educational Administration: A Management Approach* (Englewood Cliffs, New Jersey: Prentice-Hall, Inc., 1985), p. 121.
4. Donn F. Dykstra, "Accounting Starts with the Basics," *School Business Affairs*, 54, no. 10 (October 1988), p. 27.
5. Rebore, *Education Administration*, p. 123.
6. *Ibid.*
7. Ivan D. Wagner and Sam M. Sniderman, *Budgeting School Dollars: A Guide to Spending and Saving* (Washington, D.C.: National School Boards Association, 1984), p. 233.

## Selected Bibliography

Cuzzetto, Charles E., and Daniel D. Moran, "School's Still Out on Internal Auditing," *School Business Affairs*, Vol. 54, no. 10 (October 1988), pp. 37-42.

Gatti, Bernard F., "ASBO's Certificate of Excellence in Financial Reporting by School Systems," *School Business Affairs*, Vol. 54, no. 10 (October 1988), pp. 48–55.

Grace, David F., "Electronic Purchasing," *School Business Affairs*, no. 12 (December 1987), pp. 29–31.

Natale, Joseph L., "School District Purchasing," *Principles of School Business Management*, R. Craig Wood, ed. (Reston, Virginia: Association of School Business Officials International, 1986), pp. 491–518.

Rebore, Ronald W., *Educational Administration: A Management Approach* (Englewood Cliffs, New Jersey: Prentice-Hall, Inc., 1985), pp. 114–135.

Schermann, Kenneth R., "The Objective of Financial Reporting," *School Business Affairs*, 52, no. 10 (October 1986), pp. 28-31.

Seidel, Richard, "Selecting an Independent Auditor," *School Business Affairs*, Vol. 54, no. 10 (October 1988), pp. 43–47.

Tidwell, Sam B., *Financial and Managerial Accounting for Elementary and Secondary School Systems*, 3rd. ed. (Reston, Virginia: Association of School Business Officials International, 1985), pp. 547–578.

Wagner, Ivan D., and Sam M. Sniderman, *Budgeting School Dollars: A Guide to Spending and Saving* (Washington, D.C.: National School Boards Association, 1984), pp. 223–258.

Walters, Donald L., and John H. Hummel, "The Pursuit of Excellence in School Financial Reporting," *School Business Affairs*, Vol. 53, no. 10 (October 1987), pp. 50–53.

# 7

# Investing Surplus Funds

School districts have long recognized that available revenue is grossly inadequate to properly fund the various curriculum programs, salary requirements, and facility needs of the district. Added to this difficult situation is the community's interest in strengthening accountability of the allocation of tax dollars to the many categories within the budget, and the public's reluctance to approve tax levies or referendums. Budget hearings, in recent years, have been plagued with disagreements over appropriations for salary increases versus instructional materials versus building improvements and repairs. With each constituency lobbying for a "bigger piece of the budget pie," administrators have had to look at alternatives to increase available funds without requesting additional taxes. Some relief to this problem can be found in the timely investment of surplus funds.

## Cash Management

Depending on the time of the school year, surplus funds may be used to meet the cash flow requirements of the district or as an avenue for additional revenue. Until the district receives its tax receipts or state aid payments, surplus funds are often needed to meet the monthly cash requirements to operate district schools. Subsequent to the receipt of these revenues, surplus funds provide additional income through timely investments. Therefore, the different uses of surplus funds are a direct result of the timeliness of the following:

1. Tax collections
2. State aid payments
3. Federal aid payments
4. Payroll and related expenditures
5. Invoices (timing for release of checks)[1]

## Tax Collections

Property tax receipts comprise the largest single component of local revenue. For the most part, districts receive approximately 95 percent of their tax collections in January and February of each year. Early payment of taxes and delinquent taxes are paid on a monthly basis throughout the year. Since this source of funds accounts for a significant portion of the district's total revenue, sufficient cash must be available to meet operating costs until the funds are received.

## State Aid Payments

The primary types of state aid for school districts are general aid and categorical aid.[2] General aid is usually distributed to districts through a foundation or equalization program designed to insure a minimum level of education for each student. Categorical aid, on the other hand, is program specific and designed to either fund or assist in the funding of particular programs. Transportation aid, special education allocations and gifted programs in some states are examples of categorical aid. A district's total allocation of state funds is normally paid on a monthly basis in twelve equal payments.

## Federal Aid Payments

Federal funds are appropriated by the United States Congress and distributed by the Department of Education.[3] Federal program funds are largely categorical aid or block grants to assist school districts in specific areas. Chapter One, Chapter Two, Public Law 94-142, and the Federal School Lunch Program are all examples of federal funds available to school districts. These funds are normally distributed through the state departments of education on a quarterly basis each October, January, April, and July.

### Payroll and Related Expenditures

Salaries, fringe benefits, retirement contributions, and social security payments are expended on a monthly or bi-weekly basis. In some school districts, instructional personnel are given the option of receiving their salary over a nine-month or twelve-month basis, while other school personnel are paid over twelve months. Since these costs are easily identified, districts can accurately predict their payroll costs on an annual basis.

### Invoices

All other expenditures made by the school district are based on purchasing requirements, utility costs, and facility repairs and improvements. Most schools expend the greater portion of their budget allocations for instructional supplies and equipment, and building repairs during the summer months in preparation for the new school year. The timing of payment for these items will have an effect on cash availability. It is customary, and to the district's advantage, to expend these funds once a month, after approval by the board of education.

Cash management is an attempt to coordinate the receipt of revenue with the expenditures necessary to operate the district on a daily basis. Therefore, the objectives of a cash management program are twofold. First, the school district must have sufficient cash available to meet monthly expenses; and second, the district should invest unneeded funds to yield a maximum return.

## Cash Flow

In order to manage cash to the best advantage of the district, the business administrator must be able to identify the present cash flow. Exhibit 7-1 represents a model for identifying significant revenue and expenditure patterns of the district each year. Actual cash flow data is entered from district records to provide an overview of monthly cash receipts and disbursements. Dembowski, in *A Handbook for School District Financial*

EXHIBIT 7-1 • *Cash Flow Worksheet*

| | July | August | September | Octobe | November | December | January | February | March | April | May | June |
|---|---|---|---|---|---|---|---|---|---|---|---|---|
| Beginning balance | $1,500,000 | $1,900,750 | $1,984,000 | $1,020,650 | $644,200 | $218,700 | $76,700 | $1,737,658 | $3,264,669 | $2,767,754 | $2,487,818 | $2,057,770 |
| *Local* | | | | | | | | | | | | |
| Taxes | 10,000 | 15,000 | 5,000 | 20,000 | 150,000 | 400,000 | 2,000,000 | 2,000,000 | 30,000 | 1,500 | 2,000 | 1,400 |
| Invest | 8,000 | 10,500 | 10,000 | 6,800 | 2,000 | 4,500 | 1,458 | 511 | 11,584 | 21,764 | 18,452 | 16,585 |
| Stud. act. | 0 | 0 | 150 | 250 | 1,000 | 7,000 | 3,000 | 5,000 | 0 | 300 | 18,000 | 0 |
| *State* | | | | | | | | | | | | |
| Fndation program | 600,000 | 600,000 | 600,000 | 600,000 | 600,000 | 600,000 | 600,000 | 600,000 | 600,000 | 600,000 | 600,000 | 600,000 |
| Transport | 125,000 | 125,000 | 125,000 | 125,000 | 125,000 | 125,000 | 125,000 | 125,000 | 125,000 | 125,000 | 125,000 | 125,000 |
| Gifted prog. | 10,000 | 10,000 | 10,000 | 10,000 | 10,000 | 10,000 | 10,000 | 10,000 | 10,000 | 10,000 | 10,000 | 10,000 |
| Special ed | 25,000 | 25,000 | 25,000 | 25,000 | 25,000 | 25,000 | 25,000 | 25,000 | 25,000 | 25,000 | 25,000 | 25,000 |
| *Federal* | | | | | | | | | | | | |
| Chapter I | 20,000 | | 20,000 | 20,000 | | | 20,000 | | | 20,000 | | |
| Chapter II | 15,000 | | 15,000 | 15,000 | | | 15,000 | | | 15,000 | | |
| 94-142 | 50,000 | | 50,000 | 50,000 | | | 50,000 | | | 50,000 | | |
| Lunch | 40,000 | | 40,000 | 40,000 | | | 40,000 | | | 40,000 | | |
| prog. | | | | | | | | | | | | |
| *Total rec.* | $903,000 | $785,500 | $775,150 | $912,050 | $913,000 | $1,171,500 | $2,889,458 | $2,765,511 | $801,584 | $908,564 | $798,452 | $777,985 |
| *Expenditures* | | | | | | | | | | | | |
| Salaries | 150,000 | 150,000 | 900,000 | 900,000 | 900,000 | 900,000 | 900,000 | 900,000 | 900,000 | 900,000 | 900,000 | 900,000 |
| Retire | 6,000 | 6,000 | 36,000 | 36,000 | 36,000 | 36,000 | 36,000 | 36,000 | 36,000 | 36,000 | 36,000 | 36,000 |
| Social sec. | 11,250 | 11,250 | 67,500 | 67,500 | 67,500 | 67,500 | 67,500 | 67,500 | 67,500 | 67,500 | 67,500 | 67,500 |
| Fringe benefits | 35,000 | 35,000 | 35,000 | 35,000 | 35,000 | 35,000 | 35,000 | 35,000 | 35,000 | 35,000 | 35,000 | 35,000 |
| Invoices | 300,000 | 500,000 | 700,000 | 250,000 | 300,000 | 275,000 | 190,000 | 200,000 | 260,000 | 150,000 | 190,000 | 100,000 |
| *Total exp.* | $502,250 | $702,250 | $1,738,500 | $1,288,500 | $1,338,500 | $1,313,500 | $1,228,500 | $1,238,500 | $1,298,500 | $1,188,500 | $1,228,500 | $1,138,500 |
| *Ending Balance* | $1,900,750 | $1,984,000 | $1,020,650 | $644,200 | $218,700 | $76,700 | $1,737,658 | $3,264,669 | $2,767,754 | $2,487,818 | $2,057,770 | $1,697,255 |

*Management*, identifies the following four questions as the basis for developing a cash flow strategy:

1. When are cash receipts expected?
2. How long will cash be available?
3. Is borrowing required?
4. Are there opportunities for investment?[4]

Exhibit 7-1 identifies the beginning balance, revenue by source, expenditures by object and the ending balance for each month of the school year. The beginning balance of $1,500,000.00 in July, together with the revenue received during the month was sufficient to cover the expenditures. However, the monthly balance begins to decrease from November through the first of January. After the December expenditures, the balance fell to its low point of $76,700. As a result, the amount of funds available for investment decreased during the final quarter of the calendar year. This trend is reversed in January when the district begins to receive tax collections. From January through June the revenues, plus the preceding month's balance, far exceed the monthly expenditures, and therefore allow for larger investments of district funds.

Exhibit 7-2 summarizes the revenues and expenditures from the previous year, and provides a basis for the analysis and projection of cash flow. An average of the monthly balances produces an average cash availability[5] for the year. When interest income is applied to the availability figure, the business manager can identify the average return on available cash. During the previous year, the district had a 6.78 percent return on its average cash availability ($112,155/$1,654,827). This figure also allows the district to estimate yield through inserting a higher or lower interest rate. For example, an average interest rate of 9 percent would yield an investment income of $148,934 ($1,654,827 x .09), while an average interest rate of 5 percent would yield an investment income of $82,741 ($1,654,827 x .05).

## Cash Flow Projection

The previous year's data will provide the business administrator with the capability of projecting cash flow for the new budget year. Percentage increases or decreases in each of the major cash-flow categories can be applied to last year's data and provide a current-year cash-flow estimate.[6] Exhibit 7-3 demonstrates the differences in cash flow with a 5 percent increase in tax collections and state revenue, a 6 percent increase in expenditures and an average interest rate of 8 percent. The beginning

EXHIBIT 7-2 • *Cash Flow Analysis*

| | July | August | September | Octobe | November | December | January | February | March | April | May | June |
|---|---|---|---|---|---|---|---|---|---|---|---|---|
| Begin balance | $1,500,000 | $1,900,750 | $1,984,000 | $1,020,650 | $644,200 | $218,700 | $76,700 | $1,737,658 | $3,264,669 | $2,767,754 | $2,487,818 | $2,057,770 |
| Revenue | 903,000 | 785,500 | 775,150 | 912,050 | 913,000 | 1,171,500 | 2,989,458 | 2,765,511 | 801,584 | 908,564 | 798,452 | 777,985 |
| Expend | 502,250 | 702,250 | 1,738,500 | 1,288,500 | 1,338,5001 | ,313,500 | 1,228,500 | 1,238,500 | 1,298,500 | 1,188,500 | 1,228,500 | 1,138,500 |
| Ending balance | $1,900,750 | $1,984,000 | $1,020,650 | $644,200 | $218,700 | $76,700 | $1,737,658 | $3,264,669 | $2,767,754 | $2,487,818 | $2,057,770 | $1,697,255 |

*Summary*

| | |
|---|---|
| Average Annual Cash Availability | $1,654,827 |
| Investment Income | $112,155 |
| Return on Cash Availability | 6.78% |

EXHIBIT 7-3 • Cash Flow Worksheet

| | July | August | September | Octobe | November | December | January | February | March | April | May | June |
|---|---|---|---|---|---|---|---|---|---|---|---|---|
| Beginning balance | $1,697,255 | $2,113,039 | $2,193,719 | $1,168,396 | $761,461 | $306,940 | $144,706 | $1,870,543 | $3,461,697 | $2,927,258 | $2,615,401 | $2,150,806 |
| **Tax revenue** | | | | | | | | | | | | |
| *Local* | | | | | | | | | | | | |
| Taxes | 10,500 | 15,750 | 5,250 | 21,000 | 157,500 | 420,000 | 2,100,000 | 2,100,000 | 31,500 | 1,575 | 2,100 | 1,470 |
| Invest | 14,469 | 11,315 | 14,087 | 14,625 | 7,789 | 5,076 | 2,046 | 965 | 12,470 | 23,078 | 19,515 | 17,530 |
| Stud. act. | 0 | 0 | 150 | 250 | 1,000 | 7,000 | 3,000 | 5,000 | 0 | 300 | 18,000 | 0 |
| *Intermediate* | | | | | | | | | | | | |
| County | 0 | | | | | | | | | | | |
| *State* | | | | | | | | | | | | |
| Fndation prog. | 630,000 | 630,000 | 630,000 | 630,00 | 630,00 | 630,00 | 630,00 | 630,00 | 630,00 | 630,00 | 630,00 | 630,00 |
| Transport | 131,250 | 131,250 | 131,250 | 131,250 | 131,250 | 131,250 | 131,250 | 131,250 | 131,250 | 131,250 | 131,250 | 131,250 |
| Gifted prog. | 10,500 | 10,500 | 10,500 | 10,500 | 10,500 | 10,500 | 10,500 | 10,500 | 10,500 | 10,500 | 10,500 | 10,500 |
| Special ed. | 26,250 | 26,250 | 26,250 | 26,250 | 26,250 | 26,250 | 26,250 | 26,250 | 26,250 | 26,250 | 26,250 | 26,250 |
| *Federal* | | | | | | | | | | | | |
| Chapter I | 20,000 | | | 20,000 | | | 20,000 | | | 20,000 | | |
| Chapter II | 15,000 | | | 15,000 | | | 15,000 | | | 15,000 | | |
| 94-142 | 50,000 | | | 50,000 | | | 50,000 | | | 50,000 | | |
| Lunch prog. | 40,000 | | | 40,000 | | | 40,000 | | | 40,000 | | |
| Total rec. | $948,169 | $825,065 | $817,487 | $958,875 | $964,289 | $1,230,076 | $3,028,046 | $2,903,965 | $841,970 | $947,953 | $837,615 | $817,000 |

EXHIBIT 7-3 • *Cash Flow Worksheet (Continued)*

| Expenditures | | | | | | | | | | | |
|---|---|---|---|---|---|---|---|---|---|---|---|
| Salaries | 159,000 | 159,000 | 954,000 | 954,000 | 954,000 | 954,000 | 954,000 | 954,000 | 954,000 | 954,000 | 954,000 |
| Retirement | 6,360 | 6,360 | 38,160 | 38,160 | 38,160 | 38,160 | 38,160 | 38,160 | 38,160 | 38,160 | 38,160 |
| Social sec. | 11,925 | 11,925 | 71,550 | 71,550 | 71,550 | 71,550 | 71,550 | 71,550 | 71,550 | 71,550 | 71,550 |
| Fringe benefits | 37,100 | 37,100 | 37,100 | 37,100 | 37,100 | 37,100 | 37,100 | 37,100 | 37,100 | 37,100 | 37,100 |
| Invoices | 318,000 | 530,000 | 742,000 | 265,000 | 318,000 | 291,500 | 201,400 | 212,000 | 275,600 | 159,000 | 201,400 | 106,000 |
| Total exp. | $532,385 | $744,385 | $1,842,810 | $1,365,810 | $1,418,810 | $1,392,310 | $1,302,210 | $1,312,810 | $1,376,410 | $1,259,810 | $1,302,210 | $1,206,810 |
| Ending Balance | $2,113,039 | $2,193,719 | $1,168,396 | $761,461 | $306,940 | $144,706 | $1,870,543 | $3,461,697 | $2,927,258 | $2,615,401 | $2,150,806 | $1,760,996 |

FIGURE 7-1 • *Cash Availability Graph*

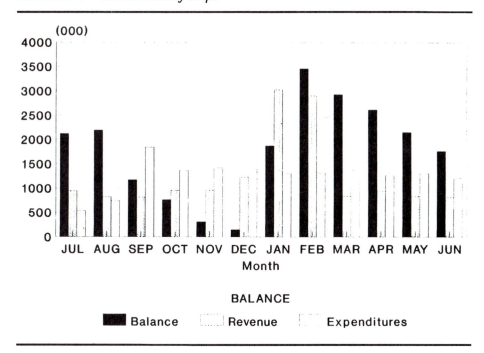

balance in January, the lowest of the year, is $144,706 or approximately $68,000 higher than the previous year. Utilizing this information, the district can time their purchases when sufficient cash is available.

The monthly cash balances can be graphed to identify time periods when surplus funds will be either needed for daily operations or available for investment. Sharp decreases can be identified, and, as updates from actual data become available, cash-flow revisions can be checked against those periods of low available cash. The business administrator may then position the district to avoid over-investment or risk not having sufficient available cash to cover necessary expenditures.[7] Figure 7-1 is a graphic representation of the data in Exhibit 7-3.

## Funds Available for Investment

Cash-flow projections identify available funds for investment. However, as noted previously, the timing of revenue receipts and expenditures plays a crucial role in both projecting cash flow and identifying available funds for investment. Exhibit 7-4 is an example how the timing of a school district's

EXHIBIT 7-4 • *Cash Available for Investment*

| Source | Day | July | August | September | October | November | December |
|---|---|---|---|---|---|---|---|
| Beginning balance | 1 | $1,697,255 | $2,113,039 | $2,193,719 | $1,168,396 | $761,461 | $306,940 |
| Balance—investment | | 97,255 | 513,039 | 1,093,719% | 568,396 | 561,461 | 306,940 |
| Bi-weekly payroll | 10 | 79,500 | 79,500 | 477,000 | 477,000 | 477,000 | 477,000 |
| Balance after payroll | | 17,755 | 433,539 | 616,719 | 91,396 | 84,461 | (170,060) |
| Revenue | 15 | 948,169 | 825,065 | 817,487 | 958,875 | 964,289 | 1,230,076 |
| Bi-weekly payroll | 25 | 79,500 | 79,500 | 477,000 | 477,000 | 477,000 | 477,000 |
| All other expenditures | 30 | 373,385 | 585,385 | 888,810 | 411,810 | 464,810 | 438,310 |
| Revenue—expenditures | | 495,284 | 160,180 | (548,323) | 70,06 | 22,479 | 314,766 |
| Ending balance | | $513,039 | $593,719 | $68,396 | $161,461 | $106,940 | $144,706 |

*Available for investment*

| | | | | | | | |
|---|---|---|---|---|---|---|---|
| Beginning of month | $1,600,000 | $0 | $0 | $0 | $0 | | |

*Investment summary, July through December*

| Amount | Number of Days | Interest Rate | Maturity Rate | Interest Income |
|---|---|---|---|---|
| $500,000 | 60 | 8.20% | 9/1 | $3,416.67 |
| $500,000 | 90 | 8.30% | 10/1 | $3,458.33 |
| $400,000 | 120 | 8.35% | 11/1 | $2,087.50 |
| $200,000 | 150 | 8.40% | 12/1 | $2,100.00 |
| $1,600,000 | | | | $11,058.33 |

payroll can affect both cash flow and investment opportunities. In this example, the district pays its employees on the tenth and twenty-fifth of each month, while all other expenditures occur at the end of the month. Revenue is received on the fifteenth of the month from local, state and federal sources. As a result, the district must have sufficient cash available at the beginning of each month to cover the payroll before revenues for the month are received. Even with a beginning balance of $1,697,255 on July 1, the district will experience a deficit in December when paying the first payroll of the month. This situation will require the district to either plan to increase its balances or to secure a short-term loan to meet the deficit.

Exhibit 7-4 also details the amount of funds available for investment. Over the six month period, the district can invest $1,600,000 with varying maturity dates and still meet the cash flow requirements each month. With this approach, the district can insure maximum return on surplus cash. However, even with the interest income, the district will still experience a deficit during the first half of December.

## Cash Control

A totally separate issue from identifying and projecting cash flow is the procedure for the protection of cash and checks coming into the district and the disbursement of funds each month. School districts receive checks routinely from local, state and federal sources, as well as actual cash through their food service and student activity accounts. The protection of these assets require specific procedures to insure against misuse or theft. Likewise, the disbursement of funds from the district's bank accounts should be safeguarded against unauthorized use.

### Cash Receipts

A division of labor among the various components of the business office will insure the safeguarding of cash receipts. The posting of cash receipts, the deposit of funds to the district's accounts and the reconciliation of the bank statement each month should be delegated to three separate individuals. This provides appropriate monitoring between the individuals and also decreases the opportunity for errors or misuse of funds. A similar procedure should be developed for the receipt of actual cash by the district. Since many of these cash items originate at each of the district's schools, one person from each school should be responsible for counting the cash, completing a deposit slip and sealing the container for delivery to either the bank or the central administrative offices. If the cash is delivered to the central office, the accounts receivable clerk should verify the amount and include the amount with the district's daily deposit. Once again, the actual deposit should be made by another individual and reconciliation by yet another person. If the cash from the individual schools is delivered directly to the bank, then verification will be conducted by an identified bank employee. While somewhat cumbersome, these procedure insure proper safeguards.

### Cash Disbursement

All disbursement of funds, with the exception of payroll, should occur on a designated day once a month. With the large number of checks required to pay the various invoices, most districts utilize a check writer with the facsimile signatures of the designated officials of the district. Separation of functions is necessary to insure non-authorized use of this equipment. Districts should require at least two signatures on valid district checks, and the check writer should be secured with two keys required for operation. The individuals responsible for preparing checks should be separate from the person who reconciles the bank statement each month. Payroll distribution should follow the same procedures. Even with the most stringent of procedures, the risk is always present that district funds will be misuse or embezzled. As a result, the district should routinely test a sample of the disbursements, both payroll and general invoices, to insure that an audit trail is present and/or that the individual receiving a payroll check actually does exist.

## Investments

### Guidelines and Policies

The board of education should take formal action to approve an investment policy for the school district. Some states regulate the investment of school funds and restrict the district to particular types of investment instruments. The following guidelines from Missouri statutes are typical of investment restraints.

> If any school district has money in the special revenue, general, capital outlay, or debt service fund not needed within a reasonable period of time for the purpose for which the money was received, the school board in the district, if it deems it advisable, may

*invest the funds in either open time deposits for ninety days or certificates of deposit in a depositary selected by the board if the depositary has deposited securities under the provisions of sections 110.010 and 110.020, RSMo; or in bonds, redeemable at maturity at par, of the state of Missouri, of the United States, or of any wholly owned corporation of the United States; or in other short-term obligations of the United States. No open time deposits shall be made or bonds purchased to mature beyond the date that the funds are needed for the purpose for which they were received by the school district. Interest accruing from the investment of the surplus funds in such deposits or bonds shall be credited to the fund from which the money was invested.*[8]

These restraints limit the district to safe, secure investments that provide the necessary protection of local, state, and federal funds. In Missouri, by law, added protection is provided by requiring banks to guarantee savings accounts and certificates of deposit purchased by school districts through the pledge of government securities equal to the investment. Absent state statute, the board of education should adopt a similar policy regulating the types of investment instruments, and thereby insuring the protection of district funds. The benchmarks for any investment policy are safety, liquidity and yield. Exhibit 7-5 reflects the most common types of investments available to school districts.

## Certificate of Deposit

A certificate of deposit is a time deposit in a financial institution for a specific period at a specified rate of interest. Denominations can be for any

EXHIBIT 7-5 • *Investment Alternatives*

| *Instrument* | *Maturities* | *Minimum Investment* |
|---|---|---|
| *Short Term* | | |
| *Banks* | | |
| Certificates of deposit | 14 Days and Over | $100,000 |
| NOW accounts | No limit | Various |
| Savings accounts | Monthly | Various |
| Repurchase agreements | 1 to 180 days | 100,000 |
| *U.S. Government* | | |
| Treasury bills | To 1 year | $10,000 |
| *Long Term* | | |
| *U.S. Government* | | |
| Treasury notes | 1 to 10 years | $1000 |
| Treasury bonds | Over 10 years | $1000 |

amount, however, the interest rate paid is generally higher over $100,000. The interest rate varies depending on the length of the investment. Interest is calculated on an actual number of days over a 360-day year. Maturities are 14 days or longer.

### Negotiable Order of Withdrawal

A negotiable order of withdrawal is a bank withdrawal ticket that is a negotiable instrument. The accounts from which withdrawals can be made, called NOW accounts, are thus, in effect, interest-bearing checking accounts.[9]

### Savings Account

A savings account is a time deposit in a financial institution. Deposits and withdrawal of cash may occur at any time, and interest is normally fixed, regardless of the size of the account. Savings accounts are primarily used to accumulate funds until a higher yielding investment can be purchased.

### Repurchase Agreements

Repurchase agreements are purchases of securities by an investor from a bank or securities dealer, with the understanding that the party will repurchase the same securities at a specific price on a specific date. Maturities usually run from 1 to 30 days.

### Treasury Bills (T-Bills)

T-bills are direct obligations of the U.S. Government. There are weekly auctions with maturities of 13 weeks (91 days), 26 weeks (182 days), and 52 weeks. The one-year T-bill is auctioned approximately once a month. These securities are issued at a discount from face value and pay face value at maturity. Minimum denomination is $10,000 in multiples of $5000. T-bills can also be purchased on the secondary market through banks and securities dealers.

### Treasury Notes (T-Notes)

T-notes are direct obligations of the U.S. Government. They are issued and redeemed at face value, and pay interest at the coupon rate semi-annually.

T-notes have original maturities of one to ten years. They are in two-, four-, and five-year maturities on a regular basis. Denominations vary from $1000 to $5000 increments.

## Security and Liquidity of Investments

### Security

All U.S. Government Securities are guaranteed by the federal government, while bank investments are insured up to $100,000 through the Federal Deposit Insurance Corporation (FDIC). Therefore, all bank investments above $100,000 should be guaranteed by U.S. securities pledged to the district through the bank.

### Liquidity

Liquidity has two dimensions: (1) how fast an asset can be converted into cash (i.e., its marketability); and (2) the risk of a realized capital loss upon the asset's cash conversion.[10] The liquidity of the short-term instruments outlined in Exhibit 7-5 are excellent. Savings accounts and NOW accounts are available at any time without penalty. Certificates of deposit and repurchase agreements will incur a penalty for early withdrawal. Treasury bills, if sold before maturity, on the secondary market will be subject to the market price at the time of sale. However, since districts tend to buy treasury bills on short duration to maturity, the loss, if at all, would be minimal.

Long-term investments in treasury notes or bonds will depend on the market conditions if sold prior to maturity. The risk of loss is greater, since bond rates tend to have an inverse relationship to market interest rates. Therefore, as interest rates rise, bond rates usually fall. However, the district takes no risk of capital loss if the notes or bonds are held to maturity. As a result, the prudent business administrator should really only consider these long-term instruments for financing pension funds or bond proceeds when the need for the funds is well-defined.

## Investment Computations

**1.** Computation of the interest income of a $100,000 certificate of deposit purchased at 8 percent for 60 days.

$$\text{Interest income} = \frac{\text{face value of certificate} \times \text{interest rate}}{360} \times \text{days to maturity}$$

$$\frac{\$100,000 \times .08}{360} = \frac{8000}{360} = 22.22 \times 60 = \$1,333.33$$

**2.** Computation of the yield on a $500,000 treasury bill purchased at a discount rate of 7.75 percent for 60 days. T-bills are purchased on a discount basis, with the face value equal to 100 and the price less than 100. The quoted rate is the discount rate from the face value.

$$\text{Income} = \frac{\text{face amount of certificate} \times \text{interest rate}}{360} \times \text{days to maturity}$$

$$\text{Cost} = \text{face amount} - \text{income}$$

$$\text{Yield} = \frac{\text{income} \times 360}{\text{cost} \times \text{days held}}$$

$$\text{Income} = \frac{\$500,000 \times .0775 \times 60}{360} = \frac{2,325,000}{360} = \$6458.33$$

$$\text{Cost} = \$500,000 - 6458.33 = \$493,541.67$$

$$\text{Yield} = \frac{\$6458.33 \times 360}{\$493,541.67 \times 60} = \frac{2,324,998.80}{29,612,500.20} = 7.85\%$$

**3.** Computation of the yield of ten-year $1000 treasury bond with a coupon rate of 8 percent. Treasury bonds are obligations of the U.S. government bearing interest payable at six-month intervals until maturity. The interest rate is called the *coupon rate*. Bonds may be purchased at discount below the face value, or at premium above the face value.

$$\text{Yield} = \frac{\text{annual interest}}{\text{cost}} = \frac{1000 \times .08}{1000} = \frac{\$80}{\$1000} = 8\%$$

If purchased at a discount of $100:

$$\text{Yield} = \frac{\$80}{\$900} = 8.88\%$$

If purchased at a premium of $100:

$$\text{Yield} = \frac{\$80}{\$1100} = 7.27\%$$

**4.** Computation of the interest income of a $200,000 repurchase agreement at 9 percent for 12 days.

$$\text{Interest income} = \frac{\text{face value} \times \text{interest rate}}{360} \times \text{days to maturity}$$

$$= \frac{\$200,000 \times .09}{360} = \frac{18,000}{360} = 50 \times 12 = \$600$$

## Selection of a Bank Depository

According to Charles K. Coe in *Public Financial Management*, public entities, including public schools, have three options for utilizing banking services:[11]

**1.** The district may use several different banks within the community by dividing its funds and accounts. Each bank would be responsible for servicing a specific fund or account (e.g., payroll account, accounts payable, or special revenue fund, debt service). As Coe stipulates, this approach has a "political benefit." In many communities bankers are often directly involved in local affairs, especially in housing and commercial development. The disadvantage to this approach is the fragmenting of the district's financial resources. With revenue spread among several firms, it becomes impossible to combine cash resources for investments. The end result is lower interest income for the district.

**2.** The district may choose to rotate its depositary on an annual basis. Each bank within the community is awarded the business on a predetermined schedule. This approach allows for the pooling of resources by placing all revenue in the same facility, but eliminates the advantages of competitive bidding.

**3.** The school district could competitively bid its depository on an annual or biannual basis. This approach provides the greatest advantage to the district. Banks within the community will often provide additional services without cost to the district in order to receive the district's accounts.[12] The following list identifies many of the more common products and services that banks have offered to school districts through competitive bidding at no cost.

    **a.** Wire transfer of funds from the state department of education to provide for same-day investment
    **b.** Wire transfer of funds to other banks to allow for same-day investment
    **c.** Investment consultation
    **d.** Acceptance of district withholding on salaries for state and federal income tax deposits and contributions to the Federal Insurance Contribution Act (FICA)
    **e.** Handling of bulk coin
    **f.** Provide deposit slips, coin envelopes, and money bags as required
    **g.** Free checking accounts for all employees
    **h.** Automatic deposit of salaries into employee accounts
    **i.** Provide all necessary checks for each checking account

Some states regulate both the selection of a bank depository and the frequency of bidding. For example, in Missouri, school districts must accept bids in each odd-numbered year, and are further limited to the selection of a bank within the county where the school district is located.[13] Furthermore, banks are often required by states to pledge securities equal to the school district deposit. On a fiscal year of July 1 through June 30, the business administrator should begin the formal process of selecting a depository through the issuance of a request for proposals (RFP) by February 1, or approximately five months before the effective day of the changeover. The formal request for proposals should include a description of the general responsibilities of the depository, a description of the products and services to be requested, at no charge, by the school district as part of the bid, and an analysis of each separate account over the past year. This analysis should include the average monthly balance, the number of deposits, and the number of checks issued each month. As part of this process, the business administrator should also request the interest rate that the bank would charge the district for short-term tax anticipation loans to meet cash-flow needs until tax collections are received. The RFP should also stimulate the procedure to be used by the district for the investment of surplus funds. It is to the benefit of the district to always invest funds, both long term and short term, on a competitive case-by-case basis. Therefore, the proposal should clearly state that the district will seek separate bids for the investment of funds. An example of a comprehensive RFP is presented Appendix A.

The evaluation of bank depository bids is often difficult and frustrating. Since the general rule of bidding is to accept the lowest and best bid, the business administrator must attempt to evaluate each proposal based on cost and expertise. The bank should be large enough to accommodate the district's volume of business and have the appropriate number of staff to service the accounts. Since the assessment of bank capability tends to be a subjective decision, the business administrator should visit each bank, discuss the district's needs, and interview the appropriate bank officers. The president of the bank and the vice-president for operations are key personnel in a successful relationship. Sufficient time should be allocated to evaluate the proposed services.

The cost of each proposal is usually contained in the amount of fees to be charged for the variety of services offered, or through the requirement of a minimum balance in each account. Exhibit 7-6 is an illustration of a bid summary sheet detailing the various services offered and fees charged.

Once the evaluation is completed and the decision rendered by the board of education, the accepted proposal should be put in writing through a contractual agreement. The primary objective of the agreement is to identify in detail the responsibilities of the bank in relation to the funds of the school district, and the consequences for failure to provide this necessary protection.

EXHIBIT 7-6 • *Banking Services to Be Provided*

| | | | |
|---|---|---|---|
| 1. Furnish necessary checks for the following Checking accounts: | | | |
| Accounts payable checks | Yes _____ | No_____ | Fee_____ |
| Bonds payable checks | Yes _____ | No_____ | Fee_____ |
| Campaign account checks | Yes _____ | No_____ | Fee_____ |
| Insurance account | Yes _____ | No_____ | Fee_____ |
| Payroll checks | Yes _____ | No_____ | Fee_____ |
| Petty cash checks | Yes _____ | No_____ | Fee_____ |
| Scholarship fund checks | Yes _____ | No_____ | Fee_____ |
| 2. Furnish necessary travelers checks | Yes _____ | No_____ | Fee_____ |
| 3. Reverse service charge on returned checks and stop payment requests | Yes _____ | No_____ | Fee_____ |
| 4. Furnish window envelopes | Yes _____ | No_____ | Fee_____ |
| 5. Bank by mail postage paid both ways | Yes _____ | No_____ | Fee_____ |
| 6. Endorsement stamps | Yes _____ | No_____ | Fee_____ |
| 7. Investment advice | Yes _____ | No_____ | Fee_____ |
| 8. Arrange for repurchase agreements | Yes _____ | No_____ | Fee_____ |
| 9. Pay interest on checking account balances | Yes _____ | No_____ | Fee_____ |
| Minimum balance requirement (if any) | _____ | | |
| Interest paid on minimum balance | _____ % | | |
| 10. Regular savings account | Yes _____ | No_____ | Fee_____ |
| Interest rate | _____ % | | |
| Minimum balance requirement (if applicable) | _____ % | | |
| Interest paid on minimum balance | _____ % | | |
| 11. Other services to be provided: | | | |

_____

_____

_____

## Cash Management Evaluation

Ultimately, the evaluation of a cash-management program is the amount of interest dollars earned by the district each year by the timely investment of available cash at the most favorable rates in accordance with the district's investment policy. Essentially, this involves the management of two dimensions: cash utilization and investment selection. The business administrator is responsible for keeping the funds invested while maintaining sufficient cash to meet the daily operating needs of the district.

One approach to the systematic evaluation of a cash-management program is to compare the average money market yields over a specified period of time. Exhibit 7-7 is a summary of the district's investments during the previous three-month period. During this period, the district had $3,493,542 invested in treasury bills and certificates of deposit. In addition to the principal cost and interest rates, an annualized yield is calculated to measure performance. The annualized yield represents the total interest income that would accrue if the funds were invested for a one-year period. This calculation provides an opputunity to measure performance. The total annualized interest is divided by the total investment ($297,250/$3,493,542) to obtain the current annualized yield of the investments. The annualized current yield of 8.51 percent could be compared to the average money market rates for the same period, thus providing the district with a measure of performance. Obviously, a current yield above the money market rate

EXHIBIT 7-7 • *Rate pf Return on Investments*

| Instrument | Face Amount | Days to Maturity | Rate | Principal Cost | Interest Earned | Annual Yield |
|---|---|---|---|---|---|---|
| Treasury Bill | $500,000 | 60 | 7.75% | $493,542 | $6,458 | $38,250 |
| Certificate of Deposit | $1,000,000 | 60 | 8.00% | $1,000,000 | $13,333 | $80,000 |
| Certificate of Deposit | $500,000 | 90 | 8.50% | $500,000 | $10,625 | $42,500 |
| Certificate of Deposit | $1,500,000 | 20 | 9.10% | $1,500,000 | $7,583 | $136,500 |
| Total Investment | | | | $3,493,542 | $38,000 | $297,250 |
| Cumulative Sum | $297,250 | | | | | |
| Total Investment | $3,493,542 | | | | | |
| Current Yield | 8.51% | | | | | |

would indicate favorable performance, while a yield significantly below the market could indicate under invesment of funds.

The use of rate of return to evaluate a cash-management program is not without its crities. Dembowski argues that the size and wealth of the district has an impact on the rate of return:

> Generally, the larger the school district, the larger the cash flows, thus the larger the cash surplus availble for investment. This problem is further exacerbated by the fact that bankers pay a premium through higher bids for the use of large amounts of cash for investments. Thus, a banker may bid only 10 percent for a certificate of deposit (CD) for 90 days on $100,000 when he may bid 12 percent for a 90-day CD on $1 million. These scale effects should be eliminated in any evaluation of cash management performance.[14]

The search for an acceptable standard to measure performance has led some writers to the expenditure side of the cash-flow statement. While accepting the fact that differences in state statutes, assessed valuation, state aid payments, and the investment expertise of the business administrator will have a definite effect on the amount of funds available for investment and the instruments selected, they agree that a typical school district could affect a rate of return equal to 1.5 percent of the district's total expenditures for the year.[15]

Erikson and Rothrock's approach to the evaluation of a cash-management program centers on the rate of return on cash availability and a cash utilization factor.[16] The return on cash availability is calculated by dividing the interest income by the cash availability. As noted earlier, cash availability is the average monthly balance for the year. The cash utilization factor is the product of the availability ratio and the return on cash availability. The availability ratio represents the relationship of the average cash availability to total revenue. Therefore, the availability ratio depicts the amount of funds available for investment and additional income.[17] The cash utilization factor is a benchmark to measure the effectiveness of the cash management program. An increasing cash utilization factor would indicate that either more funds were available for investment and/or the rate of return had increased. Exhibit 7-8 is an example of this approach to assessing the cash management program. The rate of return on expenditures is also included as a point of comparison.

The actual and estimated revenue and average cash availability over a two-year period is depicted. The return on average cash availability is 6.78 percent and 8.0 percent, respectively ($112,155/$1,654,827 and $143,166/$1,789,580) indicating a significant increase over the previous year. The availability ratios indicate that a slightly higher percent of the total revenue is available for investment during the 1989-90 school year

(11.49 percent vs. 11.84 percent). Both of these factors (increased rate of return and availability ratio) resulted in an ascending cash utilization factor.

This model provides the business administrator with a good review of the effectivenes sof the district's investment program. It clearly identifies the significant factors that ultimately result in either a successful of unsuccessful investment program. Changes in the economy, the appropriation of state aid, the district's assessed valuation, of the district's expenditure pattern may result in decreases of increases in both cash availability and/of interest rates. These changes can be easily identified through the availability ratio and return on cash availability.

The return on expenditure factor is also depicted in Exhibit 7-8. Investment income for the two years resulted in a return on expenditures of .79 percent and .95 percent, well below the targeted standard of 1.5 percent.

## Summary

One of the primary responsibilities of the school business administrator is the development and coordination of a cash-management program for the district. This includes both the timely investment of surplus funds and the protection of district funds from misuse or theft. Although lost investment opportunity through under-investment of funds will probably not be noted in the annual audit, the district is not maximizing its potential revenue if surplus funds are left in low interest-bearing accounts when higher investment-earning instruments are available.

EXHIBIT 7-8 • *Cash Management Performance Criteria*

|  |  | 88/89 | 89/90 |
|---|---|---|---|
| 1. | Total revenue | $ 14,401,775 | $15,120,511 |
| 2. | Average cash availability | 1,654,827 | 1,789,580 |
| 3. | Availability ratio (2/1) | 11.49% | 11.84% |
| 4. | Investment income | 112,155 | 143,166 |
| 5. | Return on average cash availability (4/2) | 6.78% | 8.0% |
| 6. | Cash utilization factor (3 x 5) | 77.90 | 94.72 |
| 7. | Total expenditures | 14,204,500 | 15,056,770 |
| 8. | Return on expenditures (4/7) | .79% | .95% |

# Appendix A

*Bank Depository Proposal Institution Identification Form*

Bank Name: _____

Bank Address: _____

Telephone Number: _____

Executive Officer: _____

District Contact Representative: _____

This proposal is submitted in compliance with the attached guidelines for bid proposals to serve as bank depository from July 1, 1989 through June 30, 1991. Any exceptions are noted below. Any additional information desired by the bank may also be attached.

_____

_____

_____

_____

_____
Signature of bank Official

_____
Title

_____
Date

# Bid Proposal Guidelines for Bank Depository

Please be advised that in connection with the submission of a bid proposal to furnish banking services, the following should be considered.

   **1.** Bid proposals should cover a two-year period, beginning July 1, 1989 and ending June 30, 1991.

   **2.** Projected receipt and disbursement activity for the 1989–90 school year is estimated to be $46 million. Projected activity for the 1990–91 school year is estimated to be $49 million.

   **3.** The school district reserves the right to invest surplus school funds in eligible investments on a competitive basis with other banks and/or financial institutions.

   **4.** The bank depository selected must pledge a willingness to provide the school district with short-term loans against anticipated tax revenues, needed to meet current operational expenses. The rate of interest charged will not exceed the maximum allowed under state statutes.

**5.** The school district intends to maintain eight checking accounts (accounts payable, bonds payable, campaign, payroll, petty case, scholarship fund, and two insurance accounts) and one savings account.

**6.** Deposits must be secured by collateral meeting the requirements of state statutes.

**7.** No minimum balance in any account can be guaranteed.

**8.** The school district reserves the right to reject any or all bid proposals submitted.

**9.** Any bid proposal to be considered must be submitted to the office of the Assistant Superintendent for Finance and Operations by 4:00 P.M., Tuesday, May 16, 1989.

## General Responsibilities of Depository Bank

**1.** Adhere to all state statutory provisions applicable to public school districts.

**2.** Participate in wire transfer of fund at no cost to the district from the state department of elementary and secondary education to allow for same-day investment.

**3.** Participate in wire transfer of funds at no cost to the district to other banks to allow for same-day investment.

**4.** Accept district withholding tax deposit for salaries, as well as amounts deposited under the Federal Insurance Contribution Act.

**5.** Grant short-term loans against anticipated tax revenue, if deemed necessary by the district.

**6.** Provide one large safe deposit box for district use.

**7.** Provide 24-hour depository service.

**8.** Furnish bank statements with checks sorted in numeric order by the 5th of each month.

**9.** Provide new/renewal check orders without charge.

**10.** Provide deposit slips, coin envelopes, and money bags as required by the district.

**11.** Provide handling of bulk coin without charge.

## Endnotes

1. Ronald G. Erickson and Paul D. Rothrock, *Cash Flow Management and Investments* (Association of School Business Officials, International, Seminar Presented at the Annual Meeting in Orlando, Florida, 1989), p. 9.

2. William T. Hartman, *School District Budgeting* (Englewood Cliffs, New Jersey: Prentice-Hall, 1988), p. 124.

3. Ibid., p. 128.

4. Frederick L. Dembowski, *A Handbook for School District Financial Management* (Research Corporation of the Association of School Business Officials of the United States and Canada, 1982), p. 10.

5. Erickson and Rothrock, p. 11.

6. Ibid., p. 16.

7. Ibid., p. 22.

8. Department of Elementary and Secondary Education, *The Public School Laws of Missouri* (Jefferson City, Missouri: 1988) Section 165-051, p. 84.

9. John Downes and Jordan Elliot Goodman, *Dictionary of Finance and Investment Terms* (Woodbury, New York: Barron's Educational Series, Inc., 1987), p. 250.

10. Charles R. Idol, *The Fundamentals of Credit Union Investment Alternatives, Credit Analysis, & Investment Policy* (Paper  presented at the annual meeting of the Credit Union Executives Society, 1987), p. 3.

11. Charles K. Coe, *Public Financial Management* (Englewood Cliffs, New Jersey: Prentice-Hall, 1989), p. 124

12. Ibid., p. 124.

13. Public School Laws of Missouri, Section 165.251, p. 88.

14. Dembowski, p. 7.

15. Frederick L. Dembowski and Robert D. Davey, "School District Financial Management and Banking," in R. Craig Wood, ed., *Principles of School Business Management* (Reston, Virginia: Association of School Business Officials, International, 1986). p. 240.

16. Erickson and Rothrock, p. 51.

17. Ibid., 57.

## Selected Bibliography

Berne, Robert, and Richard Schramm, *The Financial Analysis of Governments* (Englewood Cliffs, New Jersey: Prentice-Hall, 1986).

Coe, Charles K., *Public Financial Management* (Englewood Cliffs, New Jersey: Prentice-Hall, 1989).

Corrigan, Arnold and Phyllis C. Kaufman, *Understanding Treasury Bills and other U.S. Government Securities* (Stanford, Connecticut: Longmeadow Press, 1987).

Dembowski, Frederick L., *A Handbook for School District Financial Management* (Park Ridge, Illnois:  Research Corporation of the Association of School Businesss Officials of the United States and Canada, 1982).

Harrell, Rhett D., *Banking Relations: A Guide for Local Government* (Chicago: Government Finance Officers Association, 1982).

Miller, Girard, *Investing Public Funds*, (Chicago: Government Finance Officers Association, 1986).

Webb, L. Dean, and Van D. Mueller, *Managing Limited Resources: New Demands on Public School Management* (Cambridge, Massachusetts: Fifth Annual Yearbook of the American Education Finance Association, Ballinger Publishing Company, 1984).

Wood, R. Craig, ed., *Principles of School Business Management* (Reston, Virginia: Association of School Business Officials, International, 1986).

# 8

# Managing Salary, Wage, and Fringe Benefit Programs

Psychologists have recognized for a long time the importance of needs satisfaction as a motivator. The need that is satisfied might be peer recognition, a promotion, receipt of information, money, or just the feeling that comes from the knowledge that you are doing a good job at work.[1]

This self-interest motive is sometimes frowned upon because it carries a selfish connotation. However, it is a fact of life. People act in ways that they perceive to be in their own best interests. Whether a given action is truly in a person's best interest is irrelevant. What matters is that he or she believes it to be so.

Keeping this in mind, school-district administrators can affect job performance through a rewards system that ratifies what employees believe to be in their own best interests. Each individual employee may value different types of rewards. However, there are certain sets of rewards that are common to most people in our society. Obviously, it is necessary to structure a program to reward employees who, while acting in their own best interests, also act in the best interests of the school district.[2]

The most basic rewards for job performance are salaries, wages, and fringe benefits. The focus of this chapter is on the management of these rewards. However, it is very important to understand that salaries, wages, and fringe benefits are not the only kinds of rewards that are beneficial and effective. In fact, an entire array of possibilities can be classified into *intrinsic* and *extrinsic* rewards.

Intrinsic rewards are those rewards that an employee receives from doing the job itself. Employees own satisfaction on the job and their motivation to increase the level of their performance can be influenced by such rewards as: participation in the decision-making process, greater job discretion, increased responsibility, more challenging tasks, opportunities for personal growth, and diversity of activities.

Extrinsic rewards can be further divided into direct and indirect compensation. The most common forms of direct compensation are salaries, wages, overtime pay, holiday pay, and merit pay. Direct compensation is that part of a rewards system that generates the most controversy and disgruntlement among employees. Industrial psychologists have long contended that neither salary nor wage is the most important determiner of job satisfaction. However, it is an indispensable part of every rewards package.[3]

Indirect compensation usually includes protection programs, pay for time away from work, and services. There is a widespread attitude among personnel administrators, which views indirect compensation as that which helps to retain individuals. Indirect compensation is commonly referred to as *fringe benefits*. Fringe benefits can be further divided into those mandated by law and those that are offered by the school district on a voluntary basis.

In order to avoid confusion, a matter of terminology must be addressed. The most commonly used term for the subject under treatment in this chapter is *compensation*. In itself this is a legitimate term and can be substituted for the term *reward*. However, the term reward more clearly represents the reason for paying employees their salaries and for providing them with fringe benefit programs. It should be understood that effective personnel management will not permit an unproductive employee to remain on the job. Therefore, from an operational viewpoint, all salaries, wages, and fringe benefits are rewards for performance because unacceptable performance will result in termination. Also, the concept of rewarding performance is in keeping with the mandate of taxpayers that school district officials and administrators establish some method of staff evaluation that includes a performance component. A system of evaluation which is solely based on seniority, for example, runs contrary to the most current understanding of accountability.[4]

## Direct Compensation: Salary and Wage Administration

In this chapter, the term *salary* will be used to designate the amount of money that is received by an employee who is paid under an individual contract or at a set amount. Teachers, administrators, and secretaries, for example, are paid a set amount of money for a certain period of time. The term *wage* will be used to designate the hourly rate of pay received by employees such as custodians or maintenance workers. On first reading, these distinctions might seem to be unwarranted. However, salary and wage management is a very complex function and such distinctions are necessary if a fundamental understanding is to be achieved.

There are many influences that affect salary and wage programs in school districts. Among the most common are state and federal laws, collectively bargained agreements, and pay rates in the private, not-for-profit, and public sectors. The latter two influences require action on the part of school board members and administrators.

A master contract will contain either the method for determining salaries or wages or the actual salaries and wages that will be paid to the members of the bargaining unit covered by the contract. However, whether salaries and wages are collectively bargained or determined by some other process, the problem of *comparability* will surely arise. Thus, school-district administrators must continually gather data on the salaries and wages that are paid by neighboring school districts and other public, not-for-profit, and private employers in the local community, region, and state.

Most public agencies, organizations, and private companies are cooperative in sharing information concerning salary and wage programs because they too understand that their policies are influenced by others. Surveys by telephone or by questionnaire, government publications, and information published by unions and professional organizations are valuable resources in gathering this type of information.[5]

There are nine aspects of salary and wage administration that form the nucleus of direct compensation as presented in this section. It is important to keep in mind, however, that while these distinctions are rather artificial, they do allow for the orderly treatment of this subject matter. In reality, salary and wage administration is one process.

EXHIBIT 8-1 • *Salary and Wage Policy*

---

The Board of Education recognizes that quality education for the children and adolescents of this school district is directly dependent upon the quality of the staff. The Board further recognizes that the capability of the District to recruit and retain quality individuals is significantly influenced by the level of salaries and wages that are paid to employees. Therefore, the Board directs the Superintendent of Schools to create and implement a process for the research and development of a salary and wage program.

This program must be at least competitive with that of the school districts in the metropolitan area and, if financial resources permit, should provide salaries and wages that are in the upper third category when compared with other districts. This program should be reviewed annually by the Board of Education and the Board will expect the Superintendent to make a recommendation by April 1 each year setting forth whether the program should be revised to meet the objective of remaining in the top third category.

Finally, the Board of Education directs that the salary and wage program must be constructed in such a way as to reward performance.

---

## Salary and Wage Policy

It is crucial for every school district to develop a board of education policy concerning salaries and wages. Such a policy will give direction to the administration and will provide school-district taxpayers with a rationale for future board action in this area. Exhibit 8-1 is a sample board of education policy dealing with salaries and wages.

This policy contains four major elements. The first element is a recognition that salaries and wages are an important component in hiring and retaining quality individuals. The second element is a recognition that continual research concerning salaries and wages must be undertaken if a school district is to know its position in relation to other districts in the area. Such research may reveal that the salary and wage program must be changed in order to meet the objectives of the board concerning salaries and wages. Third, in this policy, the board has issued a mandate to the administration concerning the level at which the salary and wage program should be in relation to the salary and wage programs of other districts for the sake of remaining competitive. Finally, through this policy, the board has recognized the relationship between performance and financial reward.

The elements of this policy will become strategies in those districts where collective bargaining exists. Theoretically, the respective board of education and union should both be concerned with the issues that are addressed in this policy. However, the concept of a "reward" for performance and the level of salary and wage funding at which the board wishes to remain in relation to other districts are likely to become issues with the union. The union may believe that the district's employees should be the highest paid in the area. The seniority approach to setting salaries and wages, which most unions would prefer, would be threatened.

### Guidelines for the Development of a Salary and Wage Program

Program development is a lengthy and complicated undertaking. Yet, it is a task that is familiar to most administrators. Administrators also know well the effects that such a program can have on staff morale and subsequently on staff performance. There are five considerations that should be incorporated into every salary and wage program.

*Position Evaluation* A salary and wage program must recognize the skills that are required for all staff positions. Thus, every position must be evaluated in order to determine its importance in relation to all other positions. All positions can then be arranged in the order of their relative value to the school district with the position of the greatest value at the top. Therefore, a graduated classification system is established.

*Comparability* The salary and wage program must be competitive with other school districts and, as much as possible, with other public agencies and even with private industry.

*Equitable Salary and Wage Program* The Equal Pay Act of 1963 requires fiscal parity for jobs of equal skill and responsibility. There are no two jobs exactly alike because they are performed by two different individuals with different skills and, in spite of all attempts at uniformity, there usually are even slightly different responsibilities between jobs with the same title. However, there is usually sufficient similarity between categories of jobs to allow for classification. This classification process should be directed toward discovering similarities of jobs which can then become the basis for equity.

*Salary and Wage Program Review* The salary and wage program must be reviewed annually in order to ascertain if the program is competitive with other school districts and is realistic in terms of hiring and retaining personnel. The importance of this review process is in its significance for long-range planning or, to use a popular phrase, it significance for *strategic planning*. Enough justification has already been given to the importance of salaries and wages, but it is appropriate to bring this issue to the attention of administrators and the board of education as often as possible.

*Performance Incentives* A primary focus of a rewards program is the improvement of performance. Because salaries and wages are major components of a rewards program, it should be constructed so as to encourage employees both to improve performance and to assume greater responsibility. Thus, the district must establish a uniform and fair method of appraising each individual's performance.

## Effects of Salary and Wage on Motivation

An interesting question that is central to all salary and wage programs is, "Does money stimulate the employee to put forth more effort?" Earlier in this chapter the concept of rewarding performance was discussed. This question, however, captures the essence of the rewarding principle.

In order to properly understand how money acts as a motivator, it is important to keep in mind that money, per se, is rarely an end in itself but rather a means to "purchasing an end." Every person has needs, and in our society most of these needs can be satisfied only through the acquisition of money.

A self-evident concern of most, if not all, people is personal standard of living. The level of this standard becomes more critical when the person is supporting dependents who have expanding needs. We rarely find a person who is not concerned when their lifestyle deteriorates because salary or wage increases have not been keeping pace with inflation.[6]

A $2000 raise for an employee making $20,000 a year might help maintain that individual's standard of living in the face of ordinary inflation. That same raise would considerably improve the standard of living for a person earning $10,000 a year, but it would have much less effect on the lifestyle of someone earning $40,000 per year.

A study based on the responses of 157 professionals in the electronics industry showed that each dollar of merit pay had a value to employees. In fact, the research suggested that money is important to employees regardless of their job level within a company or their wage or salary level. Money also has a great deal of symbolic value in our society even though it has varying degrees of importance to individuals having different backgrounds and experiences.

If money is going to motivate individuals to greater performance, it must be made very clear that such performance will indeed be rewarded with more money. It is reasonable to suspect that the behavior thus rewarded will be repeated and the behaviors that are not rewarded with money will not be repeated.

Unfortunately, the modus operandi of most school districts has been limited to emphasizing *intrinsic* motivation. Teachers and other school district employees are expected to perform at the best of their abilities because of the importance of educating children and the resulting status afforded to them. The accountability movement which has seen taxpayers demanding a higher return on their dollar from school district employees through increased student performance, as well as the number of teacher strikes for higher salaries, should dispel the myth that the performance of any group of employees in the public sector is unaffected by money.

Statistical data also support the position that money increases intrinsic motivation under the following condition: monetary rewards must closely follow performance so as to be reinforcing, and the employee must perceive the monetary rewards as being related to work behavior.

It should be obvious from this treatment that a seniority-based salary schedule cannot reward performance except by accident and, therefore, will have little effect upon motivation.[7]

## Public Disclosure of Salaries

Salary and wage programs along with other budgetary information is often disclosed not only to school district employees but also to the general public and sometimes to the news media. This is as it should be because school districts are public agencies supported by taxes. The public has a right to know how and for what purpose their tax dollars are being spent by school-district officials.

School-district management is also affected by an open salary and wage policy. If salary and wage information becomes common knowledge among employees, people can compare their salaries and wages. Thus, inequities in the salary and wage program will soon become apparent. Also, secrecy in regard to salaries and wages may lead to misconceptions, which, in turn, may create a morale problem.

An open salary and wage policy can demonstrate that the board of education and the administration have confidence in the program and this, in turn, may increase the trust individuals have in the management of the school district.

Federal agencies have also had an impact on the public disclosure of salaries and wages. For example, the Equal Employment Opportunity Commission continues to experience an increase in the number of cases alleging that women are being paid less than men while doing the same job.

This, of course, is contrary to the provisions of the Equal Pay Act of 1963. In like manner, school districts that receive federal funds must disclose salary and wage information to demonstrate commitment to the principles of affirmative action. In regard to this issue, it is interesting to note that the National Labor Relations Board issued a decision against a company policy of Blue Cross-Blue Shield of Alabama, which stated that the company's attempt to prohibit discussion of pay during working hours was an infringement of the constitutional rights of employees.[8]

## Employee Relations in Salary and Wage Management

If employees believe that they are unfairly paid, the board of education and the administration will certainly be faced with a morale problem. The good faith of the school board and administration are the key factors. Low salaries and wages alone do not create a morale problem if employees believe that the board and the administration are doing everything possible to improve salaries and wages. Therefore, the way in which salary and wage decisions are presented to the employee is of great importance. Of course, the method will vary because of local traditions and the number of employees in a school district. However, most presentation plans will be formulated with a sensitivity to the process that is used in making salary and wage decisions. There are two commonly used processes.

In the first process, the administration analyzes the financial condition of the school district; formulates a recommendation that appears reasonable; receives approval from the board of education; and, finally, informs the school-district employees. While this method is the most efficient in terms of time spent by the board of education and the administration, it is the most vulnerable in terms of good staff morale because it is basically a unilateral approach. Unfortunately, this is a rather common approach in school districts across the country.

The second process is the most defensible. Representatives of the administration meet with representatives of employee groups to develop mutually acceptable salary and wage packages. Over half the states mandate this process in varying degrees through collective negotiations legislation. However, the essence of this process is certainly valid even in those states that prohibit collective negotiations by public school employees. Where such a prohibition exists, salary and wage decisions are the prerogative of the board of education. However, recommendations can be made by mutual agreement between the administration and employee groups.

The process of collective negotiations is the most appropriate in terms of staff involvement. It is also the most time-consuming, and disagreements between the administration and employee representatives can lead to an impasse or even a strike.

Whether the decision is made through collective negotiations or unilaterally by the board of education, the administration eventually will be charged with presenting the approved salary or wage program to the employees. The sensitive nature of a salary or wage decision cannot be overemphasized, because such a decision will necessarily affect employees' efforts to support themselves and their families. Further, the decision will affect the employee's standard of living and his or her financial security in a highly materialistic society. Consequently, effective communication is essential.

Adhering to the following guidelines will help the superintendent of schools and the superintendent's staff to explain the decision of the board of education concerning salaries and wages.

1. The administration should make complete disclosure of the fiscal condition of the school district as a prelude to explaining the board's decision. Anything less would arouse the suspicion of the employees that the administration was not being truthful.
2. The administration should avoid presenting too many technical details of the financial condition of the district which could give the impression that the administration is using this technique to confuse the salary and wage issue.
3. The administration should prepare a position statement to distribute to all employees and to the news media in which the decision of the board on salaries and wages is explained along with the process and rationale used in reaching the decision.

Likewise, it is effective in minimizing confusion and misinterpretation to invite employees to contact a designated administrator's office if, at a later time, they have questions about the content of the salary and wage position statement. The most appropriate office is that of the assistant superintendent for business and financial services. However, the office of the assistant superintendent for human resources or the director of community relations office could also be the contact point for employees with questions.

A final point needs to made concerning employee relations in salary and wage administration. The building principal in some districts is often the last person to be informed about decisions of the board of education and central office. Yet, the principal is usually the first person to be contacted by teachers and other building level employees when they have a concern or question. Therefore, it is both good administrative procedure and good internal relations to inform the principals first about salary decisions. This will also help to impress upon the principals that they are significant members of the administrative team.[9]

## Gathering Salary and Wage Data

In developing salary and wage recommendations to be presented to the board of education, the superintendent of schools and his or her staff should initiate techniques for collecting data from other school districts, governmental agencies, not-for-profit organizations, and private business and industry. Individual situations will dictate the scope of the data collection and the specific techniques to be employed. For example, in large metropolitan areas like Chicago, Illinois, the data collection process could be quite burdensome. A sampling technique would be appropriate in this situation. Whereas, in rural areas the only significant data will probably just come from neighboring school districts.

If the salaries and wages paid by a school district are to sustain a reasonable standard of living for district employees, they must be comparable to the salaries and wages received by other individuals in the same community with like education, training, experience, and responsibilities. This is the primary reason for collective salary and wage data. While the usual situation finds school-district salaries and wages below many others in a community, it is possible for school-district salaries and wages to be higher than the salaries and wages of school-district residents who are paying taxes to support the district. This can be especially true of the salaries and wages paid to secretaries, skilled maintenance employees, custodians, and other non-certificated employees. These employees who are neither certificated teachers nor certificated administrators are usually referred to as *classified* employees. A common myth is that *classified* salaries and wages paid to school-district employees are lower than comparable wages in the private sector.

A good source of information on salaries and wages paid in a given community for classified occupations is the state employment agency. The civil service commissions of state and municipal governments also have information available on their salary and wage programs.

However, the most effective way to gather data on salaries and wages is through a survey. If the survey form is accompanied by a cover letter explaining its purpose, most agencies and corporations will cooperate with school districts not only because they may need to do the same at a later date but also because they view this cooperation as a form of public service.

EXHIBIT 8-2 • *Sample Job Description*

---

*Custodian*

---

Cleans and keeps in an orderly condition work areas, washrooms, and premises of an office including hallways. Duties involve a combination of the following: sweeping, mopping, scrubbing, and polishing floors; removing trash and other refuse; dusting equipment, furniture, and fixtures; polishing metal fixtures or trimmings; and providing supplies and minor maintenance services. Workers who specialize in window washing are excluded from this classification.

---

The following guidelines for salary and wage surveys should be helpful to those administrators using this technique for the first time.

1. The answers to the survey questions must be obtained on a confidential basis. Thus, all summaries must be prepared in a manner that protects the anonymity of each respondent. In the cover letter, state that the data will be kept confidential and restricted to management personnel.

2. Every effort must be made to ensure that the survey is unbiased and objective. Therefore, statistical techniques should be used both in sampling and in analyzing the data.

3. Request salary and wage information which reflects averages for each job category. Also, for classified positions request straight-time day work rates for regularly employed full-time employees for a forty-hour work week. Requesting temporary full-time, temporary part-time, and permanent part-time wage rates will only confuse the analysis and bring into question the usefulness of the survey.

4. Job descriptions should be used in the survey in order to provide the respondent with a criteria for slotting jobs. See Exhibit 8-2.

5. The job categories selected for the survey should cover such a wide range of experience and skills that they cannot be considered typical of any one firm or group of firms. The intent is to represent job categories found widely throughout the geographical area.

Job descriptions for instructional and administrative positions generally follow the same format as that shown in Exhibit 8-2.

The attempt to keep school district salaries and wages comparable to those in the private sector is imperative not only because of labor shortages in many areas but also because more and more school-district employees are being attracted to jobs in business and industry. This is particularly true of classified employees. In fact, secretaries, electricians, cook, bus drivers, and other classified employees are sometimes "in training" with public school districts until a job opportunity becomes available in the private sector.

Therefore, a salary and wage program comparable to the private sector helps school districts to be competitive with the private sector for quality employees and also helps school districts retain employees, which, consequently, reduces the expense involved in hiring new employees.

The salaries being offered in the private sector are even attracting instructional and administrative personnel. Mathematics, industrial arts, and science teachers are finding many more opportunities in private business and industry than ever before. In like manner, this trend is reaching into the ranks of the liberal arts staff as corporations recognize that they can train an individual for almost any job if the person is motivated and has a basic college education. Some of the most creative people in a given community have been stolen away from the field of education because of the rewards programs in the private sector that recognize quality performance.

Another trend has arisen which can minimize the duplication of efforts and reduce the cost of gathering salary and wage data. Groups of school districts in the same geographical area are pooling their resources and jointly sponsoring salary and wage surveys.

## The Equal Pay Act

The United States Congress enacted the Equal Pay Act in 1963, which requires employers to pay men and women the same salary or wage for equal work. This act is part of the Fair Labor Standards Act and protects employees who work for an employer engaged in an enterprise affected by interstate commerce. The interpretation of *interstate commerce* was broadly defined by the Court in *Usery* v. *Columbia University*, 568 F.2d 953 (2d Cir.1977). In addition, the interpretation of *equal work* has been broadly defined to mean "substantially" equal and, thus, strict equality of jobs is not required. Thus, this act requires equal pay for jobs that demand equal skill, effort, and responsibility and which are carried out under similar working conditions. However, if salaries or wages are contingent upon a seniority system, a merit system, a system which measures pay by production quantity or quality, or factors other than sex, this act does not apply.

An example of a court case involving the Equal Pay Act is *EEOC* v. *Madison Community Unit School District Number 12*, 818 F.2d 577 (7th Cir.1987). In this case, a female who coached girls' track and tennis was paid substantially less than the males who coached the boys' track and tennis at the same school. In addition, a female assistant coach of the girls' basketball team was paid less than a male assistant coach of the boys' track team. Still another female coach was paid less for coaching girls' basketball, softball, and volleyball than a male coaching boys' basketball, baseball, and soccer. Finally, an assistant coach of the girls' track team was paid less than the assistant coach of the boys' track team.

The Equal Employment Opportunity Commission filed a lawsuit against the school district stating that the inequities violated the Equal Pay Act. The U.S. district court ruled in favor of the EEOC but the school district appealed to the U.S. Court of Appeals, Seventh Circuit. This court affirmed the district court's decision in the following situation: boys' and girls' track, boys' and girls' tennis, and boys' baseball and girls' softball. However, the Court of Appeals reversed the district court's decision in comparing boys' soccer to girls' volleyball, boys' soccer to girls' basketball, and boys' track to girls' basketball. The court stated that these latter situations did not require equal skill, effort, and responsibility.[10]

There is another aspect to the *equal pay* issue. When a school district has a performance-based evaluation system that is used to determine the salaries and wages of employees, the Equal Pay Act does not apply. However, in all organizations, employees tend to compare their salaries and wages with those of co-workers and also to compare how productive these co-workers are in comparison with their own productivity. The effects of this situation for school administration can be serious. It is a situation that will only fester if it is ignored. The best approach is to reemphasize the relationship between performance and reward. Also, it is important to reiterate that the performance-based evaluation process is the vehicle for determining the level of performance and the amount of reward.

Obviously, if a school district does not have an effective evaluation process, a merit-based rewards program cannot be initiated. Performance and reward are two aspects of the same process that go hand-in-hand.[11]

## Salary and Wage Program Construction

### Teacher Salary Program [12]

In public education, it has been traditional to use salary schedules as the primary method for establishing teacher salaries. Such schedules are usually divided into a number of grades, each with several step rates. For example, grade one will probably be designated for teachers with a bachelor's degree and might have ten steps. The steps may indicate a performance rating or seniority depending on the salary policy of the district. However, the number of steps usually indicates the top level or "cap" in salary that a person can achieve in that grade.

There are two major advantages to the use of salary schedules. First, recruitment of personnel could be more effective if a potential employee is able to see the possible increases in salary he or she could receive over a number of years in service. Second, the use of salary schedules will help the administration to develop long-range plans and budgets because future salary requirements are readily evident.

A major question in establishing a salary schedule is deciding on the appropriate number of steps that should be included within a grade. If the steps are numerous with small increases, employees could be unhappy because salary increases may not meet the cost of living. On the other hand, if the steps are few, even with large increases, employees could reach the maximum within a grade in a short period of time and will not have an opportunity to progress, over the long term, unless they meet the requirements to move to a higher grade such as a bachelor's degree plus fifteen hours of graduate education.

A realistic approach could be a compromise that sets forth ten or more steps within each grade with each step and grade representing a certain percentage increase. There remains, however, the problem associated with teachers who reach the top of their respective grade. Some school districts have addressed this problem with the inclusion of longevity steps at the top of a grade, offering even dollar amounts rather than a percentage increase. For example, an employee could be granted a $1000 longevity increase for every two years of service after reaching the last step within a grade.

Each teacher's salary would be indicated by placement on a grade and step. As new people are hired, they would be offered a salary that falls on the salary schedule. However, because of the shortage of teachers in some areas such as mathematics, science, industrial arts, and special education, a candidate for a position might be enticed by placement on a step above what is usual for a beginning teacher. Consistent with the philosophy that a salary and wage program should be used by a school district as a method of rewarding performance, it is not recommended that advancement from one step to another in a grade occur because that person remained with the district for another year. Advancement from one step to another should be based on performance. Consequently, an employee who is performing unsatisfactorily could remain on the same step until termination or resignation. An employee performing satisfactorily could receive a step advancement that would represent a certain percentage salary increase. A meritorious employee could be granted a two- or three-step advancement.

Some school districts have initiated a policy of placing a new employee on the first step for a probationary period and, then, advancing the person as he or she demonstrates satisfactory performance. For example, an employee might be moved to step two after six months of satisfactory performance. This method is usually applied to classified employees. Teachers and administrators are typically employed under a contract for a one-year minimum period of time.

Advancement from one salary grade to another is usually based on an increase in educational qualifications. Thus, a teacher who goes to graduate school and receives a master's degree would be advanced to that respective grade. It is important to note that advancement to a higher salary grade will not necessarily result in a higher wage for an employee. For example, step 5 of a bachelor's degree grade might indicate a salary lower that step 1 of the master's degree salary grade. Therefore, when moving a teacher to a higher grade, it is obviously important to place him or her on a step that will ensure an increase in salary for having upgraded his or her academic qualifications.

EXHIBIT 8-3 • *Teacher Salary Schedule*

| Step | Bachelor's Degree | Bachelor's Degree Plus 15 Graduate Hours | Master's Degree Plus 2 Years Experience | Master's Degree Plus 15 Graduate Hours | Doctoral Degree Plus 3 Years Experience |
|------|------|------|------|------|------|
| 1 | 17,000 | 17,765 | | 18,530 | |
| 2 | 17,765 | 18,530 | | 19,635 | |
| 3 | 18,530 | 19,295 | 19,677 | 20,740 | |
| 4 | 19,295 | 20,060 | 20,442 | 21,845 | 22,610 |
| 5 | 20,060 | 20,825 | 21,207 | 22,950 | 23,715 |
| 6 | 20,825 | 21,590 | 21,972 | 24,055 | 24,820 |
| 7 | 21,590 | 22,355 | 22,737 | 25,160 | 25,925 |
| 8 | 22,355 | 23,120 | 23,502 | 26,265 | 27,030 |
| 9 | 23,120 | 23,885 | 24,267 | 27,370 | 28,135 |
| 10 | 23,885 | 24,650 | 25,032 | 28,475 | 29,240 |
| 11 | | 25,765 | 25,797 | 29,580 | 30,345 |
| 12 | | | 26,562 | 30,685 | 31,450 |
| 13 | | | | 31,790 | 32,555 |
| 14 | | | | | 34,000 |
| 15 | | | | | 35,105 |
| 16 | | | | | 36,210 |
| 17 | | | | | 37,315 |
| 18 | | | | | 38,420 |
| 19 | | | | | 39,525 |
| 20 | | | | | 40,630 |

Exhibit 8-3 is an example of the type of salary schedule found in many school districts. There are five grades that correspond to the academic requirement necessary for placement in each grade. The grades progress from the *bachelor's degree* level through to the *doctoral degree* grade. The steps in each grade are listed on the left side of the schedule. Those teachers in grade 1 could receive a step increase with satisfactory performance up through ten steps. At that point, they would not receive a step increase until they acquired fifteen graduate hours of additional education in their subject area and, at that time, would move to step 11 in grade 2. Therefore, this method encourages teachers to upgrade their knowledge and skills. Such is the case with all grades. There are two grades that have experience requirements in addition to the academic ones. The *master's degree* grade also requires two years of successful teaching experience, and the *doctoral degree* grade requires three years. Thus, if a person pursued a master's degree or doctoral degree on a full-time basis without experience in teaching, upon employment, he or she would be placed in the preceding grade until completing the successful teaching requirement.

Exhibit 8-4 indicates the percent of increase between categories and steps. Such a salary schedule is commonly referred to as an *index system*. The designation *incremental system* refers to those salary schedules that have an equal dollar amount between grades and steps. For example, there might be $1000 difference between grades and a $500 difference between steps.

### Administrator Salary Plan [13]

Creating a salary plan for administrators is a very difficult task because the responsibilities of administrators are so diverse and so pervasive. The decisions of administrators can effect the education of hundreds and even thousands of students in addition to the working conditions of teachers and other staff members.

However, there is a gradation in position responsibilities that must be recognized as well as gradations in educational qualifications and experience. Finally, there is always a gradation in the quality of performance.

Appendix A contains a salary plan that incorporates two significant variables used in determining the appropriate salaries for various levels of administrators: position factors and incumbent factors. Position factors refer to supervisory, leadership, and administrative responsibilities. The incumbent factors are professional education and experience and the level of the administrator's performance.

EXHIBIT 8-4 • *Percent of Increase between Steps*

| Step | Index | Index | Index | Index | Index |
|------|-------|-------|-------|-------|-------|
| 1 | 1.0000 | 1.0450 | | 1.0900 | |
| 2 | 1.0450 | 1.0900 | | 1.1550 | |
| 3 | 1.0900 | 1.1350 | 1.1575 | 1.2200 | |
| 4 | 1.1350 | 1.1800 | 1.2025 | 1.2850 | 1.3300 |
| 5 | 1.1800 | 1.2250 | 1.2475 | 1.3500 | 1.3950 |
| 6 | 1.2250 | 1.2700 | 1.2925 | 1.4150 | 1.4600 |
| 7 | 1.2700 | 1.3150 | 1.3375 | 1.4800 | 1.5250 |
| 8 | 1.3150 | 1.3600 | 1.3825 | 1.5450 | 1.5900 |
| 9 | 1.3600 | 1.4050 | 1.4275 | 1.6100 | 1.6550 |
| 10 | 1.4050 | 1.4500 | 1.4725 | 1.6750 | 1.7200 |
| 11 | | 1.4950 | 1.5175 | 1.7400 | 1.7850 |
| 12 | | | 1.5625 | 1.8050 | 1.8500 |
| 13 | | | | 1.8700 | 1.9150 |
| 14 | | | | | 2.0000 |
| 15 | | | | | 2.0650 |
| 16 | | | | | 2.1300 |
| 17 | | | | | 2.1950 |
| 18 | | | | | 2.2600 |
| 19 | | | | | 2.3250 |
| 20 | | | | | 2.3900 |

This plan incorporates the essential components that should be present in every administrator salary plan. Too often school districts tie administrator salaries to teacher salaries by either giving them the same percentage of increase or by using a factor that in reality is only the extension of teacher salaries to ten or twelve months, which are the periods of time most administrators work. Thus, administrators might receive more dollars than teachers but the real differences in responsibilities are not identified.

## Classified Wages

For classified salaries, it is more effective to designate job families based on similarity in duties, responsibilities, and qualifications. From time to time, it will be necessary to reevaluate a position in order to determine if it is properly categorized. An example of a family of jobs is the designation, *secretarial-clerical personnel.*

However, not all secretaries and clerical personnel have exactly the same working situation. Therefore, a salary schedule for this designation could be constructed with grades that discriminate between the various working situations. The highest grade could be reserved for executive secretaries who work for the superintendent and assistant superintendents. Another grade could be assigned to building secretarial positions and the lowest grade might be for those in word-processing positions.

Another example of a job family designating personnel working in pupil transportation could be *transportation management personnel*. The various grades in this classification could be for the director of transportation, supervisor of drivers, and mechanic foreman.

As in the case with teacher salary schedules, each grade would have a number of steps. An employee would progress to higher steps through performance evaluations. Similar to teacher salary schedules, there would be a cap on each grade in relation to the number of steps that an employee can attain. For example, an employee in word processing could receive a starting wage of $5 per hour and move through ten additional steps to receive a maximum for that position of $10 per hour. Advancement to a high grade would depend on that person being promoted to a more responsible position. For example, promotion to a building level secretarial position would depend on a person's ability to interact with students, parents, other staff members, and visitors. Because of this additional human relations ability, the schedule might begin on step 1 with a wage of $7 per hour and progress through ten additional steps to receive a maximum for that position of $17 per hour.

### Salary and Wage Review

Approximately 80 percent of school-district budgets is spent on salaries and wages. Consequently, salary and wage review is an essential component of salary and wage administration. Some school districts attempt to *continually* review salaries and wages. These districts usually assess salaries and wages against some type of cost-of-living index. A major problem with such measures as the *consumer price index* is that it is an average and the cost-of-living in a given community may be higher or lower than the average reported. Under a continual salary and wage review process, adjustments are automatically made on salary schedules as the selected cost-of-living indicator changes. Such a process merely adjusts the base salary or wage of all employees. Performance increases are an added component to setting salary and wages for the following fiscal year. In most business and industrial situations, automatic adjustments in salaries and wages are made as the indicator changes. This is usually not the case in education. Rather, the base salary and wage is applied at the employee's yearly anniversary date or, as in the case of teachers and administrators, when their contract is renewed.

The second most prevalent process for reviewing salaries and wages occurs through a yearly review of the salaries and wages paid by other school districts, public agencies, and private business and industry in the community. The adjustments may or may not be in keeping with a recognized cost-of-living indicator but, rather, the local community becomes the appropriate measure. In like manner, performance increases must be applied separately from such adjustments.

Finally, some school districts gather data from individual employees concerning their responsibilities, the tasks they perform, and their qualifications. The data can be analyzed and used to establish salaries as part of an annual review process. The data also provide a vehicle for reevaluating jobs to ascertain if they are properly assigned to the appropriate salary schedule and in the correct range. Appendix B illustrates an employee questionnaire that can be used for this position analysis. It contains samples of job evaluation forms. The use of this questionnaire and the evaluation forms is predicated on a procedure that utilizes a salary review committee.

The decision of school districts concerning salaries and wages must always be tempered by the constraints of the budget. School districts are financed primarily through tax revenue which is usually not received on a consistent monthly basis but rather, as taxes are collected. Also, in most states, taxes can be raised to meet higher costs only by voter approval, whereas in the private sector, the price of an item can be raised at any time to offset costs.

## Payroll Deductions and Pay Periods

Making payroll deductions is such a common practice that most employees take it for granted. However, there are significant legal consequences to making such deductions. Thus, the board of education should create a payroll deduction policy covering such areas as the number and types of deductions authorized, and the opening and closing dates for entering deductions on the payroll records.

Of course, no payroll deduction should be initiated without written authorization from the employee unless authorized by law or the courts. Exhibit 8-5 is a description of the most common payroll deductions.

**EXHIBIT 8-5** • *Common Payroll Deductions*

---

I. *Income-tax deductions* Government income-tax legislation requires each employee to execute a certificate of exemptions to be used as a basis for calculating income deductions. In most instances the certificate will provide the following information:

A. *Full name* It is recommended that it be typed or printed for legibility. In the case of married women, use first name, maiden name, and last name.

B. *Employee account number* This is needed for identification on payroll tax returns as well as for employee record cards. All employees should be required to show their account card and also to copy the name as it appears on the card. The existing U.S. Income Tax Regulations require a social security (FICA) account number for all employees subject to withholding taxes. If an employee has not filed an account number, he or she should be advised to fill out an application form and send it to the nearest district office of the U.S. Social Security Administration. Forms to obtain lost account cards are also available at the same office.

C. *Home address* Print or type this information, including city, state or province, and other identifying postal information.

D. *Claim for withholding exemptions* The school district must allow exemptions to each employee on the basis of the withholding certificate. If an employee fails to furnish a certificate, the school district is required to withhold tax if the employee has claimed no withholding exemptions. A certificate filed by a new employee is to be made effective upon the first payment of salary. Once filed with the school district, a withholding exemption certificate will remain in effect until an amended certificate is furnished.

The following classifications of exemption are usually considered:

A. *Single* This refers to persons not married and who desire to claim one exemption. A mark, number, or other designation is made on the form of this claim for exemption.

B. *Married* This classification allows one exemption each for husband and wife if not claimed on another certificate. If claim is made for both exemptions, then an indication is inserted on the certificate; if one of the exemptions is claimed, or no exemptions are claimed, this is also indicated on the form.

C. *Other exemptions* This classification covers such exemptions as:
1. Age (over 65)
2. Blindness
3. Other relatives who qualify as dependents

Employees may file an amended exemption certificate, increasing the number of exemptions, at any time. Normally the deductions are reflected in the next payment of wages.

School districts will usually find it convenient to determine the amount of income tax required to be withheld from wage bracket tables. Government agencies provide these tables free of charge. Commercial tax tables may also be purchased from office supply, professional accountants' organizations, and suppliers of tax services. Tax tables are available for various pay periods: weekly, bi-weekly, semi-monthly, monthly, daily, or miscellaneous periods.

In addition to making payroll withholding as specified by Internal Revenue Service tax tables, a percentage method may be used. Additional amounts may be withheld under a written agreement between the school district and the employee. This agreement will be effective for such periods as may be mutually agreed upon.

The school district usually is assigned a reporting number for purposes of transmitting and accounting for payroll taxes deducted. Returns are usually rendered monthly or quarterly, and an annual reconciliation is required.

Some cities or local government units require collection of an occupational license or payroll tax. The law serves as the basis for the deduction and no authorizing action is required of the employee. In most instances, this tax is based on a percentage of gross salary, with no provision for exemptions.

The same employer reporting is required as mentioned above.

II. *Retirement deductions* These deductions usually come under one of three classifications: a government retirement plan for all employees; a program specifically limited to certificated or non-certificated personnel; or a commercial underwriting program. Some school districts may permit certificated employees to participate in all three plans or only one plan. This is usually determined by the school board or a governing board or bylaw. Deductions are usually based on a fixed percentage of gross salary.

III. *Court-ordered deductions* The problems of deductions relative to garnishments, bankruptcies, levies, and other deductions of this nature are sometimes vexing to school districts. Employees should be encouraged to keep their personal financial affairs in sufficient order to prevent this type of action. . . . Of course, the employee should be given every opportunity to rectify the situation if it is an oversight or an honest error on the debtor's part.

In determining this deduction, care must be taken to note the following important information:

A. Name of plaintiff or debtor
B. Date of garnishment served and received by the school district
C. Amount of garnishment
D. Court costs—advisable to verify with court
E. Amount of pay due as of date of garnishment
F. Number of days permitted to answer the garnishment

A copy of the garnishment or order should be ent to the employee for his  or her information. It is possible that a form titled *release* may be obtained by the employee which will alter the sum of money to be deducted from his salary. In no instance, should the school district accept the word of the plaintiff's or defendant's attorney, or the debtor, relative to a reduction in the principal amount of the debt unless a written form is furnished by the court responsible for the original garnishment order.

At this time, it is appropriate to stress these four points:

A. Recover the amount required by the court up to the date of the garnishment. If the salary earned is not sufficient to take care of indebtedness, there is a possibility that a subsequent garnishment will be initiated.

    B. File with court the necessary answer, within the specified time permitted. Deduction check should be made payable to the court.

    C. Always advise employees of the garnishment and give them every opportunity to clear the matter up prior to actual deduction.

    D. Establish a policy relative to the number of garnishments permitted and acquaint all employees of the policy requirements.

IV. *Miscellaneous deductions* The preceding paragraphs have dealt with deductions that are mandatory in nature and which are based on government regulations or court orders. Reference has been made to the control of deductions through an approved policy of the school district. In this connection, surveys of other school-district deduction policies may be made to assist in development of the individual district policy.

The deductions discussed in the ensuing paragraphs are on a voluntary basis, and are usually identified as fringe benefits. The types of deductions are varied in scope. However, only a few will be presented here to be used for guidance and direction.

    A. *Health, accident, and hospital plans* These deductions are based on a predetermined premium made by the underwriting company. Rates are based on the type of coverage desired by the employee—the more coverage desired the higher the premium. A part of the premium may or may not be paid by the school district depending upon the policy of the board along with applicable state laws. Some school districts may pay all of the premiums. In most instances, an applications form is required of the employee in which personal information as well as family health history is indicated. A deduction authorization form should also be signed by the employee and may or may not be included as a part of the application form. Group insurance certificates or individual policies are usually issued to the employee and confirm the coverage authorized on the deduction form.

    B. *Life insurance plans* These deductions generally follow the same outline as the plan for health, accident, and hospitalization. Many retirement plans now include life insurance as a part of their comprehensive program.

    C. *Employment association dues* Deductions for association dues are becoming increasingly popular among school districts. These include such deductions as local unit, state, or province association dues which may be paid in one or more installments out of the salary of the employee. Many associations also provide for other deductions as a part of their overall program. This could include a life insurance program, disability income protection, and personal liability insurance.

    D. *Credit union* This is becoming a more popular deduction for school district employees. The credit union has as its major purpose the encouragement of savings as well as the providing of a source of financial assistance. It is suggested that the deduction authorization form be worded in such a way that the deduction amount will not be identified as to whether it is a savings or loan payment. The treasurer of the credit union should determine the monthly amount to be paid or the savings desired and secure the signed authorization for payroll

records. Many credit unions pay for deduction service on the basis of
the number of accounts serviced.

E. *Community fund contributions* Considerable pressure is exerted on the
school districts to participate in various solicitations for the welfare of
the underprivileged in the community. Many localities have combined
all the campaigns into one, on an annual basis. It is emphasized that
every attempt be made to combine these appeals into one amount for
deduction purposes. A signed deduction form should be obtained
which would indicate the amount to be deducted, and the period
covered.

*Source*: John L. Ramsey, "Payroll Deductions" in Foster, *Wage and Salary Administration*, pp. 47–
51. Modified for this presentation.

The complexity of multiple deductions for large numbers of
employees has mandated computerization of payroll management in many
school districts which, in turn, has increased the importance of deadlines.
This situation has created an issue for school districts centered on the
number of appropriate pay periods. The basic principles for determining
the number of pay periods are the category of work performed, the amount
earned, and the cost to the school district.

Different employees have different expectations about how often they
should be paid. Custodians, bus drivers, and cafeteria workers are
accustomed to being paid on a weekly basis. These employees usually need
their money more often than skilled employees, administrators, and
teachers whose salaries and wages are higher. Skilled employees such as
plumbers, electricians, and carpenters generally receive higher wages than
unskilled workers and are accustomed to being paid on a monthly or bi-
weekly basis. Finally, professional employees, such as administrators and
teachers, are usually paid on a monthly basis.

Some school districts, by policy, allow teachers to be paid in either
nine or twelve payments, at the discretion of the individual teacher. This
same situation is true for building principals who work ten months but may
be paid in twelve payments.

The size of the school district will determine the complexity of the
payroll process. In larger school districts, of course, more people are
employed, and that usually increases the number of job classifications
having different payroll periods. This will demand more computerization
as well as more rigid deadlines and inflexible procedures for handling the
payroll. More payroll personnel specialists and equipment will also be
needed which will increase the school district's cost in managing the
payroll process.

Finally, there are a few comments that need to be made in order to
complete this section on direct compensation. First, executive salaries are

usually negotiated on an individual basis and do not fall within the limits of a salary schedule. The executive positions in school districts are relatively few and commonly pertain to the superintendent and associate or assistant superintendents.

Second, it is very important to consider each salary schedule as a separate entity. In some school districts, increases to teacher salary schedules are reflected by the same or nearly the same amount or percentage being applied to administrator schedules. This nullifies the integrity of salary schedules and defeats the objectives of salary and wage administration as set forth in this chapter.

When the process of collective negotiations is involved, such a tied-in approach also violates the distinction between management and labor. If an administrator salary schedule is affected by an increase to the teacher salary schedule resulting from collective negotiations, the administrators are in fact being represented by the teachers' bargaining agent.

Third, extra pay for extra duty, which is the common language applied to overtime pay for instructional personnel, should be determined by the same procedure used to establish regular salaries and wages. The rewards for performance and competitiveness are also primary considerations in establishing overtime pay.

## Indirect Compensation: Fringe Benefit Administration

The designation *fringe benefit* is most appropriate in describing indirect compensation because the word *fringe* indicates something that is related but not in a central position. Thus, salaries and wages are direct compensation because they are the primary vehicle for purchasing the services of employees and for rewarding employees.

Usually, fringe benefits are not contingent upon performance, and they are not motivators in the sense described earlier but, rather, are factors that affect the recruitment and retention of employees. Thus, fringe benefits are an important part of an effective compensation program. Retirement insurance, medical and hospitalization insurance, annuities, and life insurance are only a few of the many fringe benefits offered to employees in school districts across the country.

High employee turnover can cost a school district thousands of dollars each year in costs related to the recruitment and selection of personnel. Further, absenteeism also can cost a school district thousands of dollars each year. High employee turnover and absenteeism have an impact on the instructional program by creating a negative effect upon students. This effect cannot be measured in terms of dollars.

The key factor in addressing high employee turnover and absenteeism is to develop a positive approach. Attracting individuals with excellent credentials and a desire for excellence in performance will ultimately correct high turnover and absenteeism. Quality fringe benefits attract quality candidates for positions and will maintain employee commitment to the school district.

## Types of Fringe Benefits

Inflation continually eats away at real salaries and wages, which is the reason for the rapid growth in direct compensation over the last ten-year period. That same period has produced a significant increase in fringe benefits offered to employees of public school districts. The prediction made by John Sullivan has come to pass. The cost of fringe benefits has risen to approximately 35 percent of the total salaries and wages paid to employees.[14]

When school districts across the country experience financial difficulties, these districts have found that fringe benefit enrichment is an alternative when significant salary and wage increases are not feasible. Conversely, as more school districts develop elaborate fringe benefit programs, greater pressure has been placed on competing school districts to develop similar programs in order to attract and keep employees.

Another reason for the expansion of fringe benefits is that they are not taxable. If a teacher wants a certain amount of life insurance, there are two advantages in having it purchased by the school districts. First, the premium will be lower because the school district will be purchasing a large amount of protection. Second, the teacher would pay the premium for the insurance out of his or her net pay which is the dollar amount remaining after deducting taxes. If the school district pays the premium, the teacher has more money left to pay for other needs and, therefore, this becomes an attractive fringe benefit.

There is a caveat. Internal Revenue Code Section 89, which is part of the Tax Reform Act of 1986, became effective as of January 1, 1989. The purpose of Section 89 is to prevent discrimination by an employer in favor of highly compensated employees. In other words, all other employees, except the highly compensated, would be discriminated against.

If an employer does discriminate in this manner, the value of the plan can become part of the taxable income of the highly compensated employees and, in some cases, of all employees. In order for a plan not to be deemed taxable, it must meet the following requirements: (1) the plan must be set forth in writing; (2) it must be legally enforceable; (3) it must be for exclusive benefit of the employees; (4) it must be intended to be permanent; and (5) it must be communicated to the employees.

## Benefits Required by Law[15]

Certain benefits must be provided by the school district: social security premium payments, state retirement insurance, unemployment compensation, and worker's compensation. These benefits provide the employee with financial security and protection at retirement or termination or when an injury occurs in the workplace. They also provide survivors' benefits to dependents in the event of the employee's death.

The social security program usually covers classified employees. Instructional and administrative personnel are normally included in state retirement programs. Social security is the major source of income for America's retirees. This program is financed by the contributions of employees which are matched by the employer and computed as a percentage of the employee's earnings. Survivors' benefits for the dependents of a deceased employee and disability benefits for an employee who is unable to be gainfully employed are provided through the Social Security Administration.

The Social Security Act is an important aspect of the U.S. Government's attempt to care for and protect the aged by ensuring for them a minimal standard of living. Although social security is often referred to as an *insurance* program, this is a misnomer. Rather, it is a transfer program of a trust fund from one generation to another. The currently employed pay a social security tax that is used to support retired workers, dependents, and the disabled. It is important to remember that social security benefits and the program itself are subject to legislation. Thus, changes are certain to occur and must be continually monitored in order to ensure that adequate budgetary appropriations are available to meet future demands.

Unemployment compensation laws in most states provide benefits to individuals who are without a job. To qualify for these benefits, a person must usually submit an application to the state employment agency for unemployment benefits and must register with that agency for available work with a willingness to accept suitable employment offered through the agency. In addition, the person must have worked a minimum number of weeks before becoming unemployed.

Unemployment benefits are derived from a tax levied against employers calculated on a percentage of the employer's total salary and wage payroll. Benefits received by unemployed workers are calculated from the individual's previous salary or wage rate plus the length of previous employment. Unemployment benefits are provided on a limited basis, typically for a twenty-six-week period. Unemployment compensation also serves the total economy of our nation because it provides a stability in spending power during periods of high unemployment.

Worker's compensation programs provide benefits to individuals injured or disabled while engaged in a job-related activity. Benefits paid to employees for injuries are based on schedules for minimum and maximum payments, depending on the type of injury sustained. For example, the loss of a hand is compensated with a higher dollar amount than the loss of a finger. Disability payments are calculated in a like manner based on a consideration of the individual's current salary, future earnings, and financial responsibilities.

The funds for worker's compensation programs are borne entirely by the employer. While the programs are mandated by state laws, the method of obtaining worker's compensation insurance is usually left to the discretion of the employer who may buy such protection from public or private agencies or provide the protection through a self-insuring program. Like social security and unemployment insurance, worker's compensation is subject to the legislative process. Thus, requirements and benefits will certainly change with the passage of time.

Where mandated by state law, a retirement program for school-district employees generally follows the prescriptions of other protection programs. Contributions are made by the employee and are calculated on the basis of the employee's salary or wage. These contributions are usually matched by the school district. Benefits based on contributions are paid upon retirement, with survivors' benefits being available for the dependents of deceased employees.

## Voluntary Fringe Benefits

This category of benefits can be further divided into insurance programs, time away from the job, and services. Group insurance programs are available for almost every human need. Among the most common are major medical and hospitalization insurance, dental insurance, term life insurance, errors and omissions insurance, optical insurance, and annuities. The number of such programs made available to employees depends on the fiscal condition of the school district and the wishes of the employees. A school district is usually restricted by state statute to paying insurance premiums only for employees. Therefore, if an employee wishes to include dependents under such insurance programs, he or she must pay the additional premium for this coverage.

Under federal law and Internal Revenue Service regulations, school districts can design "cafeteria" fringe benefit plans that allow individual employees to choose the benefits that most meet their needs. In addition, if the employee is to bear the cost of some of these programs, the premiums can be deducted from his or her gross salary or wage before federal income taxes are levied.

This tax advantage for employees and the opportunity to choose their benefits from a predetermined list are two reasons why such programs are most desirable. The administrative expense of such a program and the availability of insurance coverage that does not demand a high percent of participation are problems. For example, a company may offer a dental insurance program to a school district only if 60 percent of its employees participate.

Federal law also requires that school districts offer a federally qualified health maintenance organization (HMO) plan if at least 25 employees are currently provided health insurance coverage. The district is exempt, of course, if it is not located in the service area of a federally qualified HMO.

There are three types of HMOs: group model, staff model, and individual practice associations. In a group model, a group or groups of physicians provide care to patients at one or more locations. In a staff model, physicians are employed by an HMO and provide services at one or more locations. In an individual practice associations model, an HMO contracts with physicians who practice out of their own offices. The federal law is satisfied by offering one of each type of HMO that has an approved service area in which the district is located. If there are more than one of each type, the school district may choose the one that will best serve the employees. However, the district may make available more than one type.

A fringe benefit that is often taken for granted by employees but creates an additional expense to a school district is paid time away from work. Therefore, sick leave, vacation time, holidays, and sabbatical leave are, in fact, fringe benefits provided at the discretion of the school district.

Corporations have long recognized the value of *services* in a fringe benefit program. Social and recreational events, employee assistance programs, wellness programs, cultural activities, credit unions, company cafeterias, tuition reimbursements, and child care centers are only a few of the services found in many large corporations. Such benefits are becoming more available in school districts.

Service benefits commonly found in school districts are expenses paid for attendance at workshops, professional meetings, and conventions.

Obviously, fringe benefits are an important component of all compensation programs, and they are becoming even more important as alternatives to large salary and wage increases.

## Summary

There are five variables that must be taken into consideration in a rewards program: employee performance, employee effort, seniority, employee skills, and job requirements. The rewarding of performance, however, must be the primary objective of a rewards program.

An effective program must include both intrinsic and extrinsic rewards. Intrinsic rewards are those that pertain to the quality of the job situation. Extrinsic rewards are divided into direct and indirect compensation. Direct compensation is referred to as *salary* or *wage* and indirect compensation is frequently referred to as *fringe benefits*.

There are many influences that affect salary and wage programs in school districts among which are the following: state and federal laws; collectively bargained agreements; and the pay rates in private, not-for-profit, and public sectors.

A master contract will contain either the method for determining salaries and wages or the actual salaries and wages that will be paid to the members of the bargaining unit covered by the contract. However, whether salaries and wages are collectively bargained or determined by some other process, the problem of comparability will surely arise. Thus, school-district administrators must continually gather data on the salaries and wages that are paid by neighboring school districts and other public, not-for-profit, private employers in the local community, region, and state.

Direct compensation, salary and wage, can be effectively administered only if the following principles are incorporated into the pay policy: skills required in various positions must be recognized; salaries and wages must be competitive; the primary focus of salary and wage increases must be improved performance; and salary schedules must be reviewed annually.

An important question central to all pay policies is, "Does money motivate?" A reasonable conclusion, supported by experience and research, is that money does affect performance if it is clear that performance is rewarded by a salary or wage increase.

There are five considerations that should be incorporated into every salary and wage program: position evaluation, comparability, equitability, annual program review, and performance incentives.

There are a number of other issues in salary and wage management that must command the attention of education administrators. These issues will have an effect on pay policy development. The issues are public disclosure of salaries and wages, equity of pay, techniques for collecting community salary and wage data, payroll deductions, pay periods, employee relations in salary and wage management, annual salary and wage review, salary and wage program development.

The U.S. Congress enacted the Equal Pay Act in 1963, which requires employers to pay males and females the same salary or wage for equal work. This act is part of the Fair Labor Standards Act and protects employees who work for an employer engaged in an enterprise affected by interstate commerce. The interpretation of *equal work* has been broadly defined to mean "substantially" equal and, thus, strict equality of jobs is not required.

In public education, it has been traditional to use salary schedules as the primary method for establishing teacher salaries. Such schedules are usually divided into a number of grades, each with several step rates.

Indirect compensation, fringe benefits, can help a school district to attract and retain good employees. Certain fringe benefits are required by law. These include social security, state retirement programs, unemployment insurance, and worker's compensation.

Voluntary fringe benefits may be divided into insurance programs, time away from the job, and services. Group insurance programs are available for almost every human need and include medical and hospitalization insurance, dental insurance, term life insurance, errors and omissions insurance, and optical insurance.

A fringe benefit often taken for granted by employees is paid time away from the job such as sick leave, vacation time, holidays, and sabbatical leave. In like manner, certain services offered by school districts are in reality fringe benefits. These include expenses paid for attendance at workshops, professional meetings, and conventions, and tuition reimbursement.

Fringe benefits, as an alternative to large salary and wage increases, will continue to play a significant role in compensating employees.

## Appendix A  Administrator Salary Plan[16]

### The Philosophy

This salary plan has been developed with the following general concepts in mind:

1. The plan should attract and retain the most competent administrative staff possible.
2. All district administrative personnel should be included in the salary structure.

3.  The salary structure should include an individual performance factor.
4.  Levels of responsibility should be taken into account in the salary structure.
5.  The salary structure should set forth a salary range for any given position.
6.  The salary structure should minimize compression between positions and contain factors to eliminate compression where it previously existed.
7.  The salary structure should include qualifications necessary for any given position, i.e., academic preparation, certification, and experience.
8.  The salary structure should take into account areas of special knowledge or preparation not covered by certification or college preparation.
9.  The salary structure should be responsive to the current state of the economy and its impact on the buying power of personnel under the plan.
10. The salary structure should be simple to compute and easy to understand.

The salary plan is based upon the above concepts. These concepts are generally principles which forward-looking private- and public-sector organizations consider foundations for administrative salary plans.

## The Plan

The salary plan consists of two factors. First, the position factor is determined entirely from the nature of the particular administrative position. This position factor changes only when the job responsibilities are changed. The position factor is composed of the following subfactors.

1.  *Supervisory responsibility* This factor refers to the following:
    a.  number of persons over whom the administrator exercises supervisory responsibility
    b.  closeness of supervision or degree of independence of those supervised
    c.  nature and difficulty of work performed by persons being supervised
2.  *Leadership responsibility* This factor refers to the following:
    a.  participation in policy and program determination
    b.  extent and nature of public contacts
    c.  independence of action in significant functions which are performed
3.  *Administrative responsibility* This factor refers to the following:
    a.  number, variety, and complexity of administrative functions for which the person is responsible
    b.  breadth of work knowledge required to appraise and make decisions with respect to administration functions
    c.  depth of work knowledge required to appraise and make decisions with respect to administrative functions performed
4.  *Conditions of employment* This factor refers to the following:
    a.  length of work year
    b.  length and nature of work week taking into account the number and regularity of working hours

*Normative Minimum Administrator Salary: $35,000*

Position Factors

| | |
|---|---|
| Elementary school principal | 1.00 |
| Middle school assistant principal | 1.04 |
| High school grade grincipal | 1.08 |
| Director of buildings and grounds | 1.06 |
| Middle school principal | 1.12 |
| High school principal | 1.20 |
| Assistant superintendent | 1.26 |
| Associate superintendent | 1.28 |

Incumbent Factors

Professional education

| | |
|---|---|
| masters + 30 hours | .02 |
| masters + 60 hours | .04 |
| doctorate | .06 |
| Quality of performance | .00–.09 |

Professional Administrative Experience

| | | |
|---|---|---|
| 1 yr. = .00 | 11 yrs. = .135 | 21 yrs. = .185 |
| 2 yrs. = .02 | 12 yrs. = .14 | 22 yrs. = .19 |
| 3 yrs. = .04 | 13 yrs. = .145 | 23 yrs. = .195 |
| 4 yrs. = .06 | 14 yrs. = .15 | 24 yrs. = .20 |
| 5 yrs. = .08 | 15 yrs. = .155 | 25 yrs. = .205 |
| 6 yrs. = .09 | 16 yrs. = .16 | 26 yrs. = .21 |
| 7 yrs. = .10 | 17 yrs. = .165 | 27 yrs. = .215 |
| 8 yrs. = .11 | 18 yrs. = .17 | 28 yrs. = .22 |
| 9 yrs. = .12 | 19 yrs. = .175 | 29 yrs. = .225 |
| 10 yrs. = .13 | 20 yrs. = .18 | 30 yrs. = .23 |

The second factor is the incumbent factor which is determined entirely from the qualifications and performance of the person in the job. The incumbent factor changes only when the incumbent changes or when the qualifications or performance of the incumbent change. The incumbent factor is composed of the following subfactors:

1. Professional education held by the incumbent. This factor refers to the scope of formal professional study in preparation for this position.

2. Professional experience of the incumbent. This factor refers to the length and nature of administrative experience in this school district.

3. Performance of the incumbent. This factor refers to the quality of services performed. This is the only factor which depends upon substantially subjective judgment.

The position and incumbent factors are assigned numerical values and then combined to produce an overall index of salary for an individual administrator. This index is then multiplied by a normative minimum administrative salary. This minimum salary would be considered for adjustment annually to reflect changes due to inflation, changes in the district's revenues, changes in the going rate for administrators in comparable districts in the area, and other variables.

## Administrative Salary Ranges

The salary plan provides for a minimum salary for each position as well as a maximum salary. It is expected that all salaries will fall within the position range; however, the plan does permit 15 percent of the administrative staff to exceed the maximum salary level.

|  | *Low* | *High* |
|---|---|---|
| Elementary school principal | $35,000 | $45,000 |
| Middle school assistant principal | 36,000 | 46,000 |
| Director of buildings and grounds | 37,000 | 47,000 |
| High school grade principal | 38,000 | 48,000 |
| Middle school principal | 39,000 | 49,000 |
| High school principal | 40,000 | 50,000 |
| Assistant superintendent | 41,000 | 51,000 |
| Associate superintendent | 42,000 | 52,000 |

The following are examples of the calculations involved in determining the salary of two administrators.

*Example # 1*

| Middle school principal | 1.12 |
|---|---|
| Masters + 60 hours | .04 |
| Quality of performance | .05 |
| Administrative experience—5 years | .08 |
| Total index | 1.29 |
| Normative minimum salary | x 35,000 |
| Salary | $45,150 |

*Example # 2*

| | |
|---|---|
| Elementary principal | 1.00 |
| Masters + 30 hours | .02 |
| Quality of performance | .05 |
| Administrative experience —2 years | <u>.02</u> |
| Total index | 1.09 |
| Normative minimum salary | x 35,000 |
| Salary | $38,150 |

*Source*: Lindbergh School District, "Administrator Compensation Plan" (St. Louis: The District, 1983).

## Appendix B  Position Description Questionnaire

### Instructions to Employee

1. Please read through the entire questionnaire carefully to familiarize yourself with all questions asked.

2. Once you have read the questionnaire, then answer each question as carefully and completely as possible. If additional space is needed to answer any question, please indicate "over" and use the back side of the sheet. If the question asked does not apply to your position, please write "does not apply" or "not applicable" in the space provided. Only in this way can we be certain you have considered each question and you can be certain that you have not missed an important question.

3. When you have completed the questionnaire, return it to your department head or supervisor.

You are urged to use care and deliberation in the completion of the questionnaire. The information you provide in your replies will be one of a number of means used to develop an official description of your position.

When this questionnaire has been completed and reviewed by your supervisor or department head, it should be forwarded to the director of personnel. After a description has been written, the job evaluation committee of the school system will evaluate the position and recommend assignment to the appropriate salary classification.

### I.    General Information

1. Your full name: _____ Date: _____
                          (First) (Middle or Maiden) (Last)

2. Title of your position: _____

When appointed to this position: _____

3. To your knowledge, is this position ever referred to by another title? _____

4. To which major division is your position assigned? (e.g., division of business administration, division of school administration, division of instruction, and so on.) _____

5. To which specific unit (office, department, school) is your position assigned?
_____

6. Regular daily hours of work:     from _____ to _____

7. What is the position title and name of your immediate supervisor? (i.e., the person or persons who assign work to you regularly and to whom you report.)

| Title | Name |
| --- | --- |
| _____ | _____ |

8. If your immediate supervisor is someone outside of your department, what is the title and name of your department head? (If same person, write "same.")

| Title | Name |
| --- | --- |
| _____ | _____ |

9. What are the position titles and names of the persons whom you supervise directly? (i.e., the persons to whom you give work assignments and from whom you receive reports on work progress. If no one, write "none.")

| Titles | Department | Names |
| --- | --- | --- |
| _____ | _____ | _____ |
| _____ | _____ | _____ |

10. Which employees do you regularly train or instruct on the job?

| Position Title | *Frequency* | | | *Only New Employees* |
| --- | --- | --- | --- | --- |
| | Weekly | Monthly | Several Times a Year | Join Department |
| _____ | _____ | _____ | _____ | _____ |
| _____ | _____ | _____ | _____ | _____ |

11. To what position, or positions, within the school system would a person normally consider a logical promotion from your position? _____

12. What jobs or positions within the school system do you feel have responsibilities about equal to yours?

_____     _____

_____     _____

13. What position in the department, bureau, section, or office to which you are now assigned is the next most responsible position? _____

## II.  Assigned Functions and Responsibilities

1. What is the basic function or purpose of your position? (e.g., to provide typing assistance to the _____ department; to receive all persons entering building and direct them to desired office; to direct and coordinate the instructional program, and so on.)

_____

_____

2. What regular duties or assigned responsibilities do you perform in your position? (Please list all of the duties you can think of, and be as specific as possible, e.g., clean windows, prepare purchase requisitions; conduct staff conferences, and so on.) Indicate frequency of performance by code letters as follows:

Daily or several times weekly          Code "D"
Weekly                                 Code "W"
Monthly                                Code "M"
Occasionally during the year           Code "Y"

              Duties                                    Code

_____          _____

_____          _____

3. What machines requiring special skills do you use in your work?

_____

_Frequency (Check one.)_

_____

                    Continuously      Frequenly      Occasionally

_____    _____    _____    _____

_____    _____    _____    _____

4. What special non-machine skills do you use in your work? (e.g., shorthand, bookkeeping, creative writing, higher mathematics, and so on.)

*Frequency (Check one.)*

|  | Daily | Frequenly | Occasionally |
|---|---|---|---|
| _____ | _____ | _____ | _____ |
| _____ | _____ | _____ | _____ |

5. What grade level of education did you complete? (Check one.)

| 8th grade (or below) | _____ | 1 yr. college | _____ |
|---|---|---|---|
| 9th grade | _____ | 2 yrs. college | _____ |
| 10th grade | _____ | 3 yrs. college | _____ |
| 11th grade | _____ | 4 yrs. college | _____ |
| 12th grade | _____ | 5 yrs. college | _____ |
| or equivalent to above grade | | 6 yrs. college | _____ |
| checked in special courses | _____ | 7 yrs. college | _____ |

Up to

| 1 year special courses after high school | _____ |
|---|---|
| 2 years special courses after high school | _____ |
| 3 years special courses after high school | _____ |
| 4 years special courses after high school | _____ |

6. If you have completed a college or university program, what degree(s) did you earn and in what major subject area?

_____

_____

7. Have you taken other courses, not covered above, to enable you to qualify for your present position or another position in the school system? (Please explain type of course, length, etc.).

_____

_____

8. Is accuracy or working within close precision limits a requirement of your job? *Yes or no.* If yes, which of the following would best describe the effect of errors you might make?

_____ Errors would be corrected early and would not be significant.

_____ Errors might involve small losses of money. Corrections can be made with minor inconvenience to other employees or supervisor.

_____ Errors might involve significant losses of money or would cause considerable delay, confusion, or bad public relations. Can be corrected but with loss of time and expense.

_____ Errors would seriously hamper financial operations of school systems or involve loss of prestige of school board. Difficult and costly to correct.

## III.  Details Concerning Responsibilities

1. For what specific activities, programs, and/or services do you have responsibilities for formulating objectives and goals? (Please list.)

_____

_____

2. What is the extent of your responsibilities for objectives? (e.g., formulate and recommend to department head; recommend to school board; establish, and so on.)

_____

_____

3. Which of the following statements best describes your responsibilities relative to objectives and goals for your program or service? (Check one.)

_____ None

_____ Opinions are sometimes requested

_____ Opinions are regularly requested

_____ Formulate and recommend objectives to supervisor or department head

_____ Formulate objectives for department, program, or service and recommend to division head

_____ Formulate objectives for division and recommend to superintendent

_____ Formulate objectives for school system

_____ Other (Specify)_____

_____

4. For which specific programs and/or services do you have responsibilities for analyzing requirements and whose requirements are analyzed for each? (e.g., purchasing and warehousing for all schools and services.)

_____

_____

5. For which department, programs, and/or services are you responsible for planning the organization, staffing, facilities, or finance? (List and describe your planning responsibilities.)

_____

_____

6. For which specific programs and/or services do you have responsibilities for evaluating effectiveness and results?

_____

_____

7. Which of the following statements best describes your responsibilities for evaluating the results of programs and/or services? (Check one.)

_____   None

_____   Opinions may be requested

_____   Opinions are regularly requested

_____   Participate in evaluation regularly with supervisor or department head

_____   Responsible for evaluation

_____   Other (Specify)_____

_____

8. For which specific activities, programs, and services do you have responsibility for developing and evaluating plans of organization?

_____

_____

9. Approximately how many staff members are included in the plans of organization that you develop and evaluate?

_____

10. If you have supervisory responsibilities, what is the nature of the tasks performed by the majority of the persons you directly or indirectly supervise?

_____   Repetitive tasks

_____   Semi-routine tasks of moderate complexity but not of a highly professional or technical nature

_____   Activities of a highly technical or professional nature

_____   Other (Specify)_____

11. For what specific activities, programs, and/or services do you have staff recruitment and/or selection responsibilities?

_____

_____

12. What type of responsibility do you have for facilities planning? (e.g., recommending amount and layouts of space)

_____

_____

13. What responsibility do you have for supervising the use of facilities and equipment? (e.g., supervising one office and office machines; supervising carpenter shop, saws, joiners, and so on.)

_____

_____

14. What responsibilities do you have for supervising the care and maintenance of buildings or equipment?

_____

_____

15. What kind of financial planning responsibilities do you have and for what programs or services? (e.g., estimating current costs, formulating budget, financial projections, and so on.)

_____

_____

16. What is the total amount of the annual budgets for which you have planning responsibility?

_____ None

_____ Less than $100,000

_____ $100,000 to $499,000

_____ $500,000 to $999,000

_____ $1,000,000 or over

Please explain: _____

_____

17. What responsibilities do you have for evaluating the management of finances; for which programs and/or services? (e.g., evaluating expenditures for maintenance or repairs; analyzing program costs, and so on.)

_____

_____

18. What is the total amount of annual expenditures for which you are responsible to evaluate financial management?

_____  None
_____  Less than $100,000
_____  $100,000 to $499,000
_____  $500,000 to $999,000
_____  $1,000,000 or over
        Please explain: _____

19. In performing your job, in what ways do you come into contact with the public, employees in other departments, other department heads, and so on? (Briefly describe.)

_____

_____

20. How would you characterize your contacts with the public, employees, and others, as you have described them? (Check one.)

_____  Little or no contact

_____  Requires only good manners, no pertinent communication

_____  Regular and frequent contact, manner and attitude important, but giving and receiving information not a principal requirement

_____  Includes giving and receiving information, requires ability to handle varied face-to-face situations

_____  A predominant feature of the job, necessitating a high degree of tact, courtesy, and ability to work effectively with individuals and groups

21. What responsibilities do you have for planning the external relations (including public relations) of your service, department, or program? (Please specify to the extent that you contribute to planning, are responsible for planning, or otherwise.)

_____

_____

22. With regard to all of your planning responsibilities, for what period of time are you usually concerned in making plans?

_____ Current academic or fiscal year

_____ Current and next academic or fiscal years

_____ Current and next 4 academic or fiscal years

_____ Current and next 10 or more academic or fiscal years

## IV.   Other Information

1.  Are there any other aspects of your responsibilities that are unusual and should be taken into account in evaluating your position?

_____

_____

2.  Are there any unique requirements not identified above that should be taken into account in establishing the qualifications of a person to fill the position you now occupy?

_____

_____

3.  How would you characterize general working conditions necessitated by the nature of your job?

_____ Work in normal temperatures, clean, comfortable surroundings—normal office conditions

_____ A few disagreeable conditions exist such as noise, congestion, drafts

_____ Several disagreeable conditions accompany the job such as: abnormal temperatures, humidity, excess noise, and dirt, offensive odors, and fumes

4.  Are there any personal hazards related to your job? (e.g., work on high ladders, use of sharp knives, electricity, and so on.)

_____

_____

## V.   Department or Supervisor's Section

(To be completed by immediate supervisor or department head.)

1.  I have read the staff members' responses to the attached questionnaire and believe they accurately reflect the duties, responsibilities, and characteristics of the position with the following exceptions:

_____

_____

2.  I believe the minimum educational requirement for this position should be:
(List grade completion such as 8th grade, 2–3 years high school, high school
graduation, A.B. degree, doctor's degree, and so on. Be realistic.)

_____

_____

3.  Which one of the following statements do you feel accurately describes the
general work schedule of this position?

_____  Normal work schedule, some gaps in the work cycle

_____  Little or no pressure

_____  Steadily paced with occasional pressure

_____  Frequent pressure of work with almost constant accumulation of tasks

_____  Very high and unusual pressure created by important decisions or frequent
emergency situations

_____
Signature, (Supervisor or Department Head)

**Score Sheet**
**Job Evaluation Committee No. 1**
**Office, Clerical and Manual Positions**

*Tally Sheet*

*Job Title* _____ *Department* _____ *Date* _____

| *Factors*<br><br>*Comittee* | *Technical Demands* | *Experience* | *Complexity* | *Accuracy* | *Supervision and Training* | *Independent action* | *Contacts* | *Mental effort* | *Physical effort* | *Working conditions* | *TOTAL* |
|---|---|---|---|---|---|---|---|---|---|---|---|
| | | | | | | | | | | | |
| | | | | | | | | | | | |
| | | | | | | | | | | | |
| | | | | | | | | | | | |
| | | | | | | | | | | | |

_____
(Signature of committee member)

Score Sheet
Job Evaluation Committee No. 2
Administrative and Professional Positions

*Tally Sheet*

*Job Title* _____ *Department* _____ *Date* _____

| Factors / Comittee | Planning responsibilities | Professional and technical demands | Supervision | Staffing | Facilities | Finance | External relations | Evaluating responsibilities | TOTAL |
|---|---|---|---|---|---|---|---|---|---|
|  |  |  |  |  |  |  |  |  |  |
|  |  |  |  |  |  |  |  |  |  |
|  |  |  |  |  |  |  |  |  |  |
|  |  |  |  |  |  |  |  |  |  |
|  |  |  |  |  |  |  |  |  |  |

_____
(Signature of committee member)

## Endnotes

1. Ronald W. Rebore, *Personnel Administration in Education: A Management Approach* (Englewood Cliffs, New Jersey: Prentice-Hall, Inc., 1987), p. 237.

2. *Ibid.*, p. 328.

3. *Ibid.*, pp. 244, 245.

4. Glen H. Tecker, *Merit, Measurement, and Money: Establishing Teacher Performance Evaluation and Incentive Programs* (Alexandria, Virginia: National School Boards Association, 1985), p. 14.

5. Rebore, *Personnel Administration*, pp. 245, 246.

6. *Wall Street Journal* (Highland), September 21, 1987, vol. LXVIII, no. 239, p. 25.

7. Steve Moore, "How To Set Up A Merit Pay Plan," *The School Administrator*, 43, no. 1 (January 1986), 18.

8. Rebore, *Personnel Administration*, pp. 246, 247.

9. *Ibid.*, pp. 249-251.

10. Data Research, Inc., *Deskbook Encyclopedia of American School Law* (Rosemount, Minnesota: Data Research, Inc., 1989), pp. 216-218.

11. "Incentive Pay Plans Full of Problems. . .," *Education USA*, Vol. 28, no. 32 (April 7, 1986), p. 248.

12. Paul D. Travers and Ronald W. Rebore, *Foundations of Education: Becoming a Teacher*, 2nd ed. (Englewood Cliffs, New Jersey: Prentice-Hall, Inc., 1990), pp. 307-309.

13. Ronald W. Rebore, *Educational Administration: A Management Approach* (Englewood Cliffs, New Jersey: Prentice-Hall, Inc., 1985), pp. 44, 45.

14. Educational Research Service, "Fringe Benefits: The Impact of Rising Costs and Increased Benefits on School Budgets," *SPECTRUM: Journal of School Research and Information*, Vol. 6, no. 4 (Fall 1988), pp. 24, 25.

15. Price Waterhouse, *Statutory Fringe Benefits* (New York, New York: Price Waterhouse, 1984), pp. 1-17.

16. Lindbergh School District, "Administrator Compensation Plan" (St. Louis: The District, 1983).

## Selected Bibliography

Educational Research Service, *Fringe Benefits for Administrators in Public Schools, Part 1* (Arlington, Virginia: Educational Research Service), 1988.

_____ , *Fringe Benefits for Teachers in Public Schools, Part 3* (Arlington, Virginia: Educational Research Service), 1988.

_____ , *Measuring Changes in Salaries and Wages in Public Schools* (Arlington, Virginia: Educational Research Service), 1989.

_____ , *Methods of Scheduling Salaries for Principals* (Arlington, Virginia: Educational Research Service), 1987.

_____ , *Salaries Paid Professional Personnel in Public Schools, 1988–89, Part 2* (Arlington, Virginia: Educational Research Service), 1989.

_____ , *Scheduled Salaries for Professional Personnel in Public Schools, 1988–89, Part 1* (Arlington, Virginia: Educational Research Service), 1989.

_____ , *Wages and Salaries Paid Support Personnel in Public Schools, 1988–89, Part 3* (Arlington, Virginia: Educational Research Service), 1989

Kienapfel, Bruce, *Merit Pay for School Administrators: A Procedural Guide* (Arlington, Virginia: Educational Research Service), 1984.

Moore, Steve, "How To Set Up A Merit Pay Plan," *The School Administrator*, Vol. 43, no. 1 (January 1986), pp. 15,18.

National School Boards Association, "Pay Equity: An Issue For The '80s," *UPDATING: School Board Policies*, Vol. 16, no. 7 (July–August 1985), pp. 1-3.

Price Waterhouse, *Statutory Fringe Benefits* (New York, New York: Price Waterhouse), 1984.

Robinson, Glen E., *Incentive Pay for Teachers: An Analysis of Approaches* (Arlington, Virginia: Educational Research Service), 1984.

_____ , *Paying Teachers for Performance and Productivity: Learning from Experience* (Arlington, Virginia: Educational Research Service), 1983.

Southern Regional Education Board, *More Pay for Teachers and Administrators Who Do More: Incentive Pay Programs* (Atlanta, Georgia: Southern Regional Education Board), 1987.

Tecker, Glenn H., *Merit, Measurement, and Money: Establishing Teacher Performance Evaluation and Incentive Programs* (Alexandria, Virginia: National School Boards Association), 1985.

Wright, Linus, "Incentive Pay: The Dallas Experience," *SPECTRUM: Journal of School Research and Information*, Vol. 4, no.1 (Winter 1986), pp. 3–8.

# 9

# Managing Ancillary Services

This chapter has four parts. The first part deals with buildings and grounds management; the second introduces the topic of pupil transportation management; the third treats food service management; and the fourth explains information management. No text in school business management would be complete without such discussions. However, these services are often overlooked and taken for granted, not only by graduate students but also by educators. Nevertheless, a disruption in the quality of these services usually brings an immediate response by everyone affected.

Buildings and grounds management receives a more detailed treatment in this chapter. It is a very complex function with issues that currently occupy the attention of many school boards and central office administrators. Space limitations prevent a similar treatment of pupil transportation, food service, and data processing management.

## Buildings and Grounds Management

The effect of school buildings and facilities on the learning-instructional process has received some attention by researchers. As may be surmised, the learning-instructional process is either enhanced or hindered by the physical environment where teaching occurs. Thus, the construction, remodeling, and maintenance of school facilities must be directed towards the mission of public school districts: to educate children and young people.

For example, we know that children have social needs that must be met via their educational experience if they are to be successful in school. A sense of belonging and companionship, therefore, must be developed. This cannot be accomplished if school facilities lack a variety of spaces for group activities. In recent years, the *commons* area, brightly decorated and comfortably furnished, has become one of the many popular architectural methods for addressing the social needs of students.

## Director of Buildings and Grounds[1]

This person should be responsible for the school district's physical plant and site program, which includes the formulation, recommendation, and administration of the school district's policies relating to facilities and their grounds.

Also, this director should be responsible for establishing effective two-way communication between the various organizational divisions of the school district. It is only through effective communication that the director will be able to administer the physical plant and site program. The director ultimately bears the brunt of criticism concerning proper maintenance of a boiler that breaks down in the dead of winter, resulting in the closing of a school until it is repaired. At such times the human relation skills of the director are most important.

The director of buildings and grounds reports to the assistant superintendent for business and financial services or another designated administrator or even the superintendent in a small school district. The director's immediate staff will include maintenance workers and custodial personnel. The director must establish procedures to make certain that the following aspects of facility and site management are being addressed: compliance with Section 504 of Title V of the Rehabilitation Act of 1973; compliance with the Asbestos Hazard Emergency Response Act (AHERA) of 1987; compliance with the Title III (the Emergency Planning and Community Right-to-Know Act of 1986) of the Superfund Amendments and Reauthorization Act (SARA) of 1986; compliance with the Lead Contamination Control Act (LCCA) of 1988; an energy conservation program; the district's construction and capital improvement programs; the school district's maintenance program; and the district's custodial program.

In terms of education and experience, the director of buildings and grounds should possess a bachelor's degree in architecture or one of the engineering sciences. Many small school districts cannot afford to pay the salaries that would attract a person with these qualifications. Therefore, an experienced maintenance person often assumes this position. In many cases, this person can do a credible job but the complexities of government regulation and the advances in technology are such that a degreed professional is the most desired person for this position.

There are many others employed in the buildings and grounds department who have supervisory responsibilities such as lead custodians, grounds keeper supervisors, maintenance supervisors, inventory managers, and so on. This chapter, however, concentrates on the director of buildings and grounds position. Many, if not all, of the employees in this department will be classified personnel with skill qualifications rather than academic credentials.

## Architectural Principles and the Learning Environment

There were no recognizable schoolhouse structures in the United States until the seventeenth century. At that time, they were neither attractive nor comfortable. They consisted primarily of one room with long tables for the pupils to sit around and a raised podium for the teacher. Until the 1850s the basic philosophy was that schoolhouses were shelters in which pupils and teachers came together. Through the efforts of eminent educators such as Horace Mann and Henry Barnard, free public education became an accepted institution in the United States and so the design of schools began to attract the attention of architects.

Shortly after the acceptance of public education, another unrelated event occurred that had a significant effect not only on the design of schools but also on the entire field of architecture. In 1880, Louis Sullivan, an eminent American architect, enunciated the principle, "form follows function." However, the planning of functional school buildings has been of primary concern to both architects and educators only since the 1940s. Until then, American architecture was more concerned with imitating what was in vogue in Europe and, particularly, in England.

The function of contemporary architecture is the design of school facilities that are as conducive as possible to the educating of children and young people. Thus, the design of school facilities must be undertaken within the context of educational concepts expressed in terms of "educational specifications." Such specifications should clearly describe the various learning activities that will take place in the proposed school facility along with special requirements. For example, the educational specifications for a senior high school home economics cooking laboratory would describe the curriculum and would project the number of students for a given class period with the number of workstations desired and the type of equipment that will be used.

There are four principles of operation mirroring the human condition that should be taken into consideration when planning an educational facility. First, the principle of gradualism dictates that the teachers, administrators, students, and parents are ready for curriculum changes that are also reflected in architectural design. The *open space* classroom is a case in point. Without proper preparation, a newly constructed school utilizing this concept will probably produce negative feelings from those teachers who have a traditional concept of how a school building should look. Indeed, partitions may gradually appear, made with bookcases and other movable objects.

Second, the principle of reversibility dictates that new dimensions in the design of school facilities which support a specific curriculum or teaching style can be changed to support a different curriculum or teaching style without extensive structural modification. Soundproof sliding partitions can be used to convert an open area into a more confined space for small-group instruction or for that teacher who is more effective in a traditional classroom setting.

Third, the maturation cycle in every community produces increases and subsequent decreases in pupil population. Thus, school facilities should be designed for more than one use. A building constructed only to be a school will require considerable structural modifications in order to convert it, for example, into an office building. A more universal design would give the district the opportunity to recoup its investment when such changes occur which, in turn, could be used for other educational purposes.

Finally, schools should be designed for people. This is so obvious that it is almost embarrassing to state but there are school buildings in many communities that appear to have been planned without consideration for the needs of students. Every child has physical, social, intellectual, and psychological needs, all of which may not be enhanced by the design of the school. For example, mental fatigue will certainly hinder a student's ability to learn. Thus, the physical conditions that cause fatigue can be minimized if a building is well ventilated and has functional heating and air-conditioning systems.[2]

### Implementing a School Construction or Remodeling Project[3]

There are four steps in the process of implementing a school construction or remodeling project. Each of these steps has a number of components which are carried out by various staff members. Each component contains a number of procedures that are very complex.

*Step One: Establishing Educational Goals and Objectives*
Strategic planning dictates that a board of education establish long range goals and objectives for the school district. A five-year plan is the most common. In this context, a goal is a broad statement of purpose or mission that gives direction to all segments of the school district. Objectives are those measurable action plans which implement the goals of the district. Of course, each year, the administration and board of education should revise the five-year plan based on the experience of the prior year so that there is always a five-year plan. A strategic five-year plan will be valid only if citizens, parents, students, teachers, staff members, and administrators have been involved in the process of developing the plan. The board of education is the decision making body that approves the goals and objectives.

The objectives are subsequently converted into a curricular plan. Curriculum development is the responsibility of the superintendent of schools and his or her staff. Certainly teachers, building level administrators, and curriculum specialists should be involved in the curriculum planning process. The curriculum is then translated into educational specifications which are used by the architect in designing the facility. The responsibility for developing the educational specifications rests with the superintendent. Of course, teachers and building level administrators along with the director of buildings and grounds will play a significant role in the development of the specifications.

*Step Two: Developing Architectural Plans*
The first concern in putting this second step into operation is the selection of an architect. Because architects are professionals who provide a service, the selection of an architect cannot be accomplished merely by taking bids. Rather, the district should advertise that the board of education is accepting proposals from interested architects and architectural firms to provide services for a specific project. Although it is time-consuming to review proposals, many architects or firms develop specialties that limit their suitability to handle all the capital projects of a given school district during a specific fiscal year.

A method that has proven to be time-saving, appropriate, and effective is the prequalification of architects or firms that have specialties. For example, a certain architectural firm may have developed an excellent reputation in the design of all-weather running tracks while another firm may have a similar reputation in the design of comprehensive high school facilities. This prequalification process would entail advertising and inviting interested individual architects and architectural firms to submit a portfolio setting forth their qualifications along with references and a listing of their most recent projects. It is important for the director of buildings and grounds to check on the following when contacting references: the number of change orders due to architect's error or omissions; project budget overruns; and the record of completing projects on time.

Further, it is advisable to ask each architect or firm about their commitment to inspection schedules. Weekly visits are not out of the ordinary for smaller projects. Staff turnover is also a signal when prequalifying a firm. A high turnover rate does not speak well for a firm. The most important concern, however, is the person who will be the project leader. This individual is the key to a successful project and the board of education, superintendent, and director of buildings and grounds should feel comfortable with him or her.

Finally, the method of payment must be explored. Traditionally, there are two: a flat fee or a percentage of the project cost. The American Institute of Architects has established guidelines which can be used as a basis for determining project fees.

The architect is responsible for taking the educational specifications and developing preliminary sketches and cost estimates for a given project. After these sketches are reviewed by the superintendent and his or her staff, the board of education should approve or reject the sketches. Not only the building principal but also teachers, curriculum specialists, and the director of buildings and grounds constitute the superintendent's staff in reviewing the sketches. When a new school is being planned, it is important for the superintendent to appoint the principal who will administer the new school before this planning process begins because he or she must be involved in every phase of this process.

The architect is the appropriate person to select a site for a new school project. Of course, an architect will probably utilize the services of a real estate agent in purchasing the property. Also, there are attorneys who specialize in the purchasing of property, and it is advisable to use the services of an attorney for such a transaction. The board of education is the legal entity responsible for approving the purchase of property upon the recommendation of the superintendent. The director of buildings and grounds should be the chief advisor to the superintendent as he or she makes the recommendation.

The architect is the professional who will develop the working drawings and architectural specifications. The architect will require the services of other professionals such as electrical and mechanical engineers to help prepare the plans.[4]

### Step Three: Developing the Financial Plan

The superintendent, assistant superintendent for business and financial services, and the director of buildings and grounds are responsible for preliminary plans for a bond issue election in order to fund capital improvements or a new facility project. The campaign should be organized and coordinated by the director of community relations. If the bond issue passes, the board of education must select an attorney who specializes in municipal bond issue projects. The various aspects involved in the bond flotation process are discussed in Chapter 7.[5]

### Step Four: Implementing the Construction and/or Remodeling

The architect is usually responsible for advertising and taking bids for a general contractor who will actually construct or remodel the building. In this model, it is more effective for the general contractor to handle the subcontracting with other construction specialists such as the electrical contractor. Approving the contract with the general contractor is the responsibility of the board of education.

Equipment lists should be prepared by the superintendent and the building principal or other appropriate staff members, such as teachers and curriculum specialists. In many cases, the architect will be responsible for taking bids on furniture and large equipment that will be used in the building.

During the construction phase, the construction site or remodeling site should be inspected on a regular basis by the architect and the director of buildings and grounds. Upon certification of the architect, monthly payments can be made to the general contractor from the money generated through the sale of the bonds. Final payment should be withheld until the board of education can make a final inspection of the new or remodeled facility.

There are two other alternative approaches to the traditional model presented above. The first is *construction management* and the second is the *design-build* approach. The construction management model brings together the superintendent or director of buildings and grounds, construction manager, and the architect during all phases of the project. Thus, a team approach, which should produce more realistic cost estimates, is used even in the design phase. Further, the construction manager could start construction and order long-delivery materials before the design phase is completed. This can save the district considerable money in case of rising costs and inflation. The setting of a schedule for completing various phases of construction becomes more accurate with this model.

The construction manager is responsible for supervising the construction phase of the projects. In some situations, the construction manager may be employed by a construction company or may be the owner of a construction company. In these circumstances, the board of education may use the construction manager's company as the general contractor. This model does not preclude competitive bidding. The architect and construction manager may be hired on the basis of their credentials. However, as an alternative the board of education may wish to seek competitive bids from construction companies that also provide construction management services.

There are companies capable of providing architectural, engineering, and construction services as a total package. The board of education, thus, seeks competitive proposals from which one company will be selected to design and construct or remodel the facility.

In the first two models, the architect and construction manager are paid a fee based on a percentage of the total cost of the project. The construction costs are based on what the market dictates in the competitive bidding process. In the design-build model, competitive bidding is the norm.

This treatment would not be complete without mentioning a practice that continues in some school districts. Through the administrative staff, the board of education can act in the capacity of a general contractor. Such a practice does not preclude the district from hiring an architect and even a construction manager. In this situation, the superintendent and the administrative staff would be required to take competitive bids for all specialties in the construction industry. For example, carpentry work, electrical work, and masonry work would be bid by the district in the same way as done by a general contractor. The obvious faults in this type of practice are the lack of expertise and the extra burden placed on school-district personnel. Except for the smallest of projects, this is not a desirable practice.[6]

### Managing the Custodial Program

There is nothing more damaging to the image of a school district than inadequate custodial services. It is a problem that exists in many school districts. However, given the tremendous problems that many districts face with respect to pupil discipline, curricular needs, and financial woes, custodial issues tend to be far down on the list of priorities that occupy the energies of administrators and school board members.

The single most difficult issue in most custodial programs is the number of custodians that are needed to clean a school. There are formulas for assigning the proper number of custodians to a facility usually calculated on a per square foot basis. For example, the March 1985 issue of *American School and University* stated that a custodian should be capable of cleaning 14,850 square feet of floor space in an eight-hour shift. However, in the final analysis there are many factors which must be taken into consideration when determining the number of custodians that should be assigned to a given facility. Some of these factors are: the number of children in the school, the design of the school, the number of after-school activities. The most effective way to address this issue is still to establish a formula, and, at the same time, to establish a performance-based evaluation program for custodians. Within a year, the adequacy of custodial staffing will become clear.

A second issue, which is a direct outgrowth of the suggestion to create a performance-based evaluation program, is the necessity to have an accurate job description for custodians. It would be impossible to evaluate custodians adequately with the hope of improving performance and with the expectation of assigning the correct number of custodians to a facility without a job description.

In like manner, the third issue is related to the first two, custodians need in-service programs as much as other employees. In addition to knowing emergency procedures, they need to be trained in the use of cleaning supplies and equipment. For example, in the event of a fire in a school building, the custodian will play a key role not only in the evacuation of students but also in shutting down systems in the facility such as natural gas.

Finally, the routine and monotony of custodial work can create morale and performance problems. When possible, it is important to develop ways of enriching custodial jobs. Preventive maintenance, health and safety management, and energy management are three areas that can be entrusted to custodians which will expand their responsibilities. Replacing windows, servicing mechanical equipment, spraying chemicals for insects and rodents, and being responsible for keeping lights and heating turned off in unused areas are tasks that can enhance the custodial position.[7]

## Managing the Maintenance Program

Students, teachers, and building administrators seldom think about the physical environment in a school until something, such as the air conditioning, malfunctions or breaks down. At that time, the maintenance staff becomes highly visible and everyone affected wants immediate action in "fixing" the problem.

Every school district will need to hire and retain skilled maintenance employees. Probably the most necessary are those employees who have training in the maintenance of boilers and air-conditioning equipment and as carpenters, electricians, and plumbers. In small school districts, it is probably more cost-effective to contract with companies that can provide these types of services.

Within the last decade, there has emerged in school facilities management a significant concept addressing long-range planning rather than just the maintenance of equipment and facilities. This emerging concept has been precipitated by the microcomputer. The challenge facing those responsible for facility maintenance is to make decisions based on accurate data. Thus, the storage, retrieval, and manipulation of data into reports has become essential in effective management. The tool that makes this possible is the computer.

The data bank should contain information concerning each facility. For example, the director of buildings and grounds and the maintenance staff should be able to generate preventive maintenance schedules for the mechanical system in a particular school building. Work orders can be entered into a computer terminal by a principal at the building site and instantly stored in the computer at the central maintenance facility. This data, in turn, can be retrieved immediately or at another time during the day by maintenance personnel. Equipment replacement schedules can be readily available when preparing the capital equipment budget for a given fiscal year. There are even software programs that will estimate the construction cost of a building renovation project.[8]

The essential ingredient is the quality of the people who are hired to manage the maintenance department. The time has long passed when such individuals can be effective and remain unschooled in the use of computers.

### Selected Issues in Buildings and Grounds Management

#### Asbestos Hazard Emergency Response Act of 1987[9]

The purpose of this act was to require school districts to identify friable and non-friable asbestos-containing building materials in each facility that is used for school purposes. The following are components of the AHERA Act:

A. *Inspection* All buildings must be inspected by an accredited inspector. Accredited inspectors are individuals who have attended and passed an Environmental Protection Agency approved asbestos inspector training program. Originally, all building inspections were to be completed by October 12, 1988. However, President Reagan signed a bill into law that extended this requirement until May 9, 1989, if the officials of a school district filed such a request by October 12, 1988 with the governor's office of each respective state. The inspections should have included not only visual but also physical assessment of asbestos-containing building materials. Samples of these materials were to be submitted to an accredited laboratory for analysis.

B.  *Response Actions* Response actions were procedures that the school district implemented if a building's assessment indicated that friable or damaged non-friable materials were present in the building. The response actions included any or all of the following: encapsulation, enclosure, removal, or repair of the damaged material. Other than small-scale or short-duration repairs, response actions were to be designed and conducted by accredited persons. The Occupational Safety and Health Administration (OSHA) and the Environmental Protection Agency (EPA) had specific standards for work practices and worker protection during the response actions.

C.  *Management Plan* An asbestos management plan had to be developed for each building by October 12, 1988 or, if extended, by May 9, 1989. Further, the management plan had to be developed by an EPA trained management planner. Management plans had to include the following: an accounting of school buildings inspected; documented locations of friable and non-friable asbestos-containing building materials; a description of sampling procedures; documented sample results; the designation of a school-district official responsible for the response action; detailed preventive measures and response actions and a schedule for carrying out the response actions; and a plan for reinspection, maintenance, and surveillance.

D.  *Operations and Maintenance* Each school district was required to implement an operations, maintenance, and repair program whenever friable asbestos was present or assumed to be present in any building.

E.  *Training and Periodic Surveillance* Each school district had to insure that all members of the maintenance and custodial staff who worked in a building containing asbestos received awareness training of at least two hours. All maintenance and custodial staff who conducted activities that could have resulted in the disturbance of asbestos-containing building materials had to receive an additional fourteen hours of training. At least every six months after the management plan was implemented, the school district must conduct surveillance in each building that contains asbestos. Each area identified must be visually inspected and a report must be submitted to the school district's asbestos manager.

F.  *Record Keeping* All records containing preventive measures and response actions to asbestos-containing building materials must be maintained in a centralized location in the administration offices of both the school affected and the school-district central office.

G. *Warning* Warning labels had to be attached adjacent to friable and non-friable asbestos-containing building materials.

### Superfund Amendment and Reauthorization Act of 1986 (SARA) [10]

Title III of SARA, the Emergency Planning and Community Right-To-Know Act of 1986, requires industry and federal, state, and local governmental agencies to participate in community-based emergency planning as preparation for a potential chemical spill or emission. Further, this law requires industry and these same governmental agencies to facilitate the reporting to the public of information about hazardous and toxic chemicals.

On August 18, 1987, the Occupational Safety and Health Administration (OSHA) issued regulations that preempted all state right-to-know laws and expanded the regulations to include all workers handling or using toxic substances.

An example of a situation that would invoke the emergency notification requirement of this law is the rupture of an underground fuel storage tank. Those school districts operating their own school buses and storing gasoline should be prepared to meet notification requirements if a spill occurs and should be prepared to initiate a clean-up process. Storing large quantities of copy machine fluids and custodial cleaning solutions also poses a risk. Other provisions of these regulations that have an impact on school districts are as follows:

> All containers of hazardous substances must be labeled, tagged, or marked, setting forth the name of the hazardous substance along with the appropriate warning and the name and address of the manufacturer or responsible party.

> Material Safety Data Sheets (MSDS) containing pertinent information about chemical substances must be made available to employees or their designated representatives.

> A training and education program must be established for employees using or handling toxic substances. This training must be specific about the chemicals in use and must clearly set forth the dangers involved in using toxic substances.

### Radon Gas [11]

This is a colorless, odorless, and tasteless radioactive gas that occurs naturally in soil, rocks, underground water, and air. The gas is produced as a natural breakdown of radium-226. Radon decay products attach themselves to particles in the air. In outdoor air, radon gas and its decay products are usually present at such low levels that there is no risk to people. However, when radon enters a building, there is a potential build-up of both the gas and its decay products. Health officials contend that breathing radon decay products can cause lung cancer. The Environmental Protection Agency has recommended the testing of school buildings for radon.

Thus, the EPA recommends that classrooms on the basement-level and ground-level floors should be tested. After examining preliminary test results from 3000 classrooms in 16 states, EPA administrator William K. Reilly made this recommendation. Of the 130 schools tested, 22 percent contained levels of radon above 4 picocuries per liter of air, which is the established safety limit. The EPA has established guidelines that explain how to conduct tests, select measurement devices, decide which rooms to test, and indicate which results suggest follow-up action.

### Lead in School Drinking Water [12]

The Lead Contamination Control Act of 1988 amended the Safe Drinking Water Act of 1974, and also required the Environmental Protection Agency to publish and distribute to the states a guidance document and testing protocol to assist schools in determining the source and level of lead contamination in school drinking water.

Medical evidence confirms that lead is a toxic metal harmful to children even at low exposure levels. Low-level exposure can cause damage to the peripheral and central nervous systems. Learning disabilities, shorter stature, impaired formation and function of blood cells, and impaired hearing in children also have been caused by comparatively low levels of exposure to lead.

This is a very complex issue. The EPA guidelines explain how lead gets into drinking water, how to develop a plumbing profile of a school, how to take samples for analysis, and how to proceed in finding a solution to this problem.

### Energy Conservation

This issue dates back to the 1970s when oil prices soared because of our dependence on foreign oil resources. At first, radical programs were developed and implemented with some degree of success but, as oil prices stabilized, the urgency seemed to fade and less radical programs replaced the original effort. The most successful programs are those which involve the monitoring of temperatures and the regulating of heating, ventilating, and air-conditioning systems through the use of computers. Also, pre-cooling and pre-heating buildings during the night hours generally costs less than during the peak periods of the day when the demand on utilities is greatest.

EXHIBIT 9-1 • *Staff Involvement in an Energy Conservation Program*[13]

---

I.  District Level
  A.  School Board
    1.  Commit school district to energy conservation ethic
    2.  Establish basic energy usage policy for school district
    3.  Authorize energy audit
    4.  Set goals for energy savings
    5.  Evaluate energy conservation efforts and results
  B.  Superintendent
    1.  Initiate and lead commitment to energy conservation ethic
      a.  Provide philosophy and rationale
      b.  Be aware of applicable funding and compliance legislation
      c.  Demonstrate impact of energy dollars exported from school district
      d.  Develop district wide, long-range energy conservation in-service educational program
      e.  Visibly reward persons and programs that meet or exceed energy conservation objectives
      f.  Set personal example of energy conservation
    2.  Establish persuasive district wide energy conservation task force or committee
      a.  Solicit energy policy suggestions
      b.  Help establish energy conservation priorities
      c.  Provide data on energy conservation performance of district
      d.  Utilize members in public information efforts
    3.  Assign specific energy conservation responsibilities to specific district individuals
      a.  Monitor their performance
      b.  Examples—building level energy manager, district public information officer
    4.  Realize energy consumption is a political and an energy matter
  C.  Assistant Superintendent for Business Affairs
    1.  Prepare technical reports for school board, superintendent, energy conservation task force, principals, physical plant staff
    2.  Monitor and report on applicable energy conservation funding and compliance legislation
    3.  Evaluate energy usage and provide factual record
      a.  Identify source, quality, and cost of each district energy source
      b.  Inspect facilities, equipment, and supplies usage
      c.  Present data in comparable forms
      d.  Establish tough yet realistic and measurable energy objectives to support district goals and priorities
      e.  Assess progress toward meeting objectives
    4.  Purchase and construct with energy savings in mind
    5.  Identify and recommend expert consultant help
    6.  Demonstrate cost-effectiveness of any energy measures
    7.  Work with building engineers in scheduling operations, maintenance, and repairs to reduce energy consumption

8.  Convey energy usage progress to school publics by:
    a.  District and by individual school buildings
    b.  Monthly, weekly, or daily energy consumption charts for principals, teachers, and pupils
    c.  Less complex charts and graphs for mass media
9.  Attend conferences and workshops on energy conservation

II.  Building level
   A.  Principals
      1.  Program and schedule to conserve energy
      2.  Participate in districtwide energy conservation conferences and workshops
      3.  Establish building energy audit and operations oversight committee
      4.  Survey teachers and staff regarding their suggestions for energy conservation in their rooms and/or building areas
      5.  Compare and compete with similar school concerning energy conservation
      6.  Report in meetings and in bulletins at least monthly about comparative energy conservation effectiveness
      7.  Prepare individual classroom energy checklists
      8.  Encourage teachers to attend conferences on energy usage
      9.  Demonstrate commitment to energy conservation ethic by setting a personal example

   B.  Teachers
      1.  Heighten pupil awareness of energy topics in imaginative ways
      2.  Put energy conservation in appropriate course materials
      3.  Program and schedule to conserve energy
      4.  Follow operational guidelines for building and district energy conservation

   C.  Physical Plant Staff
      1.  Lead or assist in collecting energy audit data
         a.  Keep accurate records
         b.  Analyze bus routes and field trip requests
         c.  Assess food services energy usage
      2.  Read and follow operational and maintenance manuals
      3.  Read and follow school district guidelines for energy conservation
      4.  Monitor and report compliance with district energy reduction objectives
      5.  Investigate alternative energy sources, especially solar, that may be used to conserve conventional sources
      6.  Suggest both short-term and long-term operational and maintenance guidelines modifications which promise energy conservation
      7.  Monitor trade journals and catalogs for energy saving tips, supplies, and equipment
      8.  Help all fellow personnel to be familiar with equipment, installations, and distribution systems
      9.  Assist in developing energy efficient purchase specifications
      10. Participate in hands-on training opportunities

D. Pupils
   1. Form committees for energy conservation awareness
   2. Act through Student Council projects
   3. Plan competition between classes, buildings
   4. Present student forums
   5. Instill awareness through curriculum projects

---

From a practical perspective, energy conservation measures can save the district large sums of money that can be redirected into other areas such as the purchase of instructional equipment. A skilled director of buildings and grounds with the assistance of his or her staff can analyze the district's energy efficiency by examining utility bills, lighting systems, major energy loads, doors, windows, roofs, and other outer building features. Such an examination should point out areas of concern.

However, an organized energy-conservation program is the only long-term solution to escalating costs. Such a program will be successful only if it is people-centered. Exhibit 9-1 presents an outline of how all members of the school community can play a part in an energy conservation program.[14]

## Managing the Pupil Transportation Program

Each school district has the obligation to provide students with the best possible instructional program. It also has the obligation to maintain a safe, effective, and efficient pupil transportation program. The ever increasing vehicular traffic on roads and highways, the lack of sidewalks in suburban areas, and the inadequacy of public transportation in many urban areas have increased the importance of pupil transportation service.

Pupil transportation is a significant extension of both the curricular and extracurricular programs. Buses are needed to transport children from their homes to school and back again. They are also needed for field trips and other excursions that certainly enrich the educational experiences of students. In addition, it would be very difficult for many students to participate in extracurricular programs, such as interscholastic athletics, if the district did not provide some level of transportation for these types of programs.

EXHIBIT 9-2 • *Guidelines to Determine the Adequacy of the School District's Transportation Program*[15]

---

1. The school board should adopt specific written policies covering the objectives of the school district's transportation program, which should include:
   a. A definition of what is considered a safe and reasonable walking distance for children
   b. Transportation of all handicapped children regardless of the distance involved
   c. A provision regarding the use of buses for noninstructional purposes
2. The administration should develop a program to teach bus safety to students at all grade levels.
3. The administration should develop a detailed written contract of responsibilities when a school district elects to provide transportation services through a private contractor. Such a contract must be executed by the board of education. This contract should contain clauses relating to the following:
   a. A performance bond to insure faithful fulfillment of the contract terms
   b. The minimum amount of insurance to be carried by the private contractor
   c. A schedule to inspect the school buses by a competent individual on a regular basis
4. The administration should provide the school board with a cost analysis of the transportation services on an annual basis that should include the following:
   a. Original cost of equipment and the date of purchase
   b. Total miles operated
   c. Miles operated on a daily basis
   d. Number of pupils transported daily and on a yearly basis by route
   e. The cost for fuel and maintenance
   f. Specific information on accidents involving school buses
   g. Specific information on property damage and traffic violations
   h. An inventory of repair parts
5. The administration is responsible for developing and maintaining the following routing information:
   a. An up-to-date map of the district's boundaries and school attendance areas
   b. The location of all roads and information relating the type and condition of roads
   c. The distance between major intersections
   d. The location of students that are transported and their grade level
   e. The exact route for each school bus
   f. The location, weight capacity, and condition of all bridges
6. The administration is responsible for selecting pick-up sites and routing buses in such a manner that:
   a. Bus stops are not on steep grades, blind curves, or near the crest of a hill
   b. The walking distance, waiting times, and riding times are reasonable
   c. Distances meet state guidelines

    d.   The time schedule is such that parents and children can be assured of a reasonable accurate pick-up and discharge time

7. The administration is responsible for establishing bus driver selection and training procedures that will insure the following:
    a.   Previous driving experience is investigated
    b.   Consideration is given to the maturity and character of each applicant
    c.   Substitute drivers meet the general requirements of regular drivers
    d.   A driver's handbook is developed that includes procedures to be followed in pupil disciplining cases and in emergency situations
    e.   A training program is developed that includes classroom instruction and actual practice in driving a school bus
    f.   Conferences are held with the bus drivers on a regular basis to discuss mutual problems and concerns

8. It is the administration's responsibility to establish rules and regulations governing pupil behavior and safety that include the following:
    a.   Procedures for reporting student misconduct, complaints from pupils and parents, bus conditions, route conditions, accidents, and injuries
    b.   Designated personnel are present to supervise the unloading and loading of pupils at school
    c.   Drivers are furnished with the names of pupils assigned to their routes
    d.   Drivers are instructed that no child should be let off the bus for any reason except at the designated stop unless special instructions have been given by the proper authority
    e.   Safe traffic patterns have been developed for approaching, parking on, and leaving the school grounds

---

Most states have statutes governing pupil transportation. It is common for school districts to be required by law to provide some pupil transportation to and from school at no direct cost to parents. However, school districts are usually permitted to charge parents for transporting their children to athletic events and for field trips.

Exhbit 9-2 provides a list of descriptors that can be used by school district administrators as they evaluate the adequacy of their school district's transportation program. Both the quality of services and the cost-effectiveness of the program are directly related to the policies created by he board of education and the procedures used by the administration.

There is a major question that will confront many school districts at one time or another: Is it better to contract pupil transportation service from a private company or is it better to have a district-operated program? The answer to this question, of course, will depend on the uniqueness of each situation. Basically, the administration must decide which approach will provide the students of the district with the best and safest service at the most reasonable cost. The director of transportation and his or her staff should be able to provide the assistant superintendent for business and financial services with data about the cost of the district-operated program along with information about the safety of the operation and long-term concerns, such as maintenance and vehicle replacement costs. In addition, a projection of the amount of funds that will be forthcoming from all sources of revenue for pupil transportation will also be an important consideration.

At that point, the assistant superintendent may have the director of transportation prepare specifications and take bids for contracted service. An analysis of the bids and a comparison of contracted service with a district-operated program then can be made in order to determine which of the two options is best for the school district.

Three issues concerned with making a pupil transportation program more cost-effective have arisen in the last decade. First, the use of alternative methods of fueling school buses has received considerable attention, which has led to experiments with gasohol and propane. Second, in those parts of the country that experience hot and humid weather, alternatives to air-conditioned buses have been explored. For example, painting the tops of school buses with reflective white paint and installing tinted insulated windows along with more fresh air vents have proven effective in reducing the heat build-up in school buses.

Third, computerized transportation programs have saved some school districts a considerable amount of money. This is particularly the case in large school districts where the establishing of routes and pupil pick-up points need to be as cost-effective as possible. Such computerized programs are available from private companies on a contract or fee basis. Medium to large school districts will probably find it more cost-beneficial to purchase their own computer hardware and software program.

The ultimate question that the director of transportation must answer is whether the initial expenditure required to convert vehicles to the use of alternative fuels, to modify buses, and to purchase or contract for computer capabilities will result in significant savings over the long term.

## Managing the Student Food Service Program

There are three reasons why a school district should provide a food service program to students: (1) students should have the opportunity during the school day to obtain the nutritional food that is needed for physical, emotional, and intellectual development; (2) the school lunch program provides students with the opportunity to learn about the quantity and kinds of food needed for good nutrition; and (3) eating in the school cafeteria provides students with the opportunity to practice desirable social behavior.

A good school food service program includes much more that just a hot lunch. Some school districts also provide breakfast especially in economically depressed areas of the country where many children are deprived of a nutritional breakfast at home. A major concern in many school districts is the level of pupil participation in school lunch programs. In some districts *a la carte* and alternative menus have significantly increased participation.

Many school districts have found that the food service program can provide a cost-effective way of enriching the interscholastic athletic program and school sponsored clubs. Every team and club in the school district looks forward to culminating the year's activities with a banquet at which individual team and club members can be recognized for their accomplishments. The cost of a banquet served at school will be much less than at a restaurant.

Like the pupil transportation program, a school district can contract with a private company to provide food service. The decision should be based on the same principle used for pupil transportation: The best option is the one that provides the students with the most nutritional and varied menu at the most cost-effective price to the district. In order to make this decision, the assistant superintendent for business and financial services can use a checklist like the one in Exhibit 9-3 which consists of a set of descriptors that can be used to evaluate the adequacy of a school district's food service program. In addition, Exhibit 9-4 provides a "blueprint" for a food service program developed by the American Food Service Association, which presents a set of objectives that will produce an effective program.

The director of food service can provide the assistant superintendent with data about pupil participation, state and federal reimbursement, menus and nutritional requirements, the cost of food products, and other direct costs. This is also the type of data that will be necessary to include in specifications if the district decides to take bids for a food service contractor.

EXHIBIT 9-3 • *Descriptors to Determine the Adequacy of a School District's Food Service Program*[16]

A school district will have an effective and efficiently managed food service program if the following questions can be answered with a "yes."

1. Are the objectives of the food service program defined in writing?
2. Is the school food service program under the direction of a competent person who is considered an integral part of the administrative team?
3. Are the food service policies, procedures, and regulations in written form and provided to all employees?
4. Are lines of authority and responsibility clearly defined in writing for the proper management of the program?
5. Does the school district have a policy regarding the sale of competitive food items such as packaged snacks, soft drinks, and candy?
6. Is the sale of all food items under the direct management of the director of food service and are all receipts deposited to the food service account?
7. Has the school district developed a policy and procedure for providing meals to needy children?
8. Is the scheduling of lunch periods well planned, and does it allow the students sufficient time to eat their lunch?
9. Is nutrition education correlated with the school food service program?
10. Is adequate supervision provided at lunchtime to students so that good food habits and social graces can be encouraged?
11. Does the administration evaluate program participation on a continual basis?
12. Are the cafeteria workers adequately supervised to insure that attractive and clean uniforms are worn by employees at all times?
13. Is there a staff development program for cafeteria workers?
14. Are all personnel required to meet locally established health standards?
15. Is the community informed of federal and state program requirements in written publications?
16. Are menus planned on a monthly basis and published a week in advance?
17. Is maximum utilization made of all food items that are not sold?
18. Are students encouraged to participate in the planning of the food service program?
19. Is the food prepared, handled, and served in a sanitary and safe manner?
20. Are inventory procedures effective in utilizing older shelf food items before they spoil?
21. Is there adequate security to protect against the possible theft of food items?
22. Is the storage space free from excessive temperature and humidity?
23. Is there a daily reading of thermostats in refrigerators and freezers to insure against spoilage?
24. Is the dining area clean, attractive, and well ventilated?
25. Are dishwashing facilities adequate and sanitary?
26. Are garbage and refuse disposed of in a sanitary manner?

27. Have rodent and insect extermination services been provided with regular applications?
28. Have procedures been established that allow for the proper handling of money?
29. Are monthly profit and loss statements prepared?
30. Are program costs calculated by using the full cost for labor, food, utilities, custodial services, capital outlay, and maintenance?

EXHIBIT 9-4 • *American School Food Service Association's Blueprint for School Nutrition Programs*[17]

Reflecting the educational potential of proper school nutrition programs, it is hereby declared to be our philosophy that food service permitted in schools shall contribute to optimum learning ability through good nutrition, good example, and good instruction.

School nutrition programs should contribute to the education of the child in three ways: 1. to his or her physical well-being, 2. to his or her mental receptivity, and 3. to his or her knowledge of food and application of good eating habits.

I. Nutrition offerings

The school, with the assistance of medical personnel, should determine the nutritional status of the individual child and his school-day nutritional needs. School food service should be expanded to those children presently excluded because of a lack of facilities and/or funds.

Provisions should be made for:

A. A meal that contains 1/3 of the child's recommended dietary allowances should be provided by the schools to all pupils without cost to the individual.

B. Two meals, each containing 1/3 of the recommended daily dietary allowances, should be available daily in all schools.

II. Nutrition curriculum

A school nutrition program should provide:

A. A sequential curriculum plan of nutrition instruction for pupils from kindergarten through high school

B. Innovative curriculum materials

C. Nutrition counseling with parents and medical personnel

D. Continuing nutrition education for teachers through regional and local workshos and courses

III. Professional education and training

The state educational agency should:

A. Establish qualifications for personnel responsible for directing, supervising, and implementing a school food service and nutrition program

B. Define criteria for pre-service and in-service training programs

C. Cooperate with educational institutions and professional organizations in developing education programs

IV. Staffing

The local educational agency should provide:

A. Direction and supervision by certificated personnel professionally trained in nutrition and/or administration and food services

B. Adequate staff, qualified through nutrition and food service training, to implement school food service programs

V. Technology

School nutrition program design should reflect the best technological research and development available to produce an optimum product at minimum cost.

VI. Research and evaluation

Continuing research and evaluation is essential to provide information which will enable school nutrition programs to define and apply practices of maximum effectiveness.

Organizations, industry, and government should combine their resources toward this purpose as well as in defining means through which this information can be effectively disseminated.

VII. Expanded use of schools

Reflecting the trend for schools to become community centers.

A. School nutrition programs should be expanded to meet the needs of all ages at all times whenever they are using school facilities.

B. Maximum use of school food service facilities and personnel may be anticipated in times of emergency.

C. School food service facilities and staff should be used for vocational training of youth and adults.

VIII. Funding

In fidelity to the premise that the school accept the responsibility for the child during the hours he or she is under its care, the school nutrition programs should meet the child's nutrition needs during the hours of the school's responsibility.

Such nutrition programs should be funded as a public responsibility, and therefore at no cost to the individual.

Taking cognizance that this goal far exceeds our present public commitment toward meeting school day nutrition needs, a timetable is needed to reach the objective.

IX. Public information

An effective school nutrition program must be understood and supported by the public. All agencies with a concern for the nutrition of children should cooperate to develop and implement a public information program.

## Managing the Data Processing Program

Ten years ago people would not have believed what has happened in relation to the use of computer technology. Almost every aspect of life in the United States is affected by computers. This has challenged the education community in regard to the use of computers in the classroom. In fact, the instructional program should incorporate three separate components dealing with computers if students are going to be able to meet the challenges facing them when they graduate from high school. Computer literacy, the first component, is usually dealt with in the elementary school program; computer usage, the second component, is taught in middle or junior high school; computer programming, the final component, is taught in high school.

This discussion, however, deals with the administrative use of data processing as a vehicle that supports the instructional program. In most school districts, data processing is used in the following areas: budget preparation, accounting, payroll, personnel, scheduling, grade reporting, pupil accounting, attendance accounting, inventory control, and enumeration census. It is also possible to *network* computer terminals by hooking them into a minicomputer or mainframe computer through a telephone modem. Through this network, messages (electronic mail) can be sent to all those having access to a terminal. Networking also allows for the input of data and the receiving of data at remote locations. This storehouse of data, thus, can be used by many more individuals more quickly than would be possible without this capability.

In small school districts, a microcomputer may be the most economical and yet effective way to handle administrative data processing. In medium to large school districts, data processing services can operate from an in-house installation or computer time can be purchased from a private service bureau. In order to handle the data processing needs of medium to large districts, a minicomputer would usually have the required capacity. In very large school districts, a mainframe computer would be necessary.

An alternative to these two approaches is for a number of school districts to form a cooperative, in which one district either purchases or merely houses the equipment and the cost is shared by the member school districts, or the districts buy time on the computer if the equipment is owned by a single district. Exhibit 9-5 is a checklist that can be used by the administration of a school district, first, to determine whether there is a need for data processing and, second, to determine the adequacy of a district's existing data processing program. It also lists those components of

EXHIBIT 9-5 • *Checklist to Determine the Need for and the Adequacy of a School-District Data Processing Program*[18]

Indicate the degree to which the district conforms to the standards as follows:
NA = not applicable; 1 = unsatisfactory; 2 = fair; 3 = satisfactory; 4 = exceptional

*Part I—Need for D.P. Services for Districts Currently Without D.P. Services.*

1.  The district has sufficient and timely accounting information.
    na   1   2   3   4
2.  The district has sufficient and timely payroll/personnel information.
    na   1   2   3   4
3.  Scheduling of students is accomplished using efficient and effective procedures. na   1   2   3   4
4.  Progress reporting of students is accomplished using efficient and effective procedures. na   1   2   3   4
5.  The district has sufficient and timely pupil information.
    na   1   2   3   4
6.  The district has adequate procedures available for meeting other informational needs. na   1   2   3   4
7.  The district has given consideration to the utilization of data processing services. na   1   2   3   4

*Part II—Descriptors for Districts Currently Utilizing D.P. Services*

*Indicate the Source(s) of D.P. Services:*

(Check One)  In-House Installation  _____
             Service Bureau/Cooperative Approach  _____

*Data Processing Goals and Objectives*

8.  Goals and objectives are formulated by the total administrative staff.
    na   1   2   3   4
9.  Objectives are prioritized by the administrative staff.
    na   1   2   3   4
10. The district has a written organizational chart for data processing.
    na   1   2   3   4
11. The district has a written job description for each D.P. employee based on written performance standards. na   1   2   3   4
12. The district has a formal education program that meets the needs of the D.P. staff. na   1   2   3   4

*Administration of D.P. Facilities*

13. The district has a written multi-year D.P. plan consistent with both short- and long-range objectives. na   1   2   3   4

14. The D.P. plan is evaluated and revised annually or more frequently.

    na   1   2   3   4

### Privacy, Security, and Confidentiality

15. The district has written procedures governing the privacy and confidentiality of data.   na   1   2   3   4
16. The district has written procedures providing for the security of software and data files.   na   1   2   3   4
17. The district has written procedures providing for the security of the computer facility.   na   1   2   3   4

### Systems and Programming

18. The district has developed written procedures for requesting and developing D.P. services.   na   1   2   3   4
19. The district has developed procedures for monitoring applications during the developmental process.   na   1   2   3   4
20. The district has written systems and programing standards that are followed in all cases.   na   1   2   3   4
21. User manuals and/or instructions are provided for each application.

    na   1   2   3   4
22. The district has developed written procedures for monitoring the effectiveness of existing applications.   na   1   2   3   4

### Computer Operations

23. The district maintains a daily and weekly machine processing schedule.

    na   1   2   3   4
24. The district has job accounting procedures relative to computer usage.

    na   1   2   3   4
25. The district maintains operator manuals adequate to schedule and process applications.   na   1   2   3   4
26. The district has a written procedure to monitor D.P. supplies.

    na   1   2   3   4

### Data Input/Output

27. The district has procedures that control and secure the processing of all incoming data.   na   1   2   3   4
28. The district maintains a daily and weekly data preparation schedule

    na   1   2   3   4
29. The data entry section has complete instructions for preparing input data.

    na   1   2   3   4
30. The district has procedures whereby new and revised forms are revised and developed jointly by the users and the D.P. department.

    na   1   2   3   4

31. The district has procedures for proper distribution of all output.
    na   1   2   3   4
32. The district has procedures for proper dispositions of test runs or other exceptional output.   na   1   2   3   4
33. The district has procedures for the verification and accuracy of all output.
    na   1   2   3   4

---

a program that must be addressed if such a program is to be effective. These major areas are: goals and objectives, proper staffing, procedures for safeguarding the security of software and files and the privacy/confidentiality of data, efficient operational procedures, and creative administration of the program.

## Summary

The importance of school buildings and facilities in the success of the instructional program is often overlooked by teachers, administrators, and school board members. The function of educational institutions is to educate children and young people. Consequently, the design of school facilities must be viewed within the context of educational concepts.

The director of buildings and grounds is the administrator who should be responsible for the district's physical plant and site program. Thus, he or she also should be responsible for formulating, recommending, and administering the school district's policies relating to facilities and their sites. The director is also responsible for establishing effective two-way communication between all the various organizational divisions of the district and the department of buildings and grounds.

Further, the director must establish procedures which will ensure that the following aspects of facility and site management are being addressed: compliance with Section 504 of Title V of the Rehabilitation Act of 1973; compliance with the Asbestos Hazard Emergency Response Act (AHERA) of 1987; compliance with the Title II (the Emergency Planning and Community Right-To-Know Act of 1986) of the Superfund Amendments and Reauthorization Act (SARA) of 1986; compliance with the Environmental Protection Agency guidelines for dealing with Radon Gas; compliance with the Lead Contamination Control Act (LCCA) of 1988; an energy conservation program; the district's construction and capital improvement program; the school district's maintenance program; and the district's custodial program.

In terms of education and experience, the director of buildings and grounds should possess a bachelor's degree in architecture or one of the engineering sciences.

Historically, schoolhouses as such did not appear until the seventeenth century, and consisted primarily of one room, with long tables for the pupils and a raised podium for the teacher. In 1880, Louis Sullivan, an eminent American architect, enunciated the principle, "form follows function." The planning of functional school buildings has been the continual concern not only of architects but also of educators.

There are four principles of operation mirroring the human condition that must be considered when planning an educational facility: (1) gradualism, (2) reversibility, (3) dual-purpose design, and (4) people centered design.

In addition, there are four steps in the process of carrying out a school construction and/or remodeling program: First, establish educational goals and objectives; second, develop architectural plans; third, develop a financial plan; and fourth, implement the construction and/or remodeling project. Each of these steps has a number of components implemented by various staff members. Each component involves, in turn, a number of procedures and subprocesses.

A school district has an obligation not only to provide students with the opportunity to be taught by competent professionals at school but also to provide and maintain a safe and effective pupil transportation program. The pupil transportation program can enhance curricular and extracurricular activities by providing transportation for field trips and interscholastic athletic events. Some school districts have found that contracting transportation services from private companies can be the most efficient and effective way to meet this responsibility.

Every school district should provide a food service program for three reasons: (1) Pupils should have the opportunity to obtain nutritional food during the school day; (2) the school lunch program provides students with the opportunity to learn about good nutrition; and (3) eating in the school cafeteria provides pupils with the opportunity to practice desirable social behavior. Some school districts have found that contracting with private companies can be the most economical and effective way to meet this responsibility.

The management of all school programs can be enhanced by data processing. In most districts, data processing can be applied to the following areas: budget preparation, accounting, payroll, personnel, scheduling, grade reporting, pupil accounting, attendance accounting, inventory control, and enumeration census. It is also possible to *network* computer terminals by hooking them into a minicomputer or mainframe computer through a telephone modem. Through this network, messages (electronic mail) can be sent to all those having access to a terminal. Networking will also allow for the input of data and the receiving of data at remote locations. This storehouse of data, thus, can be used by many more individuals more quickly than would be possible without this capability.

## Endnotes

1. Ronald W. Rebore, *Educational Administration: A Management Approach* (Englewood Cliffs, New Jersey: Prentice-Hall, Inc., 1985), pp. 137–138.

2. George J. Collins, "School Design Then, Now . . . And Soon To Be," *American School and University*, Vol. 60, no.4 (December 1987), p. 17.

3. Glen I. Earthman, "Facility Planning and Managemet," *Principles of School Business Management*, R. Graig Wood, ed. (Reston, Virginia: ASBO International, 1986), pp. 614–617.

4. C. William Day, "What Should Clients Expect from their Architects?" *American School and University*, Vol. 59, no. 3 (November 1986), pp. 11–12.

5. Earthman, pp. 617–619.

6. *Ibid.*, pp. 636–639.

7. Arthur W. Steller, "Cleaning up Your Custodial Program." *UPDATING: School Board Policies*, Vol. 17, no. 11 (December 1986), pp. 1–3.

8. Nancy Sanquist, "Facility Management: A Strategic Function." *The Office*, Vol. 105, no. 3 (March 1987), pp. 71–72.

9. Kristin Olson, *Legal Aspects of Asbestos Abatement* (Topeka, Kansas: National Organization on Legal Problems of Education, 1986), pp. 1–27.

10. Federal Register, *Hazard Communication: Final Rule*, Part III, Occupational Safety and Health Administration (Washington, D.C.: Department of Labor, Monday, August 24, 1987), p. 31–52.

11. U.S. Environmental Protection Agency, *Radon Measurement in Schools: An Interim Report* (Washington, D.C.: Office of Radiation Programs, 1989), pp. 1–8.

12. U.S. Environmental Protection Agency, *Lead in School Drinking Water* (Washington, D.C.: The Office of Water, 1989), pp. 1–23.

13. Dale E. Kaiser and James C. Parker, "Staff Involvement in Energy Programs," *School Business Affairs*, Vol. 47, no. 7 (June 1981), pp. 10, 11, 23.

14. Arthur Steller, "Put the Heat on Cutting Energy Costs," *UPDATING: School Board Policies*, Vol. 16, no. 9 (October 1985), pp. 1, 2.

15. Rebore, pp. 128–129.

16. *Ibid.*, pp. 130–131.

17. American School Food Service Association and Association of School Business Officials, *A Guide for Financing School Food and Nutrition Services* (Denver: The Association, 1979), pp. 69–71.

18. Missouri Department of Elementary and Secondary Education, *Checklist to Determine the Need for and the Adequacy of a School District's Data Processing Program* (Jefferson City, Missouri: The Department, 1982).

## Selected Bibliography

Castaldi, Basil, *Educational Facilities Planning, Modernization, and Management*, 2nd ed. (Boston: Allyn and Bacon, Inc., 1982).

Coley, Joe D., "A Practitioner's Perspective on School Facilities Problems," *School Business Affairs*, Vol. 54, no. 8 (August 1988), pp. 20–24.

Donn, George E., "A Brief History: The National Conference on School Transportation," *School Business Affairs*, Vol. 55, no. 4 (April 1989), pp. 26–28.

Federal Register, *Hazard Communication: Final Rule*, Part III, Occupational Safety and Health Administration) Washington, D.C.: Department of Labor, Monday, August 24, 1987).

Kimbrell, David W., "Planning for AHERA Compliance," *School Business Affairs*, Vol. 54, no. 2 (February 1988), pp. 23–26.

Miller, Anthony R., "Contractor Relationships," *School Business Affairs*, Vol. 55, no. 4 (April 1989), pp. 40–44.

Reecer, Marcia, "Get Ready for Radon: Brace for the Next Threat to a Safe School Environment," *The Executive Educator*, Vol. 10, no. 2 (February 1988), pp. 13–16, 55.

Tanner, Kenneth C., and C. Thomas Holmes, *Microcomputer Applications in Educational Planning and Decision Making* (New York: Teachers College Press, 1985).

U.S. Environmental Protection Agency, *Lead in School's Drinking Water* (Washington, D.C.: Office of Water, 1989).

U.S. Environmental Protection Agency, *Radon Measurements in Schools: An Interim Report* (Washington, D.C.: Office of Radiation Programs, 1989).

Van Egmond-Pannell, Dorothy, "Food Services at School," in *Principles of School Business Management*, ed. R. Craig Wood (Reston, Virginia: Association of School Business Officials International), pp. 381–407.

Watkins, Shirley Maree, "Give Everyone a Vested Interest in Food Service," *The School Administrator*, Vol. 44, no. 5 (May 1987), pp. 10–12.

Wold, Geoffrey H., "Strategic EDP Planning," *School Business Affairs*, Vol. 54, no. 10 (October 1988), pp. 10–12.

Zeitlin, Laurie S., "Pupil Transportation and Fiscal Responsibility," *School Business Affairs*, Vol. 55, no. 4 (April 1989), pp. 35–39.

# 10

# Risk Management

During the 1950s, a significant advance took place in the commercial insurance industry. The insurance companies allowed business and industrial corporations and companies to draw together all their property and casualty insurance coverage into one package. Ultimately this approach provided businesses with the opportunity to develop convenient and cost-effective insurance programs along with improved coverage.

However, insurance coverage is only one aspect of a total risk management program. The contemporary milieu which consists of large dollar claims against school districts due to legal liability and the cancelling of insurance coverage of school districts because of large dollar losses are the reasons for the emphasis on risk management. This situation is as significant as what happened in the 1950s in terms of commercial insurance packaging. From this has arisen the new administrative position of *risk manager*.

This individual should be someone who has broad experience in the insurance industry. In terms of organizational structure, the risk manager should report to the assistant superintendent for business and financial services. The risk manager should be responsible for coordinating the insurance programs in the district, and should be a resource person to all the other divisions and departments in the school district concerning the identification and resolution of risk to property and people. It is important to note that accidents on the job that result in worker's compensation claims should be of particular concern to the risk manager. The position of risk manager will enlarge in scope and responsibility if the school district is self-insured. This treatment, however, is geared towards a situation in which the school district purchases insurance coverage from private companies.

The inability of some school districts to acquire insurance coverage because their loss experience indicates that they are high risks is certainly a good argument to establish the position of risk manager. This same situation has also produced the *insurance cooperative* by which several school districts join together in establishing a self-insured pool that will provide them with some coverage. While this has proven to be successful in some situations, it is not the ideal. Therefore, this text does not address such coverage.

It is recognized that some school districts are too small to hire a person whose sole responsibility is to administer the risk management program. However, a group of school districts might cooperatively hire a person who has the expertise that would allow them to have these necessary services at a reasonable cost. Of course there are consultants who can also be hired for this purpose. In some situations, the superintendent or an assistant superintendent might pursue the educational programs offered through many professional school administrator organizations, such as ASBO and AASA, that will help them develop and administer a risk management program.

## Principles of Risk Management[1]

The very act of living is a risk. It does not matter what you do or how careful you are, there is always the possibility that an accident will cause injury to you or damage to your property. The situation in school districts and in private business and industry is similar. Over time, these entities have developed certain principles for handling risks that have proven to be successful.

First, identify and evaluate the school district's exposure to risks. It is possible to ask the district's insurance agent or broker or underwriter to help the risk manager or other administrators conduct an audit of the school district's facilities in order to ascertain what potential risks might be present.

If such a service is not available from the school district's agent, broker, or underwriter, there are consulting firms that employ *safety engineers* who can advise the administration about hazards. Even districts with a risk manager may need the services of consultants when it comes to evaluating risks associated with asbestos, toxic chemicals, and radon gas.

The identification of exposure to risks, for example, might reveal that steps do not have slip-retarding strips or adequate handrails to protect students as they move from one floor to the next. Custodial chemical storage areas may need additional ventilation to prevent the accumulation of fumes that may be sparked into an explosion. Driver's education cars should have dual steering mechanisms to prevent an accident, if a student driver loses control of the vehicle. While numerous additional examples could be given, the following questions explain what needs to be considered in identifying a school district's potential risks. What are the causes of the potential risks? How serious are the consequences of these potential risks?

The second step in managing risks should be an attempt to eliminate or minimize potential risks. Repairing defective handrails and installing slip-retarding strips on steps are easy and relatively inexpensive ways of minimizing potential risks. Solutions that require a major building modification would be more costly. However, the expense of installing a new and more effective fire alarm system is much more cost-effective than rebuilding a facility extensively damaged by fire.

The magnitude of the risk, of course, is a critical aspect of this second step. To continue with the example above, if the fire alarm system is adequate but just not "state of the art," a large expenditure to replace the system would not be fiscally prudent. Safety, however, is always the major determining factor. If the fire alarm system is not adequate, it should be replaced.

Finally, if it is impossible to eliminate or significantly minimize a risk, it will be necessary to transfer that risk to another party. Purchasing insurance is the most common method of doing so. There are, however, other circumstances when a school should transfer a risk to another party through a contractual agreement. Many school districts in metropolitan areas have seen enrollments decrease resulting in the closing of schools. Many of their facilities have been leased to private firms and to other public institutions. The lease agreement should contain a provision requiring the lessee to indemnify the school district and to protect the property through property and casualty insurance. Further, it is important for the district to require the lessee to have the school district designated as a *named insured* on the lessee's insurance policies. This could prevent the school district from being sued, in addition to the lessee, if an accident occurred that damaged property or injured a person. A second example of transferring risk through a contractual agreement involves the usual requirement of a performance bond from a contractor who is building or remodeling a school facility.

### The Value of Deductibles

The insurance premium paid by a school district is a direct measure of the transferred risk. The greater the risk, the more it will cost the district in premium. If the risk assumed by the insurance company is reduced, not only will the premium be reduced but also the competition between insurance companies to acquire the account will be increased.

The most effective way to reduce premiums is to increase the deductible. In other words, if the deductible in an insurance policy on property damage is $5000, the premium will be less than if the deductible is $1000. Obviously, the insurance company is more likely to pay out claims with the $1000 deductible and, therefore, will charge the district a larger premium. It is good management for a school district or for any business to retain some portion of a risk because this encourages a continual effort to eliminate or reduce risks. In addition, higher deductibles eliminate nuisance claims and reduce internal administrative costs.

Although there is no magic formula for determining the appropriate size of a deductible, there are some guidelines that can be followed in analyzing a school district's situation. First, determine the district's loss expectancy from past history. Second, determine how much loss can be absorbed through the school district's budget. This determination should be calculated on a per occurrence and on an aggregate basis. For example, could the district absorb a $5000 loss if this occurred an average of ten times per year which would be equal to $50,000 per year? Third, calculate how much money could be saved in reduced premium costs if the district assumed a portion of the risk.

There are many different types of deductibles. The most commonly used are the *straight-dollar* and *percentage* deductibles. The straight-dollar deductible is the amount that is subtracted from every loss while the percentage deductible is the amount that the district assumes on a percentage basis of the loss or of the value.

## Commercial Package Insurance Policies

As stated in the first part of this chapter, packaged commercial insurance policies were nothing more than separate property and liability coverages brought together under one cover. The true commercial package combines both property and liability coverage offering broader based protection.

## Property Insurance

Of course, property insurance constitutes the most extensive part of the school district's insurance coverage. Damage to buildings and the contents of buildings can be disastrous financially. Basic property coverage insures the facilities and the contents of these buildings against damage caused by fire, lightning, windstorm, hall, smoke, vandalism, explosion, a riot, and by a vehicle or aircraft. This coverage can be extended through what is termed an *endorsement* to include glass breakage and damage caused by ice, snow, water, and earthquakes. A more common approach today in providing property coverage is the *all risk* policy which is broader than the most inclusive *named peril* policy. All risk protection means that a loss is covered unless it is clearly excluded in the policy.

Most property insurance policies limit the amount of recovery on losses to *actual cash value,* which is defined as the current replacement cost minus actual physical depreciation. However, it is possible to have property insurance endorsed to provide coverage for *replacement cost.* A school district will probably be able to acquire property insurance only equal to 80 or 90 percent of replacement value even with such an endorsement. This is because insurance companies want the insured to assume some of the exposure, which usually causes the insured to institute risk management principles. Most insurance companies will also cover furniture, machinery, and equipment on a replacement cost basis.

## Liability Insurance

The liability part of an insurance package should be written on a *comprehensive* basis, which provides automatic coverage for newly acquired or rented premises. The standard liability protection covers claims of bodily injury or property damage arising out of the facility. For example, if a student slips on a loose floor tile and breaks an arm and damages a wristwatch, the hospital costs, physician's fee, and the cost of a new wristwatch should be covered under the liability portion of the property insurance coverage. The limits of coverage are determined by the history of claims but protection under one million dollars in the aggregate is very risky for a school district.

## Additional Types of Coverage

Many additional types of insurance coverage can be included in a package. Some of the more common types in a school district package are: crime coverage for loss of money occurring inside or outside the school-district premises; boiler and machinery insurance for losses and injuries sustained in a boiler explosion or because of failure of major machinery such as a high-voltage electrical panel; automobile and vehicle insurance coverage for driver's education cars and district-owned vehicles; and insurance on specialty items, such as musical instruments, that an insurance company might exclude in the regular policy. Errors and omission liability insurance for teachers, administrators, and members of the board of education is also very important coverage given the current amount of litigation concerning education.

## Selecting an Agent or Broker

Through competitive bidding, the school district will receive proposals from insurance companies. These proposals will be submitted by either an insurance agent or insurance broker. The majority of insurance companies operate under the American Agency System by which the company contracts with an individual who is authorized to issue policies, collect premiums, and solicit renewals within a given geographic territory. An *independent* agent may represent several companies while an *exclusive* agent will represent a single company. In either situation, the agent is a legal representative of the insurance company and can interact with the school district on behalf of the insurance company.

An insurance *broker* is not the legal representative of any insurance company. He or she acts on a free-lance basis. The broker may place business through an agent or go directly to an insurance company. The significant difference between an agent and a broker, therefore, is the ability of the agent to legally represent an insurance company. If an agent endorses additional insurance coverage for a school district, the district has the coverage. The broker must first obtain approval from the insurance company. The broker, however, can construct an insurance package by incorporating the best coverages from a number of companies.

## Selecting an Insurance Company

While there are hundreds of insurance companies providing property and casualty insurance to school districts throughout the country, these companies differ significantly in the quality of service they provide and in their financial ability to pay claims. A good reference concerning the quality and financial stability of an insurance company is the rating service, A.M. Best Company.

The A.M. Best Company provides an independent evaluation of approximately 1700 property and casualty insurance companies on a continual basis. The evaluation process categorizes each insurance company based on service provided policy holders and relative financial size. The overall review of an insurance company's management takes the following into consideration: profitability, leverage, liquidity, amount and soundness of reinsurance, adequacy of reserves and experience, and the integrity of the management team. The A.M. Best Company then assigns an alphabetical rating based on this review. The rating scale is as follows:

A+ = Superior
A = Excellent
B+ = Very good
B = Good
C+ = Fairly good
C = Fair

Approximately 25 percent of the companies reviewed do not qualify for a rating and are classified as "non-assigned."

The financial size of an insurance company is calculated through a formula which uses a *policyholders' surplus* criterion. Roman numerals indicate the financial size category beginning with I through XV which corresponds to the adjusted policyholders' surplus range listed in millions of dollars. Each company receives a Roman numeral rating. Obviously, the larger the Roman numeral, the larger the surplus and the more financially sound is the company. Exhibit 10-1 presents the financial size rating scale.

EXHIBIT 10-1 • *Financial Size Rating Scale*

| | |
|---:|:---|
| I | = Less than 1 |
| II | = 1-2 |
| III | = 2-5 |
| IV | = 5-10 |
| V | = 10-25 |
| VI | = 25-50 |
| VII | = 50 -100 |
| VIII | = 100-250 |
| IX | = 250-500 |
| X | = 500-750 |
| XI | = 750-1000 |
| XII | = 1000-1250 |
| XIII | = 1250-1500 |
| XIV | = 1500-2000 |
| XV | = 2000 or more |

The A.M. Best ratings are invaluable in analyzing the proposals that are submitted by insurance companies in a competitive bidding process. Before the request for proposals is publicized, it is necessary for the school district to have up-to-date appraisals of school buildings and their contents. A land appraisal is not necessary for insurance purposes but would be necessary, if the district is considering the sale of a school site.

The services of a professional appraiser are easily obtained. Appraisal is a subjective process, and thus, the risk manager must thoroughly understand the criteria and procedures that the appraiser will use in establishing values. In fact, it is good business practice to acquire more than one appraisal. The appraised values will have a significant effect on the financial condition of a school district if a catastrophe occurs and the district needs to replace a building and its contents. The coinsurance provision in most insurance policies by which an insurance company will assume 80 to 90 percent of the risk and will require the school district to assume the remaining risk, makes it imperative for a district to keep its appraisal values consistent with replacement cost. Otherwise a school district may be underinsured.

Appendix A contains specifications for the taking of bids for insurance coverage. In analyzing the proposals, the risk manager should seek an answer to the following questions. First, does the insurance company write all the forms of coverage needed by the school district? Second, is the insurance package flexible enough to include optional coverages that are not available in conventional packages and which the district may request during the contract period? In other words, is the company's underwriting philosophy progressive enough to consider new types of insurance risks? Third, does the insurance company have nearby offices staffed by professionals who can process all types of claims in an expeditious manner?

Exhibit 10-2 is an instrument that was developed by the Missouri Department of Elementary and Secondary Education which has been slightly modified for this presentation. This instrument was meant to be used by administrators as they evaluate their district's insurance program. Each descriptor is a criterion for evaluating the management of the program. Whether the school district's management procedures conform to each descriptor is evaluated by a yes or no response.

EXHIBIT 10-2 • *Checklist to Determine the Adequacy of a School District's Insurance Program*[2]

| Yes | No | |
|-----|-----|---|

*Legal Requirements*

_____ _____ The school district has developed policies and procedures which comply with common understandings of the state statutes as they apply to school insurance.

_____ _____ The school district utilizes open competition to determine who carries their insurance; also the board accepts the lowest responsible bid.

_____ _____ The school district's total insurance program is open for inspection.

*Responsibility*

_____ _____ The school district has developed a policy which places the responsibility for managing the insurance on the central office administration.

_____ _____ The school district maintains adequate records of the total insurance program.

_____ _____ The school district utilizes professional assistance as needed in evaluating the total insurance program.

_____ _____ The school district reviews the total insurance program annually.

*Procedures*

_____ _____ The school district has developed a standard operating procedure utilizing a definite set of written criteria for awarding insurance on the basis of competition.

_____ _____ The school district recognizes that the continuity of the insurance program is important and changes in the program or carriers are made on the basis of substantial improvement of coverage or cost reduction.

_____ _____ The school district utilizes acceptable business principles in developing its risk management program.

_____ _____ The school district has developed procedures to follow for insurance losses.

_____ _____ The school community in general and interested local insurance agents and brokers in particular are well aware of the objectives of the program.

_____ _____ The school district's policy on insurance matters neither favors nor discriminates against local insurance representatives.

*Risk Management Identification*

_____ _____ The school district has a clearly defined, written and legally defensible policy for liability coverage.

_____ _____ The school district has developed a clearly defined, written policy for providing adequate protection for all school properties.

_____ _____ The school district's policy provides for a definite procedure for periodically appraising replacement cost and the insurable value of buildings and contents.

_____ _____ The school district keeps a current listing of all buildings and/or additions for insurance purposes, including details such as dates of construction, condition, and square footage.

_____ _____ The school district, for insurance purposes, classifies as building-fixed equipment: laboratory tables, built-in cabinets, and other items that are attached to the building.

_____ _____ The school district keeps a current inventory of all school supplies and equipment classified as contents for insurance purposes, including such details as current market value, date of purchase, and condition.

_____ _____ The school district keeps a current listing of all school vehicles for insurance purposes, including details such as model, purchase price, and current value.

_____ _____ The school district has a standard procedure to account for depreciation on the various types of property.

_____ _____ The school district's vehicle coverage includes comprehensive, liability, personal injury, property damage, fire, theft, collision, and uninsured motorist types where applicable.

_____ _____ The school district provides a bond on the treasurer.

_____ _____ The school district provides burglary insurance.

_____ _____ The school provides broad-form coverage on money and securities.

_____ _____ The school district carries broad-form boiler insurance.

_____ _____ The school district boiler insurance includes a provision for regular inspection and reports.

_____ _____ The school district reports crimes and vandalism to the proper policy authorities.

_____ _____ Employees and supervisors are familiar with reporting procedures in the event of accidents.

_____ _____ The school district is prepared to cover all of the risks which have been determined as responsibilities of the school system, i.e., fire, and extended floater, boiler, liability, worker's compensation, vehicle, crime, athletics, honesty bond, health and medical for employees and student, builder's risk, and sprinkler.

*Risk Reduction*

_____ _____ The school district has cooperated with outside agencies such as the insurance carriers, fire department, police department, and others in developing policies and procedures to eliminate hazards to human life and property and for possible reduction in insurance premiums.

*Risk Assumption*

____ ____ The school district is aware of all coverage that is not transferable and also of limitations on insurance coverage.

____ ____ The school district utilizes coinsurance coverage on property.

____ ____ The school district includes a deductible clause in its insurance policy or policies where the premium difference is favorable.

*Risk Transfer*

____ ____ The school district has considered the possibility of transferring some risks to contractors or lessors. Transportation is an area where this might be considered.

____ ____ The school district's policy statement on insurance outlines an approach which provides effective coverage at a minimum cost for those risks that have been classified as responsibilities to be transferred from the district.

____ ____ The school district schedules premium payments in such manner that approximately equal amounts are paid each year and ensures that policies are written for a specified period of time.

____ ____ The school district has insured property on the basis of insurable value and/or replacement cost.

____ ____ The school district includes an agreed amount clause in the carrier's written policy or policies if coinsurance is utilized.

____ ____ The school district has considered a package plan that combines coverages.

____ ____ The school district utilizes blanket coverage, schedule coverage, and/or specific coverage plan in its insurance program.

____ ____ The school district endeavors to engage a minimum number of agencies and companies in its insurance program.

____ ____ The school district uses services such as A.M. Best's Rating Guide to determine the managerial and financial status of the insurance companies with which it deals.

## Loss Control

This is the last section of this chapter and was reserved for this position because it is better understood after the previous treatments on the various aspects of risk management. It is a continuation of the first two principles of risk management. The goal of a loss-control program is the conservation of assets which in this context means people, property, and cash. In order to achieve this goal, it is imperative that the risk manager initiate the following tasks.

## Loss Identification

The most obvious strategy in controlling losses is the elimination of a circumstance which could produce a loss. This is also the most effective risk-management technique. The risk manager should be involved as a resource person in all aspects of planning in the school district whether the planning is concerned with a new curriculum or in the remodeling of a school building. If potential risks can be uncovered before an activity begins, it will be less of a problem to initiate corrective measures than will be the discontinuance of the activity after problems arise. Information about previous losses is essential if such losses are to be avoided in the future.

This information will not be available unless there is extensive training for staff members about post-incident reporting. This training should center on what procedures must be undertaken that will ensure the gathering of relevant information. Also, it is important to train staff in what to do after an incident that will minimize claim loss. For example, if a building is damaged due to a fire, there must be procedures initiated after the fire is out that will recover salvageable material and prevent further losses. In addition, the checking of inventory lists must take place as soon as possible after the incident.

There are many computer programs that can be purchased to help in the organization of loss information. Most of these programs use a matrix format which is valuable in the analysis of losses. The frequency and severity of losses will readily identify problem areas in the district. A requirement that places the responsibility for filling out loss reports on supervisors is also a way to sensitize them to what factors cause claims incidents.

## Loss Control Programming

No loss-control program will be successful unless it is sanctioned and encouraged not only by the superintendent of schools but also by the board of education. The most difficult task is not the formulation of a loss-control program but rather the communicating to the staff of what needs to be done. The following are aspects of a loss-control program which have proven to be successful in the prevention of losses:

> Requiring pre-employment physical exams
> Developing job-related safety training
> Developing an accident investigation procedure
> Establishing safety committees

Designating certain staff members as safety inspectors

Requiring the use of safety equipment

Developing an easily retrievable loss claims record system

Making safety performance a part of an employee's performance evaluation

Developing adequate inventory procedures[3]

Appendix B is a checklist that can be used as an audit instrument to determine the degree of safety and security that exists in a school. Also, it is a document that exhibits the scope of loss control administration in relation to safety and security.

## Occupational Safety and Health Act (OSHA) 1970

This law enables individual states to enact their own laws concerning safety in the workplace. However, state law must be no less stringent than the federal law. There are civil and criminal penalties attached to violations of OSHA standards. According to the general procedural requirements of OSHA, a school district is responsible for informing workers about the intent and coverage of this law. The most common manner of informing employees is through the posting of this information in the workplace. Further, the district must post annual summaries concerning occupational injuries and illnesses and must post citations received from either the federal or state OSHA agency.

OSHA agencies may enter the workplace to ascertain if proper safety measures are in place and, of course, may enter the workplace to investigate complaints. The district may appeal any complaint. The OSHA appeals board may affirm, modify, or cancel the citation. Public employers are exempt from civil penalties that may be levied because of a code violation. However, criminal penalties may be levied against specific managers.[4]

## Summary

During the 1950s a significant advance took place in the commercial insurance industry. The insurance companies allowed business and industrial corporations and companies to draw together all their property and casualty insurance coverage into one package.

Insurance coverage is only one aspect of a total risk-management program. The contemporary milieu which consists of large dollar legal claims against school districts and the cancelling of insurance coverage of school districts because of large dollar losses are the reasons for the emphasis on risk management. From this, has arisen the new administrative position of risk manager.

The risk manager should be an individual who has broad experience in the insurance industry. The risk manager should report to the assistant superintendent for business and financial services. The risk manager should be responsible for coordinating the insurance programs in the district in addition to being a resource person to all the other divisions and departments in the school district concerning the identification and resolution of risk to property and people. Some school districts are too small to hire a person whose sole responsibility is administering the risk management program. However, a group of school districts might cooperatively hire a person who has the expertise that would allow them to have these necessary services at a reasonable cost. There are also many consultants who can be hired for this purpose.

It does not matter what you do or how careful you are, there is always the possibility that an accident will cause injury to you or damage to your property. The situation in private business and industry is similar. Over time, these entities have developed certain principles for handling risks that have proven to be successful. First, identify and evaluate the school district's exposure to risks. Conducting a safety audit is the most effective way to implement this first principle. Second, eliminate or minimize potential risks. Third, if it is impossible to eliminate or significantly minimize a risk, it will be necessary to transfer that risk to another party. Purchasing insurance is the most common method of transferring risks.

In purchasing insurance, the premium paid by the school district is a direct measure of the transferred risk. The greater the risk, the more it will cost the district in premium. If the risk assumed by the insurance company is reduced, not only will the premium be reduced but also the competition between insurance companies to acquire the account will be increased. The most effective way to reduce premiums is to increase the deductible. The insurance company is likely to have to pay out more money for claims if the district has a small deductible, which, obviously, will affect the amount of the premium.

The true commercial package combines both property and liability coverage thus offering broader based protection. Of course, property insurance constitutes the most extensive part of the school district's insurance coverage. A common approach today in providing property coverage is the all risk policy which means that a loss is covered unless it is clearly excluded in the policy. It is better for a school district to have property insurance coverage on a replacement cost basis rather than on an actual cash value basis.

The liability part of an insurance package should be written on a comprehensive basis that provides automatic coverage for newly acquired or rented facilities. The standard liability protection covers claims of bodily injury or property damage arising out of the facilities. Errors and omissions liability insurance for administrators and members of the board of education is also very important given the amount of litigation that school districts encounter.

Through competitive bidding the school district will receive proposals from insurance companies. These proposals will be submitted by either an insurance agent or insurance broker. An independent agent may legally represent several companies while an exclusive agent will represent a single company. An insurance broker is not the legal representative of any insurance company and may place business through an agent or go directly to an insurance company.

While there are hundreds of insurance companies providing property and casualty insurance to school districts throughout the country, these companies differ significantly in the quality of service they provide and in their financial ability to pay claims. A good reference concerning the quality of service and financial stability of an insurance company is the rating service, A.M. Best Company.

Before a request for insurance proposals is publicized, it will be necessary for the school district to have up-to-date appraisals of school buildings and their contents. The appraised values will have a significant effect on the financial condition of a school district if a catastrophe occurs and the district needs to replace a building and its contents. The coinsurance provision in most insurance policies by which an insurance company assumes 80 to 90 percent of the risk and requires the school district to assume the remaining risk, makes it imperative for a district to keep its appraisal values consistent with replacement costs.

The goal of a loss-control program is the conservation of assets, which, in this context, means people, property, and cash. The most obvious strategy in controlling losses is the elimination of circumstances that could produce losses. If potential risks can be uncovered before an activity begins, it will be less of a problem to initiate corrective measures than will be the discontinuance of the activity after problems arise. Information about previous losses is essential, if such losses are to be avoided in the future. No loss-control program will be successful unless it is sanctioned and encouraged not only by the superintendent of schools but also by the board of education.

The Occupational Safety and Health Act (OSHA) of 1970 enables individual states to enact their own laws concerning safety in the workplace. This is the most significant law dealing with loss control.

## Appendix A  Insurance Specifications

### All-Risk Coverage on Building and Contents

All-risk coverage including theft and sprinkler leakage must be provided on the buildings and their contents as listed in the attached schedule of buildings and contents values on a blanket basis without a prorata distribution clause. Coverage must be 90 percent of replacement value of all property. Coverage must be provided on a 90 percent coinsurance basis. Replacement value coverage must be endorsed to void any requirement to replace a damaged structure *on the same site* of the loss occurrence. An *agreed value* endorsement for one year must be included to permit the district to review the values of its property.

Coverage must include $25 million of flood and earthquake insurance with a 2 percent deductible. The flood and earthquake coverage may be provided by a separate policy or on a special *difference in conditions* form if necessary.

Coverage must be written with a flat $25,000 deductible. Alternate deductibles of $5000 and $10,000 are also requested. An *inflation guard* provision must be included to provide an annual increase in property values and coverage thereof equal to 8 percent (2 percent per quarter).

Off-site coverage of contents and equipment of $25,000 must be included with an applicable deductible of $1000.

### Property Floater

An all-risk inland marine floater or equivalent form written on a broad-form and blanket basis must be provided for replacement values of the listed property. Floater coverages must include a $250 deductible per occurrence (not per item).

General or miscellaneous mobile equipment (office, shop, audio-visual, laboratory, photographic, sound, lawns and grounds, and athletic equipment, etc.) not included in above building and content coverage must be covered.

Total coverage amount: $96,000

### Computer and Data Processing Coverage

An all-risk EDP form must be written on computer and data processing equipment. Equipment must be insured for 100 percent of replacement values totaling *$1.2 million*. Coverage must be written on a blanket basis and include a $250 per occurrence deductible on equipment, and include an *extra expense* coverage for $7500 with a $100 deductible and *transit* coverage of $10,000 with a $100 per occurrence deductible.

## Boiler and Machinery Insurance

Broad-form boiler and machinery insurance must be written to cover all district objects as listed herein on a blanket-group basis for a limit of $5 million per accident on a repair and replacement basis and the legal liability for the property of others in the care, control, or custody of the district. Bodily injury and furnace explosion should be omitted to the extent such perils are covered under other insurance requested within these specifications. Coverage must include a $5000 deductible and expediting expenses of $10,000.

Coverage must include blanket boiler, fired vessels, unfired pressure vessels, refrigerating systems, compressors, and air-conditioning units.

Automatic coverage of newly acquired objects and loss adjustment provisions must be included. Equipment must be inspected annually, internally and externally, by a qualified inspector.

## General Liability Insurance

General liability coverage must be written on an occurrence basis on a comprehensive general liability broad-form or its equivalent for a *single limit* of $1 million and an aggregate limit of $2 million for bodily injury, property damage, and personal injury liability resulting from district premises, operations, products and completed operations, owner protective and independent contractors, owned and non-owned watercraft up to 26 feet, incidental and nurse malpractice, broad and blanket contractual, employee discrimination, garage keepers legal liability, teachers' liability including corporal punishment, fire legal liability, employee benefit liability, host liquor liability, and student athletic participants. Coverage must include parties using or leasing district property on an occasional basis. Coverage must be broadened to either liberalize or eliminate (eliminate preferred) the exclusion of property in the care, custody, and control of the insured bidder. Coverage must include medical payments of $5000 per person and $250,000 per occurrence.

Bidders are requested to submit a quotation for adding asbestos and sexual molestation liability coverages.

In addition to insuring the district as the policyholder, the coverage must insure all board members, school officials, and all district employees while acting within the scope of their responsibilities, duties, or employment. Coverage must be endorsed to insure those individuals performing services for the district as *volunteers* without receiving remuneration of any kind. Also, all activities under the supervision and control of the district must be covered.

An endorsement must be included to eliminate any exclusion of personal injury sustained by a person(s) as a result of an offense directly or indirectly related to the employment of such person(s) by the policyholder or district employees or officials.

The present public liability coverage of the district is a claims-made form with a retroactive date of July 1, 1986. The bidder is requested to submit a *buy-out* or retroactive date provision or prior coverage of unknown claims provisions to the retroactive date that would in effect convert the liability coverage to an occurrence form dating back to the retroactive date (with a $100,000 SIR). The cost of this provision must be stated on a separate page and attached to the rate-premium bid quotation form.

Coverage must include all stadiums, bleachers, grandstands, swimming pools, cafeterias, and lunchrooms. Coverage must extend to cover the policyholder when premises are leased to other parties.

## School Board Legal Liability Insurance

Legal liability insurance for errors and omissions (*wrongful acts*) must be written on a broad-form basis for a per claim limit of $5 million and annual aggregate limit of $5 million with a $2500 per claim retention. Coverage must include a *prior acts* endorsement. Bidders are requested to submit alternate quotations on larger coverage limits than those cited above. An errors and omissions application will be supplied or completed for the bidder upon request.

## Umbrella Liability Insurance

Umbrella liability insurance on an occurrence basis must be written with a per occurrence limit of $5 million and an annual aggregate limit of $5 million with a retention of $10,000. All underlying liability coverages must be included, except school board legal liability. If school board liability can be included, it should be and the cost of doing so must be stated on the rate-premium bid quotation form.

## Crime and Bond Coverages

A broad-form *money and securities* coverage must be written for a limit of $5000 for on-and-off-premises coverage. Premises are defined to include premises of the administration building and those schools with cafeterias (# schools). Coverage must include a $500 deductible per occurrence.

A *public employees bond* for faithful performance on a blanket basis must be written for a penalty of $200,000 and should define the term *employee* to include any student under the jurisdiction of the district while having control or possession of property or funds in connection with school activities. Coverage must include a $5000 deductible.

A *depositor's forgery bond* must be written to cover the district for $25,000 for outgoing items only. Coverage must include a $1000 deductible.

A *public officials' bond* must be written on behalf of the district for $50,000 for the treasurer of the board of education.

## Automobile Insurance

Automobile insurance must be written to cover the district for liability arising from bodily injury and property damage, for uninsured motorists, for medical payments, and for physical damage for owned, leased, hired, and temporarily used vehicles according to the limits cited below.

*Liability Limits*
   Bodily injury and property damage—single limit of $1 million.
   Medical payments—$5000 per person.
   Uninsured Motorists—$25,000 per person and $50,000 per occurrence.

*Physical damage*
   Private passenger vehicles must be insured for actual cash values for comprehensive and collision coverage. Both coverages, comprehensive and collision, must include a $500 deductible.
   Commercial vehicles must be covered for comprehensive and collision. Both comprehensive and collision coverages must include a $1000 deductible.

No physical damage coverage should be written for any vehicle valued at $3000 or less.

Coverage must be written on a blanket-fleet basis for vehicle acquisition and disposal premium adjustments during the policy period.

Automobile liability insurance must be endorsed to cover the lessee and the lessor as a person or organization legally responsible for use of a leased vehicle by an individual who is an insured under the coverage.

The term *insured* must be defined to include the members of the board of education, school officials, all district employees, and individuals serving the district as *volunteers* without remuneration of any kind while such parties are acting within the scope of their responsibilities, duties, employment, or volunteer activities.

## Garage Keepers

Garage keepers insurance must be written for $120,000 per location. Comprehensive coverage must include a $500 deductible for theft, mischief, and vandalism subject to a $1000 maximum deductible for all such loss in any one event. Collision must include a $500 deductible for each covered auto.

# Appendix B  Safety and Security Audit

*School and Administration Building(s)*

Rating System
   0 = Not Able To Judge
   1 = Low
   2 = Some
   3 = High

Level of Concern

*Access by persons other than students, faculty, or staff.*

_____  1.  There is control over visitor access to buildings.

_____  2.  Visitor ingress limited to a single door at each building.

_____  3.  Sign in/sign out log maintained (and used for visitors at all locations).

_____  4.  Unrecognized persons dressed as repair, custodial, mail delivery, etc. personnel are challenged for identification and authority to be in buildings or on grounds.

_____  5.  Other unidentified persons in hallways, offices, or rooms are challenged for identification.

_____  6.  Periodic checks are made of restrooms for suspicious persons/objects.

_____  7.  The central office administration center maintains a current list of all active employees.

_____  8.  Duress alarms are in office areas. Note: These alarms can sound within the building only to summon assistance from staff members.

*Ingress/egress: Buildings, rooms, offices*

_____  9.  Doors of metal or solid core construction are used in perimeter areas.

_____  10.  Perimeter doors do not have exposed hinges which can be removed.

_____  11.  Locked doors are propped, tied, or wedged open.

_____  12.  Hallway access is closed, limited or controlled via gates or doors.

_____  13.  Existing door locks can be retracted by insertion of a narrow instrument to *slip* them.

14. Fire doors and panic bar hardware (including that on seldom-used doors) are frequently inspected.

15. Perimeter walls of important rooms are constructed slab-to-slab in order to defeat entrance via a dropped ceiling.

16. All offices and exits are secured promptly at the end of the school/business day.

17. One employee (at each location) is designated to check and secure all appropriate offices and exits promptly at the end of the school/business day.

18. A log is maintained that indicates precisely who has keys, what key(s) each individual has, and how long they have had them.

19. Extra building/room keys are maintained in a secure environment and are controlled by one individual.

20. Keys are given or loaned out on a temporary basis to students, employees, or non-employees who need them.

21. Master keys are accorded a higher degree of control than non-masters.

22. If keys are given/loaned on a temporary basis, a procedure exists to ensure their timely return.

23. A procedure is used to ensure that terminated employees turn in all keys.

24. Locks are rekeyed or cores rotated frequently.

25. High security or non-duplicable keys are used for sensitive areas.

*Ability to physically secure and protect equipment and supplies*

26. There is control over equipment/materials leaving buildings via service doors.

27. All custodial personnel are strictly forbidden to park their personal vehicles adjacent to any building.

28. All custodial personnel follow a schedule so that their whereabouts are known at all times.

29. All supply rooms, closets, and file areas are locked at all times when unattended.

30. All typewriters, adding machines, dictaphones, calculators, etc., are property tagged and inventoried.

31. A log is maintained indicating which personnel have what equipment, by serial number.

_____ 32. Equipment/supply inventory records are frequently reviewed and reconciled to what can actually be located (random sample method).

_____ 33. There is an awareness that school and office supplies have a significant dollar value in aggregate.

_____ 34. There is an awareness that portable electronic equipment carries a very high susceptibility to theft.

_____ 35. Portable electronic equipment (VCRs overhead, film and slide projectors, etc.) is secured to carts by means of anchor pads, cables, wires or chains.

*Ability to physically secure and protect equipment and supplies*

_____ 36. Anchor pads are used to secure typewriters, computers, and other desktop electronic equipment.

_____ 37. Smaller electronic articles are kept secure when not in use.

_____ 38. Policy mandates that all electronic and high-value (including uncrated) equipment is locked in a secure room with limited key access when not in use.

_____ 39. Sufficient secure storage space exists for this type of equipment.

_____ 40. Fire detectors are installed in areas designated for storage of this type of equipment.

_____ 41. Materials are optimally protected against misplacement, accidental loss, or theft.

_____ 42. It is policy to lock all desks, file cabinets, credenzas, etc., while unattended.

_____ 43. All keys are removed from desks, file cabinets, credenzas, etc., when unattended.

_____ 44. The school district encourages a *clear desk* policy at the end of each business day.

_____ 45. The security of confidential records/forms is adequate.

_____ 46. Consistent efforts are made to maintain secure conversations.

_____ 47. There are safes at schools and/or offices to provide necessary temporary storage of tuition/fees, etc.

_____ 48. Checks are stamp-endorsed upon receipt and deposited the same day as received.

_____ 49. Check-writing machines are maintained in secure areas with keys removed.

_____ 50. Blank checks are strictly controlled, kept in a safe, and treated as cash.

_____ 51. Critical records are stored off-site or in environmentally secure on-site area.

_____ 52. Backup media has been created and backup EDP facilities are available for data processing used in critical administrative operations.

_____ 53. A determination has been made of the maximum length of time that the school district can survive without financial or administrative operations/facilities.

_____ 54. Classes can continue in the event of the destruction of one or more buildings or schools.

_____ 55. Procedures exist for immediate evacuation of buildings in all types of emergencies.

_____ 56. These procedures are frequently practiced.

_____ 57. Emergency medical facilities and transportation have been identified in the event of a disaster.

_____ 58. Drills have taken place to ensure the availability of these facilities/equipment and the feasibility of their use.

_____ 59. Each appropriate building has an emergency power source.

_____ 60. Students/faculty/staff are aware of bomb-threat procedures.

_____ 61. Written guidelines are available to assist employees in asking the right questions and capturing the right information at the time of receipt of a bomb-threat or extortion demand.

## Endnotes

1. Ronald W. Rebore, _Educational Administration: A Management Approach_ (Englewood Cliffs, NJ: Prentice-Hall, Inc., 1985), pp. 144–151. Many of the concepts in this chapter have been gleaned from this previous work by the author.

2. Missouri Department of Elementary and Secondary Education, _Checklist to Determine the Adequacy of a School District's Insurance Program_ (Jefferson City, MO: The Department, 1982).

3. L. Nathan Randal, "Risk Management," _Principles of School Business Management_, R. Craig Wood, ed. (Reston: Association of School Business Officials International, 1986), p. 353.

4. _Ibid._, pp. 356, 357.

## Selected Bibliography

Ailes, Jim, "Umbrella Coverage: Keeping Your Entity Safe and Dry," *Public Risk*, Vol. 3, no. 1 (November/December 1988), pp. 8–10.

Gallagher, Patrick, "Our Policy: Where Does a Risk Manager Start?" *Public Risk*, Vol. 1, no. 4 (May/June 1987), pp. 4–8.

Grasley, Sheldon W., "What's Ahead in General Liability and Property Insurance," *The School Administrator*, Vol. 42, no. 9 (October 1985), pp. 8, 9.

McConnell, James G., "Claims Made Insurance Requires Thoughtful Consideration," *School Business Affairs*, Vol. 52, no. 6 (June 1986), pp. 16–20.

Michelson, Richard S., "Crime Prevention on Campus," *American School and University*, Vol. 59, no. 10 (June 1987), pp. 45–48.

Randal, L. Nathan, "Risk Management," *Principles of School Business Management*, R. Craig Wood, ed. (Reston, Virginia: Association of School Business Officials International, 1986), pp. 345–380.

Rebore, Ronald W., *Educational Administration. A Management Approach* (Englewood Cliffs: Prentice-Hall, Inc., 1985), pp. 144–151.

Stover, Del, "Your Staff is the Target of Violence," *The Executive Educator*, Vol. 10, no. 10 (October 1988), pp. 15–21, 33.

# 11

# Legal Considerations in School Business Management

School-district business officials, in addition to their primary role as the chief fiscal agent of the district, must be cognizant of both current legal issues and emerging federal and state trends regarding district taxing powers, state funding, and facility requirements. The mechanics of school business management are dictated by a myriad of federal and state legislation, policies, and regulations. The traditional issues of equity of educational opportunity, while primarily a state matter, continuously affect the amount of state dollars available to local school districts. The many facets of state educational reform place greater financial demands on school districts without corresponding increases in funding. Issues involving tax-payer equity appear to be re-emerging as wealthier districts are able to fund local programs with a lower tax rate than property-poor districts. Compliance with federal environmental regulations regarding drinking water, storage tanks, radon exposure, and asbestos removal have placed a heavy financial burden on districts.

With the exception of reviewing the Supreme Court's landmark decision in *San Antonio Independent School District* v. *Rodriguez* in 1973 regarding state equity issues, this chapter will concentrate on major legal issues affecting school business management during the past ten years.

## Financial Equity Issues

The legal power of taxation is an inherent power of the state limited only by the constitutional provisions of the state and the Fourteenth Amendment to the U.S. Constitution. The Equal Protection Clause prohibits the state from taxing through unreasonable classification. Therefore, the state may not levy a discriminatory tax only on one segment of the population. While the state may not discriminate within classifications, there is no constitutional prohibition against different taxing policies between classifications. For example, the state may impose different income tax rates based on levels of income. Likewise, the state may choose to assess commercial property at a higher rate than residential property for taxing purposes.

As agents of the state, school districts are granted the right of taxation through specific authorization of the state legislature. The courts have held that legislative authority to establish and maintain local school districts does not imply taxing powers unless specifically mandated by statute. As a result, the state legislature may decide to fund education by a statewide tax or other applicable system.[1]

The issues of fiscal equity are not easily summarized since states approach the equity issue through several channels. Walters, in "Equity and Diversity: A Challenge for the Allocation of Financial Resources," maintains that there are basically two conflicting standards of equity.

> *One equity theme is equalization of fiscal outcomes (Revenues, Expenditures, and Tax Rates). A pure version of this standard would not permit any student to obtain a more expensive education than that afforded to others. The second equity standard, fiscal neutrality, holds that the quality of public education may not be a function of wealth, other than the wealth of the state as a whole. According to this standard, fiscal outcomes may vary among school districts according to local willingness to pay for public schooling. The definition of fiscal neutrality includes two different, and possibly conflicting, concepts also. The ex ante variety of fiscal neutrality maintains that districts levying equal tax rates should have equal revenue and expenditures regardless of their tax base wealth differences. The goal here is an equitable school finance process that equalizes the ability of districts to earn educational funds. The concern of ex post fiscal neutrality is not with the process but with the end products of a school finance system. Ex post neutrality holds that wealthy districts should not have more educational funding than poor districts. The second kind of fiscal neutrality requires that there be no systematic relationship between district tax base wealth and each district's fiscal outcomes.[2]*

During the 1970s, challenges to state aid distribution systems centered on the equalization of fiscal outcomes. Litigants argued that the failure of state aid programs to ensure equal access to educational dollars constituted a violation of the *Equal Protection Clause* of the Fourteenth Amendment of the U.S. Constitution. As a result, federal remedies were sought to rectify this concern. In a landmark decision of the United States Supreme Court in *San Antonio Independent School District* v. *Rodriguez*, the Court addressed the equal protection clause as it applies to state distribution of funds to local school districts.

The case involved a suit against the Texas system of distributing state aid by a group of Mexican-American parents whose children attended the elementary and secondary schools in the Edgewood Independent School District. They filed a class action suit on behalf of all minority school children who were educated in school districts with a low property tax base. The federal district court held that the Texas school finance system was unconstitutional on the grounds that it violated the *Equal Protection Clause* of the Fourteenth Amendment. The state appealed and the Supreme Court reversed the decision. The following paragraphs represent some of the more important excerpts from the decision.

*San Antonio Independent School District v. Rodriguez*

*Mr. Justice Powell delivered the opinion of the Court*

First, in support of their charge that the system discriminates against the "poor," appellees have made no effort to demonstrate that it operates to the peculiar disadvantage of any class fairly definable as indigent, or as composed of persons whose incomes are beneath any designated poverty level. Indeed, there is reason to believe that the poorest families are not necessarily clustered in the poorest property districts. . . .

Second, neither appellees nor the District Court addressed the fact that, unlike each of the foregoing cases, lack of personal resources has not occasioned an absolute deprivation of the desired benefit. The argument here is not that the children in districts having relatively low assessable property values are receiving no public education; rather, it is that they are receiving a poorer quality education than that available to children in districts having more assessable wealth. Apart from the unsettled and disputed question whether the quality of education may be determined by the amount of money expended for it, a sufficient answer to appellees' argument is that, at least where wealth is involved, the Equal Protection Clause does not require absolute equality or precisely equal advantages. Nor indeed, in view of the infinite variables affecting the educational process, can any system assure equal quality of education except in the most relative sense. . . .

This brings us, then, to the third way in which the classification scheme might be defined—district wealth discrimination. Since the only correlation indicated by the evidence is between district property wealth and expenditures, it may be argued that discrimination might be found without regard to the individual income characteristics of district residents. . . .

We thus conclude that the Texas system does not operate to the peculiar disadvantage of any suspect class. But in recognition of the fact that this Court has never heretofore held that wealth discrimination alone provides an adequate basis for invoking strict scrutiny, appellees have not relied solely on this contention. They also assert that the State's system impermissibly interferes with the exercise of a fundamental right and that accordingly the prior decisions of this Court require the *allocation of the strict standard of judicial review. It is this question—whether education is a fundamental right, in the sense that it is among the rights and liberties protected by the Constitution—which has so consumed the attention of courts and commentators in recent years. . . .*

*We hold that the Texas plan abundantly satisfies this standard.*

*Reversed.*[3]

Having failed to receive a favorable decision from the Supreme Court, the litigants turned to the state courts on the premise that existing distribution systems violated the equal protection clause found in state constitutions. Most state constitutions included an equal protection clause similar to the Fourteenth Amendment, as well as an implied guarantee of equality and uniformity of taxation. Specifically, challenges were based on the premise that a state financial plan that allows per pupil revenue, based on the individual wealth of the district rather than the collective wealth of the entire state, is a violation of the states equal protection clause. Counterbalancing this challenge was the position that local control of school districts is the prime objective of state policy, and therefore local responsibility for financing education is a necessary corollary of that policy. Rossmiller, in "School Reform through Litigation: Expressway or Cul-de-Sac," provided the following summary of state equal protection litigation.

> *Whether or not the local control argument will prevail depends upon whether a court finds that the state constitutional provisions for education create a fundamental interest in education, thus subjecting the state's arrangement for providing and financing education to stricter scrutiny than would otherwise be required.*[4]

Another challenge to state funding was tied to the *education clauses* of state constitutions relative to the development of a free and gratuitous system of public education for all citizens of the state. The challengers argued that the disparity between local districts, and the heavy dependence on local property wealth to fund educational programs, was a violation of the state's responsibility to provide equitable educational opportunities. For example, in *Edgewood Independent School District* v. *Kirby*, the Texas Supreme Court ruled that the "state's school financing system is neither financially efficient nor suitable in the sense of providing for a 'general diffusion of knowledge' statewide."[5] In a similar case, *Abbott* v. *Burke*, the New Jersey Supreme Court found the state's finance system unconstitutional on the grounds that it violated the *Education Clause* through a failure to provide poorer districts with funding equal to the property rich districts in the state. This decision resulted in the passage of the *Quality Education Act of 1990* by the New Jersey Legislature. This act appropriated an additional $1 billion for education to rectify these inequities.[6]

A third approach to rectifying educational inequities is based on the special educational needs of specific students. Proponents of this strategy argue that the *special needs* of particular students demand additional financial resources. Educational programs in school districts with a large population of at-risk students are more costly and demand greater resources. In some cases, these arguments have led to changes in the state funding through mechanisms such as *pupil weighting* to provide additional funds for students with special needs. (See Chapter 2.)

In those states where the school finance systems have been overturned, the court has ruled that education was a fundamental right subject to either the state's equal protection and/or education clauses. Therefore, the court reasoned, all students within the state are guaranteed an equitable educational program regardless of the individual wealth of the local districts. In states where the current finance systems were upheld, the courts concluded that education was not a fundamental right and inequitable funding was not a violation of the equal protection or education clauses. In almost all of these cases, the issue of local control formed the basis of the decision. For example, the Oregon Supreme Court, in *Olsen* v. *Oregon* (1976), ruled that the prominence of local control outweighed the plaintiff's contention that the state's flat grant program was the result of inequity between districts.[7]

Litigation regarding equity and related issues will continue to be the subject of state court deliberations during the decade of the 1990s. With the state's contribution so critical to the funding of local district programs, school districts with limited resources have no other choice than to attempt a redistribution of wealth.

## Special Education

The *Individuals with Disabilities Education Act*, formally named the *Education of All Handicapped Children Act*, passed by Congress in 1975 requires that all handicapped children be identified and provided with an appropriate education in the least restrictive environment. This act clearly places the responsibility for providing such programs on states and local school districts. Federal appropriations for special education each year do not legally establish a ceiling for special education program expenditures. Even in the absence of federal funding, the state and school districts are required to provide the appropriate level of services.[8] While the issue of program cost is not specifically addressed by the act, and is not considered a legal defense for not providing the service, the courts have attempted to deal with the issue in some respects.

Rothstein, in her book entitled, *Special Education Law*, addresses the issue of program cost in her review of the Supreme Court Case, *Irving Independent School District* v. *Tatro* (1984). The Court was asked to determine whether catheterization was a related health service, or not required under the act. The Court ruled that since the parents were not requesting the purchase of any equipment, and that a school nurse, not a physician, could perform the service, catheterization was a related service under the act.[9]

Two other significant cost issues have been decided by the Court. The first concerns the quality of the program provided by the school district. The Supreme Court, in *Board of Education* v. *Rowley*, concluded that the primary issue was the *appropriateness* of the service. The law requires each district to provide an appropriate education for each handicapped student. When more than one approach is available, the district may choose the less expensive program. The Court ruled that the act does not guarantee the "best available program, but an appropriate program." As long as the district can prove that the service offered will address the student's handicap, the more cost-effective program can be implemented.[10] The second issue involved ultimate responsibility for providing special education services. The Ninth Circuit Court of Appeals, in *Doe* v. *Maher*, concluded that the state must assume ultimate responsibility if the district cannot provide the program. When appealed to the Supreme Court for ruling, the Court was split evenly regarding fiscal responsibility. As a result, that portion of the case was affirmed.[11] Absent of a clear ruling by the Supreme Court, this issue will continue to receive attention until ultimately decided.

## Tax Increment Financing

Many states have recently enacted, through state legislation or constitutional amendment, tax increment financing plans. While specific requirements vary from state to state, the primary objective of these acts is to provide funds for the development of blighted areas, for the removal of structures which constitute a threat to the public health and safety, or for the redevelopment of areas within a municipality to attract or retain industry. In order to fund these projects, the ad valorem taxes collected by each of the taxing authorities are frozen at the dollar amount collected prior to the development of the plan. When the area is redeveloped, the increase in property taxes as a result of the higher assessed valuation is used to pay for the improvements or to retire revenue bonds issued to fund the approved projects. The local taxing authorities only receive the prior development taxes until the redevelopment costs are paid. In some states, the funding for each project may extend up to twenty-five years. In many states, ad valorem taxes represent the largest source of local income for school districts. As a result, tax increment financing adversely impacts school districts more than any other local governmental plan.

In 1987, the City of El Paso created a tax increment district in the central business area. The school districts within the reinvestment zone claimed that the act was unconstitutional on the grounds that the city cannot use school district ad valorem tax revenues for noneducational purposes.

The Texas Supreme Court, in *City of El Paso* v. *El Paso College District*, ruled that the legislators were aware of the impact of the act on school districts and upheld its constitutionality.[12] The procedural requirements for most tax increment financing plans usually require notification of all taxing authorities involved, and a reasonable time frame for comment. The district business administrator should be aware of the procedural requirements. District challenges to these plans, for the most part, are limited to procedural compliance and statutory use of the funds.

## Tax-Exempt Bonds

In 1982, Congress passed the *Tax Equity and Fiscal Responsibility Act* (TEFRA). Section 310 of this act modified one of the most significant characteristics of general obligation bonds issued by school districts. Specifically, the act removed the tax-exempt status of any general obligation bond issued in *bearer form* after 1983.[13] Since the passage of TEFRA, school districts are now required to issue bonds in registered form to retain the tax-exempt status of the issue. With registered bonds, the paying agent for the district maintains a list of bond holders, and pays the semi-annual interest and annual principal payments on behalf of the school district.

South Carolina decided to challenge the constitutionality of Section 310 on the grounds that it violated the Tenth Amendment and the doctrine of intergovernmental immunity.[14] The Tenth Amendment limits the authority of the federal government over the states to only those areas specifically mentioned in the U.S. Constitution. Regarding the doctrine of intergovernmental immunity, South Carolina argued that a tax on a municipal bond is a direct tax on the state, local government, or school district. The Supreme Court, in *South Carolina* v. *Baker*, concluded that the owner of a municipal bond has no constitutional protection against the payment of taxes. Likewise, the Court reasoned that Section 310's provision to tax municipal bearer bonds after 1983 was a tax on the individual and not a direct tax on the state or local government.[15] Through this decision, the

Court established constitutional authority allowing Congress to tax municipal bonds. Although Congress has never indicated an interest in taxing general obligation registered bonds, the authority to do so has been established. The imposition of a tax on municipal bonds would result in the loss of lower interest rates available on tax-exempt bonds, and also would directly affect the total interest cost of the issuing agency.

## Federal Environmental Issues

Since 1986, federal mandates regarding specific environmental issues have required local school districts to take corrective measures without additional funding. In most cases, local districts were unprepared for the tremendous costs of compliance and monitoring activities required by existing law.

### Safe Drinking Water Act Amendments of 1986

This act stipulates different requirements based on whether or not the school district is its own water supplier. If the district supplies its own water, the regulations require that lead levels of water entering the distribution system must be below 5 ppb (parts per billion). Furthermore, water samples must be tested at laboratories certified by the state. The Environmental Protection Agency (EPA) requires notification if the school's distribution/plumbing system contains any materials that can be a source of lead contamination.[16] The EPA requires that the notice of contamination be conveyed to the public through one of the following four vehicles.

1. Three newspaper notices (one for each of three consecutive months)
2. Once by mail
3. Once by hand delivery
4. By continuous posting in a conspicuous place for three consecutive months

Exhibit 11-1 is a checklist provided by the EPA to alert districts for possible contamination and the development of a plumbing profile.[17] Schools that purchase their water should contact their supplier to ascertain what steps are being taken to reduce lead contaminants.

The *Lead Contamination Control Act of 1988* requires that states provide direction to local districts to test and correct any lead contamination in drinking water from water coolers. The EPA, under this act, must publish a list of each brand of water cooler which is known to contain a lead-lined storage tank. Water coolers found to be contaminated, according to the

EXHIBIT 11-1 • *Lead Contamination*

---

*When to Expect Lead Contamination*

---

*In general, you can expect widespread lead contamination in your school's drinking water if:*
1. The building's plumbing is less than 5 years old and lead solder was used in the construction
2. The water is corrosive
3. Sediment in the plumbing and screens contains lead
4. Lead pipes are used throughout the building
5. The service connector is made of lead

*In general, you can expect localized contamination if:*
1. The building's plumbing is more than 5 years old
2. The water is non-corrosive
3. There are pipes or fittings containing lead in some locations
4. Recent repairs or additions to plumbing used materials containing lead (solder, brass, etc.)
5. Numerous solder joints are installed in short sections of pipe
6. There are areas of low flow or infrequent use
7. Sediment in the plumbing and screens at isolated locations contains lead
8. Water coolers have tanks lines with lead or other construction materials made of lead

*Developing a Plumbing Profile of Your School*
Completing a survey of your school's plumbing is an essential part of an overall program to identify high risk areas for lead in your drinking water. In addition, this survey will help you:

Make decisions about water supply and pipe materials in the school;
Make overall policy decisions regarding steps to initiate remedial action;
Inform parents and employees about what the school system is doing about lead in the drinking water.

---

Consumer Product Safety Act, should be immediately considered hazardous and taken out of service until repaired or replaced. The effective date of these regulations is March 1, 1990.

## Toxic Substances Control Act of 1988

The Environmental Protection Agency published the following remarks concerning Radon-222.

*Radon-222 is a colorless, odorless, tasteless, radioactive gas that occurs naturally in soil, rocks, underground water, and air. It is produced by the natural breakdown of radium-226 in soil and rocks. . . . Breathing radon decay products increases the chance of developing lung cancer. In outdoor air, radon is usually present at such low levels that there is very little risk. However, when radon enters a building, it and its decay products can accumulate to high concentrations.*[18]

While school districts are not required to conduct radon testing, the issue has received substantial public attention. Many schools are currently being pressured by parents and staff to conduct the testing at district expense. The cost of radon testing is relatively insignificant in relation to building modifications if radon contaminants are confirmed. The following guidelines are recommended by the EPA.

*1. If a confirmatory measurement is greater than 20 pCi/L (picocuries per liter of air), school officials should take action to reduce levels as much as possible. EPA recommends that action be taken within several weeks. The urgency of corrective action is greater as the levels increase. For example, if levels are about 100 pCi/L or greater, school officials should consult with appropriate state or local health officials to consider temporary relocation until the levels can be reduced.*

*2. If a confirmatory measurement is about 4 to 20 pCi/L, school officials should take action to reduce levels as much as possible. EPA recommends that actions be taken within a few months.*[19]

At the present time, no financial assistance is being offered to schools found to be highly contaminated.

## Resource Conservation and Recovery Act

This act requires the Environment Protection Agency to protect both people and the environment against contamination from leaking underground storage tanks. School districts are required to comply with the provisions of the act by October 26, 1990. While the act covers several different underground storage containers, the following are the most common ones found in school districts.

1. Farm or residential tanks with capacity of 1100 gallons or less storing motor fuel which is not for resale
2. Tanks for storing heating oil which is used on-site
3. Septic tanks
4. Surface impoundments, pits, ponds, or lagoons
5. Storage tanks on or above the floor of an underground area, such as a basement or tunnel[20]

The regulations require that each school district demonstrate fiscal responsibility through one or a combination of the following mechanisms.

1. Insurance coverage from an insurer or risk retention group plan
2. A surety bond
3. A letter of credit
4. State fund
5. Any other method of coverage approved by the state[21]

At the present time, districts are not approved to self-insure against loss. However, the EPS is considering guidelines over and beyond what is required of private suppliers wishing to self-insure. The current limits of financial exposure for school districts is $500,000 per occurrence for districts using 10,000 gallons or less each month, and $1 million for more than 10,000 gallons per month. Aggregate coverage is $1 million for owners of 1 to 100 separate tanks, and $2 million for more than 100 separate tanks.[22]

## Summary

With the complexities of state aid, local tax rates, special education programs, taxing schemes, and environmental issues, the courts will continue to play a significant role in education at both the state and local level. The continuing federal agenda regarding environmental issues impacts schools either through direct regulations for compliance, or through stringent notification requirements that pressure districts into compliance.

## Endnotes

1. Kern Alexander and M. David Alexander, *American Public School Law* (St. Paul, Minnesota: West Publishing Company, 1985), p. 710.

2. David L. Walters, "Equity and Diversity: A Challenge for the Allocation of Financial Resources," Paper presented at the meeting of the International Intervisitation Programme in Educational Administration (Honolulu, 1986), p. 3.

3. *San Antonio Independent School District* v. *Rodriguez*, 411 U.S. (1973).

4. Richard A. Rossmiller, "School Finance Reform Through Litigation: Expressway or Cul-de-Sac," in *School Law Update*, Thomas N. Jones and Darel P. Semler, eds. (Topeka, Kansas: National Organization on Legal Problems in Education, 1986), p. 194.

5. John Augenblick, Steven D. Gold, and Kent McGuire, *Education Finance in the 1990s* (Denver, Colorado: Educational Commission of the States, 1990), Appendix 1.

6. *Ibid*.

7. *Ibid*.

8. Laura F. Rothstein, *Special Education Law* (White Plains, New York: Longman Press, 1990), p. 32.

9. *Ibid.*, pp. 140–143.

10. *Board of Education* v. *Rowley*, 458 U.S. 176 (1982).

11. Laura F. Rothstein, *Special Education Law*, p.189.

12. Bruce Beezer and Bettye MacPhais-Wilcox, "Finance" in Stephen B. Thomas, ed., *The Yearbook of Educational Law, 1988* (Topeka Kansas: National Organization on Legal Problems in Education), p. 213.

13. The Internal Revenue Service, Section 149 (A).

14. Karl R. Ottosen, "Tax Exempt Municipal Bonds—An Endangered Species," *School Business Affairs*, Vol. 54, no. 11 (November 1988), p. 42.

15. *Ibid.*, p. 43.

16. U.S. Environmental Protection Agency, *Lead in School Drinking Water* (Washington, D.C.: Office of Drinking Water, United States Environmental Protection Agency, 1989), p. 7.

17. *Ibid.*, p. 10.

18. U.S. Environmental Protection Agency, *Radon Measurements in Schools* (Washington, D.C.: Office of Radiation Programs, 1989), p. 1.

19. *Ibid.*, p. 14.

20. U.S. Environmental Protection Agency, *Dollars and Sense* (Washington, D.C.: Office of Underground Storage Tanks, 1988) p. 2.

21. *Ibid.*, p. 6.

22. *Ibid.*, p. 5.

## Selected Bibliography

Alexander, Kern, and M. David Alexander, *American Public School Law* (St. Paul, Minnesota: West Publishing Company), 1985.

LaMorte, Michael W., *School Law, Cases and Concepts* (Englewood Cliffs, New Jersey: Prentice-Hall, Inc.), 1987.

Ottosen, Karl R., "Tax Exempt Municipal Bonds—An Endangered Species," *School Business Affairs*, Vol. 54, no. 11 (November 1988), pp. 42–43.

Rothstein, Laura F., *Special Education Law* (New York: Longman Publishing Company), 1990.

Wheeler, Robert, "Radon Testing in Schools," *School Business Affairs*, Vol. 55, no. 7 (July 1989), pp. 20–23.

# 12

# Ethical Considerations in School Business Administration

The last few years have brought to public attention the vulnerability of those in leadership positions. No segment has been left unscathed. Disheartening have been the revelations about elected officials, but particularly disturbing have been those failings of religious personalities like the Reverend Jimmy Swaggart.

On a much larger scale, the Contra arms scandal was surpassed only by Watergate. Further, nothing rocked Wall Street harder than the guilty plea of Ivan Boesky to trading on inside information.

Every parent who read about Baby M must have debated with himself or herself, at least somewhat, about that most basic of human notions, kinship.

Many of the popular magazines have devoted extensive coverage to these concerns and a few have even entitled their lead story with that often misunderstood word, ethics.[1]

Educators employed by private schools and public school districts have also encountered outrage because of misdeeds. Nothing is more embarrassing to the vast majority of conscientious and upright educators than when a colleague is convicted of the heinous crime of sexually abusing a child.

The litany could be continued for many pages but the point has been made. It must also be obvious that the question of ethics must be addressed in all books dealing with school administration and particularly public school administration because of the *public* accountability required in this sector of education.

On first glance, the study of ethics seems to be a rather straightforward task. However, the term has been uttered for centuries with a variety of meanings. Aristotle in the *Nicomachean Ethics* treats ethics as a practical science with application to the social and political aspects of human existence, while Friedrich Nietzsche contended that believers in traditional ethics had no grasp of the psychological needs of the individual. Thus, the task is arduous but necessary.

There is also a caveat that must be stated here at the beginning of this treatment. Of all the contemporary issues that face the educational administrator, the understanding of the question of ethics in administrative practice is the most susceptible to continual interpretation. However, there are certain principles and practices of behavior that can be labeled either as appropriate or inappropriate given the common understanding of our society. Such is the basis of the material presented in this chapter. Also, this chapter does not address the tenets of moral conduct set forth in particular religions. Rather, a philosophical approach is utilized.

The philosophical bases for ethical conduct are grounded in an understanding of human nature and the nature of human institutions.

It is impossible to elaborate on all the systems of philosophy or even all of the major concepts adhered to by contemporary philosophers and, indeed, it is not necessary in this text.

Moreover, what educational administrators are most concerned about are the beliefs of the citizens who live in their school districts. Citizens have impressions and opinions about human nature and the nature of school districts that are not always expressed and, perhaps, not even well organized in their own minds. However, they certainly do know when the conduct of administrators, teachers, and staff members is contrary to what they believe to be appropriate.

It is also reasonable to expect that constituents do accept the concepts underlying our cultural heritage. That heritage rests firmly upon the Declaration of Independence, the Constitution, and the Bill of Rights. Almost no one would deny that these documents embody the spirit by which all citizens should live.

It is also undeniable that there are definite concepts concerning human nature and the nature of government in these documents that should influence the conduct of educational administrators.

For the purposes of this chapter, it is sufficient to identify Aristotle (384 B.C.–322 B.C.), John Locke (1632–1704), and Jean Jacques Rousseau (1712–1778) as having had a great influence on those who wrote and approved the Declaration of Independence, the Constitution, and the Bill of Rights. In this context they, as well as others, contributed to the doctrine of natural rights.

It is interesting to note that the idea of *natural rights* was such a central concept in the thinking of the people living at the time of the Revolutionary period that the Declaration of Independence refers to these rights as *self-evident*.

Natural rights presuppose a natural law from which these rights emanate. The natural law becomes evident through the use of reason, which enlightens all human beings. The primary realization is that each person is free to determine his or her own goals in life. This freedom is not blind without limits. Human reason makes known to the individual the order of reality and helps the person to discern that to which he or she should conform.

Further, the political philosophy at the time of the American Revolution posited that natural rights existed before all civil governments. The basic rights inherent in human nature are the rights "to life, liberty, and the pursuit of happiness." These rights are dependent upon no government!

Government is brought into existence for the common good by agreement between those to be governed. This consent theory is best illustrated by the slogan, "no taxation without representation."

The objective of government is human development and well-being. It is a contradiction to hold that such an end can be attained when individual freedom and rights are restricted. The preamble to the Constitution reinforces these notions:

> We the People of the United States, in Order to form a more perfect Union, establish Justice, insure domestic Tranquility, provide for the common defense, promote the general Welfare, and secure the Blessings of Liberty, to ourselves and our Posterity, do ordain and establish this Constitution for the United States of America.

If a government breaches the compact with the people who have established it, its authority is illegitimate and the people have a legitimate right to revolution as set forth in the Declaration of Independence:

> . . . whenever any Form of Government becomes destructive of these ends, it is the Right of the People to alter or to abolish it, and to institute new Government, laying its foundation on such principles and organizing its powers in such form, as to them shall seem most likely to effect their Safety and Happiness.

The monarchical societies at the time of the Revolution did not recognize the dignity of the ordinary person. In fact, the ordinary person had no rights except those bestowed upon him by the monarchy. The natural rights philosophy was the antithesis of the monarchy because it focused on the ordinary person and his personal welfare. Thus, we have the perfect explication of this self-realization principle in the Declaration:

*We hold these truths to be self-evident, that all men are created equal, that they are endowed by their creator with certain unalienable Rights, that among these are Life, Liberty and the pursuit of Happiness.*

The implications of these philosophical notions for educational administration are many. First and foremost is the notion that public schools exist by and for the citizens of each school district because they emanate from state government. In almost every state, legislatures have enacted statutes which establish local school districts and provide for the election of school board members who are charged with the governance of these districts.

In fact, school districts are very responsive to the wishes of the local community because school board members are easily accessible to their neighbors who can exert considerable influence on their thinking. In addition, a significant amount of revenue for public schools is raised through a tax on local property. In most states, the school board must seek voter approval in order to change the tax rate.

If the citizens of a school district are unhappy with the curricular program, with district policies, or with the manner in which the budget is spent, they can elect new board members and/or refuse to approve increases in taxes. Regardless of the inconvenience that is caused board members and administrators, this is how it should be. Accountability to citizens is immediate.

A second major implication of the philosophical notions set forth above concerns the personal treatment given each student, teacher, staff member, and administrator. It seems perfectly logical to expect the local, state, and federal governments to be concerned about the welfare of each individual citizen.

Thus, we have seen a proliferation of federal laws, state statutes, and board policies that reaffirm the rights of students and employees. The emphasis on fair treatment for handicapped students and staff members that occurred through legislation in the 1970s (Rehabilitation Act of 1973 and Public Law 94-142 of 1975) are good examples of how government reacts to situations when individual rights are infringed upon.

Affirmative action requirements that must be followed in the hiring of staff members and the due process required in the termination of employees are also logical outgrowths of the "life, liberty, and pursuit of happiness" notion.

In concluding this section on historical antecedents, it should be obvious that *ethics* originates from the religious and philosophical beliefs of people. Those who reside in public school districts place expectations that issue forth from their beliefs on school administrators.

## A Code of Ethics and Standards of Conduct

"Ask yourself why you're doing things you want to hide," is good advice for someone who begins to question the appropriateness of his or her behavior![2] However, administration is a complex responsibility in contemporary society. Not a day passes without at least one issue or problem appearing in almost every newspaper or on almost every local television news program dealing with public education.

In the midst of daily responsibilities and tasks, administrators are required to make decisions that have far-reaching and severe consequences.[3] They do not have time to calmly analyze the ethical implications of their decisions.

Therefore, it is extremely helpful for administrators to have available guidelines that can be consulted when they have questions concerning ethical conduct.

### A Code of Ethics

The Association of School Business Officials International has a *code of ethics*, reprinted in Appendix A, which has been selected as an example of the kind of codes that are available. It has been selected also because it is an excellent code that is very pertinent to the responsibilities of school business administrators.

It is interesting to note that ASBO promotes not only a code of ethics but also a *standards of conduct* that appears in Appendix B.

The *code of ethics* serves not only as a guide but also establishes an ideal that all administrators should strive to reach in their professional careers. Identifying the ideal is the significant difference between a code and standards of conduct. Many administrators may not appreciate this distinction and see the two as one which is certainly understood by this author. However, a more critical appraisal of ASBO's *code of ethics* and *standards of conduct* should point out the value in making this distinction which is the purpose of the following sections.

In the *code of ethics*, administrators are asked to acknowledge that they must be committed to the idea of universal educational opportunity. This

This certainly includes not only the education of the typical student but also students with special needs and interests. Thus, the education of children with a handicap, children who are at risk, in addition to students who have vocational interests and abilities must be understood and fostered by all administrators.

In our complex educational institutions, it is very easy to plead specialization as an excuse for not actively promoting the best educational opportunity for all children. Thus, a school business administrator might leave the issue of providing special counseling for students with a drug problem to the director of pupil personnel services.

Business administrators should never think that they are *treading on someone else's turf* by promoting the welfare of students at risk, if they believe that such children are being neglected.

This code also places significant emphasis not only on obeying local, state, and federal laws but also urges the administrator to become involved in trying to change laws that do not promote sound educational goals.

It goes without saying that civil and human rights must be respected and promoted. Such goals are impossible, unless the school administrator fulfills his or her professional responsibilities with honesty and integrity.

These personal qualities of honesty and integrity mitigate against using an administrative position for personal gain outside of the compensation that is agreed upon in the administrator's contract with the district.

Further, these personal qualities should prevent the school administrator from using political, social, economic, or other influences to further personal career goals.

An experienced school administrator is capable of manipulating the tasks of his or her position in such a manner as to hinder the proper implementation of school board policies and administrative rules and regulations. Such actions are certainly unacceptable under this code.

ASBO, as a professional organization, has recognized for many years the necessity of ongoing professional development and has consistently promoted this among its membership. However, academic degrees and programs that are available from unaccredited colleges and universities do not meet the standards of integrity and honesty which are fundamental qualities underlying this code.

There is a very interesting aspect of ASBO's code that addresses the need to improve the effectiveness of the school business profession through research. Thus, it is recognized that the school administrator must be not only a consumer of research but also a producer. Too often, administrators believe that research is the perogative of just university professors. This misconception occurs because many administrators do not have a proper understanding of the meaning of *research*. They conceive of research in a very narrow sense that superimposes the experimental method upon the definition of research.

Gaining new insights from the practice of business administration is a form of research that can be shared with colleagues through the publication of articles in professional journals or through developing and leading seminars or workshops at national or state conventions as well as for local associations and organizations.

It is refreshing to find a code of ethics that does not consist of a long list of do's and don'ts. ASBO's code, rather, addresses those issues that are certain to impinge upon the practice of school business administration, and clearly establishes the need for the guiding principle of *the education of students*. This rests upon the two personal qualities of honesty and integrity that must be possessed by school administrators if the student welfare principle is to succeed.

## Standards of Conduct

The standards, of course, deal with the behavior of the school business administrator within the school district, in relation to colleagues in other districts, and behavior in professional associations.

In regards to relationships within the school district, this section of the standards charges the school business administrator with the responsibility of providing personal and professional support to fellow workers. It is obvious that this means refraining from publicly criticizing school board members, other administrators, and, in fact, all other staff members regardless of position within the organization.

Private criticism is also inappropriate and can even be more insidious than public criticism because people against whom statements are being made may have no opportunity to defend themselves.

The obligation, however, is also stated in a positive manner. The school business administrator is responsible for assisting fellow administrators as they work toward fulfilling their obligations and duties, and also is responsible for helping subordinates to achieve their maximum potential.

In addition, this section of the standards places the obligation on the school business administrator to support the goals and objectives of the school district, and to fairly interpret district policies to the community and to those whom he or she supervises. This, in turn, will help to maintain and build a positive image for the district.

Finally, this section calls for the school business administrator to implement, to the best of his or her ability, the administrative regulations of the district. A dilemma arises when an administrator finds that the policies or administrative regulations of the district do not conform to personal beliefs and, in some cases, what the administrator sees as detrimental.

There are two possible courses of action that can be taken. First, the administrator should confront the appropriate supervisor with these concerns. In most school districts, the school business official will probably report to the superintendent of schools. It is important for the administrator to strictly adhere to the chain of command in the district in presenting personal views. Of course, if the immediate supervisor does not agree with the administrator, he or she can bring the matter to the next level of command and ultimately to the board of education.

The second course of action is to resign. That is not always a practical solution to the problem especially if the administrator has financial and family obligations. However, it is better to find alternate employment as soon as possible rather than remain in a position that presents an ethical dilemma. No one can maintain a healthy outlook on life and live contrary to his or her principles.

The second major section of the *standards of conduct* deals with the manner in which the business administrator carries out the business function of the school district. Once again, honesty and integrity are the keystones.

The last ten years, however, have sensitized the public toward the potential for corruption in the discharge of business. Therefore, many corporations and even many not-for-profit foundations have found the need to demonstrate that the officials and staff of their organizations are expected to maintain the highest standards of ethical conduct. The most common way to demonstrate this commitment is by establishing a *conflict of interest* policy and by requiring top-level administrators to actually sign a *disclosure statement*.

School districts should not be the exception with regard to conflict of interest.[4] In fact, many major auditing firms annually make recommendations to their clients, school boards, to formally adopt a conflict of interest policy and to require administrators as well as board members to sign disclosure statements.

Exhibit 12-1 is a typical example of an employee conflict of interest policy. In substance, it sets forth that it is unethical for an administrator to realize personal financial gain if that person's position with the school district was the direct or even indirect cause for such financial gain. Exhibit 12-2 is an example of a disclosure statement which calls for the employee to

EXHIBIT 12-1 • *Conflict of Interest Policy*

---

Employees shall not engage in, or have direct financial interest in, any activity that raises a reasonable question of conflict of interest with their duties and responsibilities as members of the Lindbergh School District staff. In addition, staff members are required to adhere to the following policies:

1. Employees will not participate for financial remuneration in outside activities wherein their position on the staff is used to sell goods or services to students or their parents/guardians.
2. Employees who have patented or copyrighted any device, publication, or other item will not receive royalties for use of such item in the district schools.
3. Employees will not engage in any type of work where the source of information concerning customer, client, or employer originates from information obtained through the school district.
4. Employees shall not act as agents or accept commissions or other rewards for books or other school materials, the selection or purchase of which they may influence. The school district will not purchase products distributed directly or indirectly by employees of the district.

---

*Source*: Lindbergh School District, *Staff Conflict of Interest Policy* (St. Louis, MO: The District, 1988), GBCA.

declare by signature that personal financial gain will not be made through his or her position with the district.

One other observation should be made concerning the business operations of a school district. As a public entity, all business must be conducted in an atmosphere of openness. For example, while bids for services and goods must be *sealed* so that no one knows what a competitor is bidding, after the bids are opened, they become public and can be reviewed by all interested parties, including citizens who were not a party to the bidding process.

The final section of the *standards of conduct* deals with the school business administrator's relationship to administrators in other districts and participation in professional associations.

School business administrators are encouraged to refrain from publicly criticizing other administrators and elected school officials. Further, business administrators are expected to offer assistance and guidance to colleagues whether requested or not, if there appears to be a need.

Participation in professional associations is a responsibility of all administrators. Accepting leadership positions within such associations is likewise an expectation because associations like ASBO are actively promoting the improvement of school business administration, in particular, and education, in general. All associations need to instill within their membership a sense of perpetuation, if these associations are to advance their missions. Thus, it is incumbent upon all members to encourage colleagues to join professional associations.

A final aspect of this section deals with refraining from using a leadership position or just membership in professional associations for personal financial gain. Very rarely does such a situation arise. However, there is a potential for abuse in relation to the attending of professional meetings, workshops, and conventions. It is not unheard of for an administrator to charge inappropriate expenses to a school district that where incurred while attending a convention, workshop, or meeting.

Exhibit 12-3 sets forth a business expense policy that fosters attendance at professional gatherings because such experiences help administrators to keep current on issues facing the administration which, in turn, will be beneficial to the school district.

EXHIBIT 12-2 • *Disclosure Statement*

---

I have read the foregoing conflict of interest policy and as a result, I am making the following disclosure.

I do not directly or indirectly have a material financial interest in any firm doing business with the school district except as follows: _____

To the best of my knowledge, neither I nor my immediate family have received any profit or gain from my position with the school district except as follows: _____

I am not an officer or employee of any organization or business with which the school district obtains goods or services except as follows: _____

I have not received any gifts, special payments, or favors greater than a nominal value from any organization providing goods or services to the school district except as follows: _____

Any other situation, not covered above, which might be interpreted to be a conflict of interest or about which there is any question or doubt as to proper conduct, should be disclosed.

I understand that the above statements will be received by the board of education and all existing conflicts of interests disclosed herein will be reviewed and disposition thereof will be indicated in the minutes of the board at least annually.

---

| _____ | _____ |
| Date | Signature |

---

*Source*: Lindbergh School District, *Disclosure Statement* (St. Louis, MO.: The District, 1988).

Exhibit 12-3 • *Administrator Business Expenses Policy*

___

The board of education recognizes the value of professional meetings, seminars, workshops, and conventions for the administrative staff. Such experiences help to keep administrators informed and updated on issues facing schools and school districts. This, in turn, benefits the school district because administrators are better able to meet the challenges of the contemporary educational environment.

Therefore, the board of education authorizes the superintendent of schools to develop and implement guidelines and procedures for administrator business expenses.

___

*Source:* Lindbergh School District, *Administrator Business Expenses Policy* (St. Louis, MO.: The District, 1987).

Exhibit 12-4 consists of guidelines that explain what expenses are appropriate and the manner in which these expenses can be reimbursed to the administrator. All the figures in this chapter were developed by the author for the school district so cited and therefore, they are consistent with the philosophical foundations presented in his chapter.

Exhibit 12-4 • *Administrator Business Expenses Guidelines*

___

1. All requests to attend conventions, conferences, and workshops must be approved by the superintendent of schools or his or her designee.
2. Expenses will be paid only for prior approved conventions, conferences, and workshops. In order to receive approval, the proper form must be completed.
3. Cash advances will be issued upon submission of the appropriate form which shall be limited to:
    The total projected cost of lodging
    The total projected cost of airfare or automobile mileage
    Fifty percent of other projected expenses
4. Air travel will be by coach only.
5. If available, lodging will be at a major hotel/motel chain.
6. Meal expenses will be reimbursed, not to exceed fifty dollars per day.
7. Entertainment expenses that are not a part of the convention, conference, or workshop will not be allowed.
8. Expenses for an accompanying spouse will not be paid.
9. Incurred expenses will be verified by receipts. Exceptions are auto mileage and tips.
10. Expenses must be verified on the appropriate form within five working days after returning from the convention, and so on.

___

*Source:* Lindbergh School District, *Administrator Business Expenses* (St. Louis, MO.: The District, 1987).

## A Postscript

The question of ethical behavior in the private business sector has become a major issue not only with corporations but also with schools of business administration.

General Dynamics is a good example of how companies are responding to this issue. In 1985, General Dynamics launched an improved ethics program which is the first of its kind in the defense industry. The first step was to create a written document that institutionalized a code of ethics and conduct. The company then appointed ethics program directors at all company locations. These directors provide information and guidance, gather facts about allegations, and may initiate investigations.

Throughout 1986, the company conducted ethics awareness workshops that were designed to help employees identify situations of an ethical nature in the workplace. After the training, employees who needed additional assistance in identifying and dealing with situations of an ethical nature could call hotlines installed at approximately forty company locations.[5]

In 1988, Arthur Andersen & Company, a major public-accounting firm, announced that it would spend $5 million over the next five years developing case studies on ethics for business schools.

The new program is called PACE. In addition, Arthur Andersen & company will provide free training to college professors who are interested in teaching the cases. This company also plans to develop a series of conferences on ethics for business college faculties, students, business executives, and company clients.

The PACE program presents case studies in the areas of accounting, economics, finances, marketing, and management; the program emphasizes situations that entry-level employees might face.

It is clear that ethical conduct will continue to be an area of concern not only to the profession of school administration but also to the public in general. Therefore, it is imperative that school business administrators provide leadership in this area within their school districts. Administrators can best accomplish this by carrying out their responsibilities in a manner that clearly demonstrates their ethical beliefs.

## Summary

The last few years have brought to the public's attention the vulnerability of those in leadership positions. The scandal of T.V. evangelism, of the Contra arms deal, and the insider trading on Wall Street are only a few examples of why public confidence has been shaken.

In addition, the periodic news stories about educators who have been convicted of crimes, especially those convicted of sexually abusing children, shock and embarrass all members of the education profession.

Thus, it is imperative for educational administrators to investigate and study the discipline of ethics. They should also contemplate their own personal notions of ethics in order to be better prepared to sort out the daily ethical issues that are always present in the administration of schools and school districts.

Almost all recognized philosophers have addressed the question of ethics in one or more of their writings. Most people have certain philosophical notions that they adhere to even if they seldom or never verbalize them. Thus, it is difficult to center on a given set of principles that administrators can use as guidelines in conduct.

However, there are sources of principles that can meet this need because they form the very bases of our way of life. They are the Declaration of Independence, the Constitution, and the Bill of Rights.

The principles set forth in these documents rest upon the doctrine of natural rights which was a central concept in the thinking of the people living at the time of the Revolution.

Natural rights presupposes a natural law from which these rights emanate. It was firmly held by our forefathers that natural rights existed before all civil government. The basic rights inherent in human nature are the rights to life, liberty, and the pursuit of happiness. The precursor to the stating of these rights was the concept that all men are created equal. The objective of government is human development and well-being.

The implications for educational administration are numerous. First, school districts are agents of government, which exists for the welfare of the people. Therefore, the school administrator must be publicly accountable to the citizens of the school district.

The second implication centers on the responsibility of every administrator to safeguard the personal rights of students, teachers, and staff members.

It is not enough for a school administrator to know the foundations of religious and ethical expectations. Administration is a very complex responsibility and it is extremely helpful for administrators to have available guidelines that can be consulted when they have questions concerning ethical conduct.

The *Code of Ethics* of the Association of School Business Officials International is an excellent guide particularly for school business administrators as they carry out their responsibilities. The code also establishes an ideal that administrators can strive to achieve.

The code asks administrators to be committed to the idea of universal educational opportunity and it places emphasis on obeying local, state, and federal laws. The personal qualities of honesty and integrity, of course, are unquestioned necessities as is a respect for human and civil rights. Using the position of school business administrator for personal financial gain beyond the compensation contracted for is unethical, as is using political, social, economic, or other influences to further an administrator's career.

School business administrators are asked to recognize the need for continuing education and the obligation of being both a consumer and producer of research.

ASBO's *Standards of Conduct* deals with the school business administrator's behavior within the school district, in relation to colleagues in other districts, and in professional associations.

The last ten years have sensitized the public toward the potential for corruption in the discharge of school business. A common way to demonstrate a commitment to honesty is through establishing a conflict of interest policy and requiring top-level administrators to actually sign a disclosure statement.

In conclusion, the private sector is slightly ahead of public education in dealing with ethics from an organizational perspective and there are very good models available from corporations that could be modified for school districts.

## Appendix A  Code of Ethics

An educational administrator's professional behavior must conform to an ethical code. The code must be idealistic and at the same time practical so that it can apply reasonably to all educational administrators. The administrator acknowledges that the schools belong to the public they serve for the purpose of providing educational opportunities to all. However, the administrator assumes responsibility for providing professional leadership in the school and community. This responsibility requires the administrator to maintain standards of exemplary professional conduct. It must be recognized that the administrator's actions will be viewed and appraised by the community, professional associates, and students. To these ends, the administrator subscribes to the following statements of standards.

### The Educational Administrator

1. Makes the well-being of students the fundamental value in all decision making and actions

2. Fulfills professional responsibilities with honesty and integrity
3. Supports the principle of due process and protects the civil and human rights of all individuals
4. Obeys local, state, and national laws and does not knowingly join or support organizations that advocate, directly or indirectly, the overthrow of the government
5. Implements the governing board of education's policies and administrative rules and regulations
6. Pursues appropriate measures to correct those laws, policies, and regulations that are not consistent with sound educational goals
7. Avoids using positions for personal gain through political, social, religious, economic, or other influence
8. Accepts academic degrees or professional certification only from duly accredited institutions
9. Maintains the standards and seeks to improve the effectiveness of the profession through research and continuing professional development
10. Honors all contracts until fulfillment or release

*Source:* Association of School Business Officials International, "Code of Ethics," *School Business Affairs,* Vol. 54, no. 3 (March 1988), pp. 54–56.

## Appendix B  Standards of Conduct

Now, especially in this age of accountability, when the activities and conduct of school business officials are subject to greater scrutiny and more severe criticism than ever before, standards of conduct are in order. The association cannot fully discharge its obligation of leadership and service to its members short of establishing appropriate standards of behavior.

In relationships within the school district, it is expected that the school business official will:

1. Support the goals and objectives of the employing school system
2. Interpret the policies and practices of the district to subordinates and to the community fairly and objectively
3. Implement, to the best of the official's ability, the policies and administrative regulations of the district
4. Assist fellow administrators as appropriate in fulfilling their obligations
5. Build the best possible image of the school district
6. Refrain from publicly criticizing board members, administrators, or other employees
7. Help subordinates to achieve their maximum potential through fair and just treatment

In the conduct of business and the discharge of responsibilities, the school business official will:

1. Conduct business honestly, openly, and with integrity

2. Avoid conflict of interest situations by not conducting business with a company or firm in which the official or any member of the official's family has a vested interest
3. Avoid preferential treatment of one outside interest group, company, or individual over another
4. Uphold the dignity and decorum of the office in every way
5. Avoid using the position for personal gain
6. Never accept or offer illegal payment for services rendered
7. Refrain from accepting gifts, free services, or anything of value for or because of any act performed or withheld
8. Permit the use of school property only for official authorized activities
9. Refrain from soliciting contributions from subordinates or outside sources for gifts or donations to a superior

In relationships with colleagues in other districts and professional associations, it is expected that the school business official will:

1. Support the actions of a colleague whenever possible, never publicly criticizing or censuring the official
2. Offer assistance and/or guidance to a colleague when such help is requested or when the need is obvious
3. Actively support appropriate professional associations aimed at improving school business management and encourage colleagues to do likewise
4. Accept leadership roles and responsibilities when appropriate, but refrain from "taking over" any association
5. Refrain from using any organization or position of leadership in it for personal gain

*Source:* Association of School Business Officials International, "Standards of Conduct," *School Business Affairs*, Vol. 54, no. 3 (March 1988), pp. 54-56.

## Endnotes

1. "What Ever Happened to Ethics," Time, 129, no. 21 (May 1987), pp. 14–35.
2. *Wall Street Journal* (Highland), May 18, 1987, p. 28.
3. J. Ronald Buschmeyer, "Focus on School Business Officials," *School Business Affairs*, Vol. 54, no. 4 (April 1988), pp. 10–12.
4. Ralph B. Kinbrough, *Ethics: A Course of Study for Educational Leaders* (Arlington, Virginia: The American Association of School Administrators, 1985), p. 15.
5. *St. Louis Business Journal* (April 11–17, 1988), sec. A, p. 5.

# Selected Bibliography

American Association of School Administrators, *AASA Statement of Ethics for School Administrators and Procedural Guidelines* (Arlington, Virginia: The Association, 1976).

Aristotle, *The Nicomachean Ethics*, trans. J.E.C. Welldon (Buffalo, New York: Prometheus Books, 1987).

Bayles, Michael D., and Kenneth Henley, *Right Conduct: Theories and Applications* (New York: Random House, 1983).

DeGeorge, R.T., *Business Ethics* (New York: Macmillan Publishing Co., 1982).

Goldman, A.H., *The Moral Foundations of Professional Ethics* (New Jersey: Rowan and Littlefield, 1980).

Gonsalves, Milton A., revised by, *Fogothey's Right and Reason: Ethics in Theory and Practice*, 8th ed. (Columbus, Ohio: Charles E. Merrill Publishing Co., 1986).

Grassian, V., *Moral Reasoning* (Englewood Cliffs, New Jersey: Prentice-Hall, Inc., 1981).

Johnson, Oliver A., *Ethics: Selections from Classical and Contemporary Writers* (New York: Holt, Rinehart and Winston, 1984).

Kimbrough, Ralph B., *Ethics: A Course of Study for Educational Leaders* (Arlington, Virginia: The American Association of School Administrators, 1985).

Mappes, Thomas A., and Jane S. Zembathy, *Social Ethics: Morality and Social Policy*, 3rd ed. (New York: McGraw-Hill Book Co., 1987).

Norman, R., *The Moral Philosophers* (Oxford: Clarendon Press, 1983).

Purtill, Richard L., *Moral Dilemmas: Readings in Ethics and Social Philosophy* (Belmont: Wadsworth Publishing Co., 1985).

Strike, Kenneth, Emil Haller, and Jonas Soltis, *The Ethics of School Administration* (New York: Teachers College, 1988).

Weinrelch-Haste, H. and D. Lock, eds., *Morality in the Making* (New York: John Wiley and Sons, 1983).

# Epilogue

As the nation moves into the last decade of the twentieth century, education finds itself involved in a variety of *reform programs* as a result of both state and federal agendas emphasizing outcomes and accountability of local school districts. Neither one of these two items are revolutionary. Accountability movements have surfaced often during the past 25 years. What made the 1980s so unique were the solutions discussed and implemented by state legislatures. The traditional methods of resolving differing educational outcomes were limited to attempts to provide equity programs for all students, and categorical aid for students needing specialized programs. While these issues are certainly still being discussed and litigated, state reform has concentrated on increasing graduation requirements, lengthening the school day, testing programs, and so on. As a result, one may suspect that this movement will continue throughout the 1990s. Taking the two concepts of reform and accountability and applying these issues to a variety of programs currently being discussed, or recently implemented to some degree, it would be possible to consider the following issues as definite possibilities for major issues during the 1990s.

1. *Choice* Allowing parents and students to select the school within the district, or in another district for educational programs, regardless of the parent's residency within the state.
2. *Pre-School Programs* The development and delivery of pre-school programs to all members of the community under the umbrella of the local school district.

3. *Equity Issues* The expansion of equity to taxpayers, regardless of residency within the state.
4. *Specialization* Greater emphasis on the preparation of administrators regarding school business management.

## School Choice

The recent publication of *The School Match Guide to Public Schools* by Bainbridge and Sundre, identified school choice as one of the major issues facing schools in the 1990s. The authors found that 68.9 percent of parents surveyed indicated that their first choice of a school would be one demonstrating average or above average performance on achievement tests. Parents were more concerned with the individual child's success than with the school receiving the highest rating.[1] The traditional discussion of *choice funding* is centered around the voucher system. Each child represents the amount of dollars contributed on a per pupil basis by the state, as well as the property taxes paid by the parents to the local school district. Therefore, the school accepting the student would receive both the state and local revenue due to the child. Proponents of inter-district choice funding argue that competition will have a positive effect on the quality of each local district. School boards will take the necessary steps to ensure that district programs are meeting the needs of the students and efficiently operated. Kiplinger, in *America in the Global '90s*, maintains that public education is suffering from the same calamities of any monopoly, "high-priced and a lack of incentive to innovate for improved quality."[2] There is no incentive to improve because there is no link between funding and excellence. School districts continue to receive additional funds from state and local sources without any accountability regarding educational excellence. Minnesota currently has a *pick-your-school* program whereby each district receives $2800 per pupil.

The opponents of choice argue that competition will do no more than siphon off needed funds from schools requiring the most help. The increased competition will require districts to mount expensive public relations campaigns to attract students. As a result, districts will be more concerned with keeping students than with increasing standards. Therefore, choice programs will hinder the excellence movement rather than help it.

Intra-district choice programs do not have the same financial ramifications for the local district. Parents are given the option of choosing any school within the district for their children. The district receives that same amount of funding since the aggregate number of students within the district is not altered. While this process does create competition between schools in the district, many districts already allow students to enroll in any of the district's schools. Usually, the only restriction is transportation. Parents wishing their children to attend a school outside the current boundaries for that attendance area are required to provide their own transportation. However, even proponents of choice express concern regarding the implementation of programs within districts. If not careful, intra-district choice can create inequality of programs. Many districts have experimented with *magnet schools* dedicated to one or more specialized areas. Students are allowed to attend the schools regardless of the location of their residence within the district. The fear is that districts, in an attempt to develop specialized programs, will underfund the regular school programs. Sylvester identified three goals and three dangers of choice programs.

*Goals*
1. It can revitalize school programs by giving teachers the freedom to be creative.
2. It can make schools better places for children to be.
3. It can break down the barriers of segregation because of its power to draw students across political and economic boundaries.

*Dangers*
1. It can resegregate schools when choices are limited or available only to the elite.
2. It can create new kinds of inequities by funding schools unequally or segregating students within schools by tracking them by ability.
3. It can lull politicians and educators into believing they have found the answer to the problems of education.[3]

As of 1989, intra-district choice programs have been implemented in Seattle, San Jose, San Francisco, Boston, and East Harlem.

## Pre-school Programs

The preponderance of evidence indicating that pre-school programs can effectively remediate some learning problems before the child enters kindergarten provides a persuasive argument for expanding these programs. Legislatures are beginning to pay attention to the many groups lobbying for extending the right to a free and gratuitous education to three-year-olds. While most agree that these should be voluntary programs, all proponents agree that public funds should be used. The outcomes of these programs fit easily into the *excellence movement* with their emphasis on early detection of learning problems and on remediation before entering kindergarten.

## Equity Issues

State equity programs to fund local education have been under close scrutiny throughout the 1980s. This trend will continue as more state plans are challenged through litigation and legislative action. The equity issue regarding tax payer equity is beginning to reemerge as property valuations in many states lack consistency. Also, tax rates in commercially poor districts far exceed the rates in districts with substantial commercial properties. Taxpayers recognize the inequity of differing property taxes on residential property of the same value as an accident of their location within a particular school district. As a result, the reluctance of communities to increase their property taxes will result in districts seeking alternative methods of increasing local revenue. Odden, in "Sources of Funding for Education Reform," identifies three major sources of local funds under consideration:

1. Donor funds, including direct cash donations to local districts, indirect cash donations through locally created educational foundations, and donations of goods and services

2. Enterprise activities, such as leasing school services and facilities or charging user fees for various school materials and activities

3. Shared or cooperative activities with community colleges, other colleges and universities, and local government agencies, including sharing buses, parks, recreational centers, and pools.[4]

## Specialization

Twenty-five states currently require specific certification for school business administrators. With the emphasis on fiscal accountability and efficiency so prevalent throughout the country, more states will move toward specific certification standards for the chief fiscal officer of the local district. The Association of School Business Officials (ASBO) is currently in the process of developing a "Model Preparation Program for School Business Officials." The primary objective of the program is to provide guidelines to universities in the development of curricular programs in school business, as well as some direction to states considering certification standards. While the program is intended to be voluntary, the National Council for the

Accreditation of Teacher Education (NCATE) has adopted the program as part of the certification of educational administration programs.

## Endnotes

1. William Bainbridge and Steven Sundre, "School Choice: The Education Issue of the 1990s," *School and College* (March 1990), pp. 21–23.

2. Austin H. Kiplinger and Knight A. Kiplinger, *America in the Global '90s* (Washington, D.C.: Kiplinger Books, 1989), p. 151.

3. Kathleen Sylvester, "Schools of Choice: A Path to Educational Quality or 'Tiers of Inequality'?" *School Business Affairs*, Vol. 55, No. 11, (November 1989). pp. 10–14.

4. Allan Odden, "Sources of Funding for Educational Reform," in *Innovations in Education: Reformers and Their Critics*, 5th ed., ed. John Martin Rich, (Englewood Cliffs, New Jersey: Prentice-Hall, Inc., 1988), p. 145.

## Selected Bibliography

Bacharach, Samuel B., ed., *Educational Reform: Making Sense of It All* (Needham Heights, Massachusetts: Allyn and Bacon), 1990.

Rich, John Martin, ed., *Innovations In Education: Reformers and their Critics*. 5th Ed. (Englewood Cliffs, New Jersey: Prentice-Hall, Inc.), 1988.

# INDEX